1999-00
EDITION

MOTOR MUSEUMS

of the British Isles and Republic of Ireland

David Burke & Tom Price

VELOCE PUBLISHING PLC
PUBLISHERS OF FINE AUTOMOTIVE BOOKS

Other Veloce publications -

Colour Family Album Series
Bubblecars & Microcars by Andrea & David Sparrow
Bubblecars & Microcars, More by Andrea & David Sparrow
Citroën 2CV by Andrea & David Sparrow
Citroën DS by Andrea & David Sparrow
Fiat & Abarth 500 & 600 by Andrea & David Sparrow
Lambretta by Andrea & David Sparrow
Mini & Mini Cooper by Andrea & David Sparrow
Motor Scooters by Andrea & David Sparrow
Porsche by Andrea & David Sparrow
Vespa by Andrea & David Sparrow
VW Beetle by Andrea & David Sparrow
VW Beetle/Bug, Custom by Andrea & David Sparrow
VW Bus, Camper, Van & Pick-up by Andrea & David Sparrow

SpeedPro Series
How to Blueprint & Build a 4-Cylinder Engine Short Block for High Performance by Des Hammill
How to Build a V8 Engine Short Block for High Performance by Des Hammill
How to Build & Modify Sportscar/Kitcar Suspension & Brakes for High Performance by Daniel Stapleton
How to Build & Power Tune Weber DCOE & Dellorto DHLA Carburetors by Des Hammill
How to Build & Power Tune Harley-Davidson 1340 Evolution Engines by Des Hammill
How to Build & Power Tune Distributor-type Ignition Systems by Des Hammill
How to Build, Modify & Power Tune Cylinder Heads by Peter Burgess
How to Choose & Time Camshafts for Maximum Power by Des Hammill
How to give your MGB V8 Power Updated & Revised Edition by Roger Williams
How to Plan & Build a Fast Road Car by Daniel Stapleton
How to Power Tune BMC/BL/Rover 998cc A Series Engines by Des Hammill
How to Power Tune BMC/BL/Rover 1275cc A Series Engines by Des Hammill
How to Power Tune the MGB 4-Cylinder Engine by Peter Burgess
How to Power Tune the MG Midget & Austin-Healey Sprite by Daniel Stapleton
How to Power Tune Alfa Romeo Twin Cam Engines by Jim Kartalamakis
How to Power Tune Ford SOHC 'Pinto' & Sierra Cosworth DOHC Engines by Des Hammill

General
Automotive Mascots: A Collectors Guide to British Marque, Corporate & Accessory Mascots by David Kay & Lynda Springate
Bentley Continental Corniche & Azure 1951-1998 by Martin Bennett
Alfa Romeo Giulia Coupe GT & GTA by John Tipler
British Cars, The Complete Catalogue of 1895-1975 by Culshaw & Horrobin
British Trailer Caravans & their Manufacturers 1919-1959 by Andrew Jenkinson
Chrysler 300 - America's Most Powerful Car by Robert Ackerson
Cobra - The Real Thing! by Trevor Legate
Cortina- Ford's Best Seller by Graham Robson
Daimler SP250 'Dart' by Brian Long
Datsun/Nissan 280ZX & 300ZX by Brian Long
Datsun Z - From Fairlady to 280Z by Brian Long
Fiat & Abarth 124 Spider & Coupé by John Tipler
Fiat & Abarth 500 & 600 (revised edition) by Malcolm Bobbitt
Ford F100/F150 Pick-up by Robert Ackerson
Jim Redman - Six Times World Motorcycle Champion by Jim Redman
Grey Guide, The by Dave Thornton
Lea-Francis Story, The by Barrie Price
Lola - The Illustrated History (1957-1977) by John Starkey
Lola T70 - The Racing History & Individual Chassis Record New Edition by John Starkey
Mazda MX5/Miata 1.6 Enthusiast's Workshop Manual by Rod Grainger & Pete Shoemark
Mazda MX5/Miata 1.8 Enthusiast's Workshop Manual by Rod Grainger & Pete Shoemark
Mazda MX5 - Renaissance Sportscar by Brian Long
MGA by John Price Williams
Michael Schumacher - Ferrari Racing 1996-1998 by Braun/Schlegelmilch
Mini Cooper - The Real Thing! by John Tipler
Porsche 356 by Brian Long
Porsche 911R, RS & RSR New Edition by John Starkey
Porsche 914 & 914-6 by Brian Long
Prince & I, The (revised edition) by Princess Ceril Birabongse
Rolls-Royce Silver Shadow/Bentley T Series, Corniche & Camargue by Malcolm Bobbitt
Rolls-Royce Silver Wraith, Dawn & Cloud/Bentley MkVI, R & S Series by Martyn Nutland
Singer Story:Cars, Commercial Vehicles, Bicycles & Motorcycles by Kevin Atkinson
Taxi! The Story of the 'London' Taxicab by Malcolm Bobbitt
Triumph TR6 by William Kimberley
Volkswagen Karmann Ghia by Malcolm Bobbitt
VW Bus, Camper, Van, Pickup by Malcolm Bobbitt

First published 1999 by Veloce Publishing Plc., 33, Trinity Street, Dorchester DT1 1TT, England.
Fax: 01305 268864/e-mail: veloce@veloce.co.uk/website: http://www.veloce.co.uk
ISBN: 1-901295-39-7/UPC: 36847-00139-1

British Library Cataloguing in Publication Data -
A catalogue record for this book is available from the British Library.
Typesetting (AGaramond), design and page make-up all by Veloce on AppleMac.
Printed in Hong Kong.

Contents

Introduction

Welcome to this guide to transport museums. Motoring in Britain has produced many famous names: Rolls-Royce, Jaguar and MG are just some of the well known marques of today. But what of the past? Names like Armstrong-Siddeley, Railton, Jowett, Humber, Alvis, Guy and Cotton belong to but a few of the makes that are no longer in production.

Fortunately, we have a great variety of transport museums in these islands where you can still admire fine examples of cars, trucks, buses and motorcycles produced by manufacturers who have either gone out of business, or who have amalgamated with larger firms.

Thriving clubs devoted to single marques or models are a testimony to the esteem in which older marques are held today. Club meetings, rallies, concours and other events take place throughout the year at venues where proud owners display their much-loved motors.

Motor museums in Britain range from the National Motor Museum at Beaulieu, open every day and with a vast collection on display, to the Bugatti Trust near Cheltenham which may have only two cars on display for limited opening hours.

We have sought to list all the museums with their relevant details, such as opening times, refreshment facilities, etc., together with the machines that are usually on display. Many museums have collections greater than the available display space so the exhibits may change from time to time. Many vehicles are on loan from their owners so, again, may be absent from a display for various reasons. Opening times/days may change. If you are planning, therefore, to make a visit to a specific museum it is always a good idea to phone beforehand to check your timetable, and especially whether a specific vehicle which you want to see is on display. Many of the museums are shown as being open on New Year's Day; however, on January 1st 2000, some museums may be closed. The admission prices quoted are the latest available at the time of compilation. Registration numbers, where available, have been included in the guide. When visiting Tourist Information Offices, look out for motor museum brochures as these very often carry a money-off voucher.

There are many museums in this guide, including some specialist ones where collections can only be seen by appointment.

If we have left a collection out, or should you find an incorrect entry, please write to us with details c/o Veloce Publishing. Any other comments and suggestions you may have would also be welcome.

Our sincere thanks to all who have helped in the compilation of this guide, especially Michael Ware, Director of the National Motor Trust. Most of all, thanks to our long-suffering wives who have put up with our passion for old vehicles.

David Burke and Tom Price

Note: From 1st June 1999, new STD codes will come into effect for several places in the UK. London - 0171 becomes 0207; 0181 becomes 0208; Cardiff - 01222 becomes 02920; Coventry - 01203 becomes 02476; Portsmouth - 01705 becomes 02392; Southampton - 01703 becomes 02380; Northern Ireland will have 028 plus a different two numbers for each county. Between 1.6.99 and 22.4.2000 both old and new STDs will work; after 22.4.2000 only the new code will work.

STOP PRESS: A report in the March 30th 1999 issue of *The Times* states that the Government intends to make entry to all national museums and galleries free of charge to the public. Starting in April 1999, children are to be admitted free to these museums, which include the Imperial War Museum and the Science Museum listed in this guide. In 2000, OAPs will have free entry and it is intended to do away with all remaining charges by the end of 2001/beginning of 2002.

Foreword by Nick Scheele, former Chairman and Chief Executive, Jaguar Cars

I was asked to contribute this foreword some months ago, at the time when we were preparing to open our new heritage vehicle centre in Coventry. Like so many other museums, the Jaguar Daimler Heritage Trust Centre is helping to preserve this country's rich automotive history. During the past one hundred years, Britain has played a leading role in the development of the motor vehicle and commercial transport industry. It is an integral, vital and fascinating component of twentieth century culture and we are extremely fortunate that so many of the vehicles which have contributed to our industry's progress have been preserved for the interest and enjoyment of future generations. David Burke and Tom Price's informative and well-researched book gives details of over one hundred transport museums, and is an invaluable guide to all those who are interested in looking at the history of a machine and an industry which has influenced the lives of us all.

Nick Scheele
Coventry, England.

The Shuttleworth Collection, Old Warden Aerodrome, Near Biggleswade, Bedfordshire, SG18 9ER.

Tel. 01767 627288. Marketing: Tony Podmore.
Web site: www.shuttleworth.org/html/main.htm

Old Warden Aerodrome is 2 miles west of the A1, where it bypasses Biggleswade, and approximately 30 miles from Junction 23 on the M25. It can also be accessed by air, with prior permission ,via the above telephone number.

Famous for its magnificent collection of vintage aircraft, the Shuttleworth Collection also has a superb range of equally old cars and motorcycles on display. The aerodrome, which has seven hangars and workshops (some of which are open for viewing engineering activities), is situated on the edge of Old Warden Park, adjacent to a Victorian mansion and the 'Swiss Garden'. Flying displays and special events provide a full calendar throughout the year. There is also a childrens' playground. Motoring enthusiasts cannot fail to appreciate the quality of the aircraft. Open daily, except for one week from Christmas Day to New Year's Day (inclusive). Open: April to October 10.00am to 4.00pm; November to March 10.00am to 3.00pm. Facilities include gift and bookshop, ample free parking, restaurant by Hudson Rowe, toilet and facilities for the disabled.

MOTORCARS			MOTORCYCLES	
1898	Benz 3.5hp 2 seater dog cart	T 274	1900	Singer motor wheel
1899	Mors model A Petit Duc 4hp	F7	1900	March Gordon Quadricycle
1898	Panhard Levassor 12hp	TM 19	1904	Aurora 2.25hp
1900	Marot-Gordon 2.5hp	DPC489	1921	Scott combination
1901	Arrol-Johnson 12hp		1924	Triumph SD 550 cc
1901	Locomobile Stanley steam car	FM 63	1927	Raleigh-type 14
1902	Baby Peugeot 5hp	AA 1417	1927	Raleigh-type 14
1903	De Dietrich 24hp	A 1853	1929	Ariel 550 cc
1903	Richard Brazier 24hp	H 127	1940	BSA WD
1912	Wolseley 24/30 BM	2181	1938	Rudge 500 cc
1912	Crossley 15hp Model	T5 Y 1616	1962	Norton combination ex RAC
1913	Morris Oxford 10hp			
1918	Ford Mod T chassis, Hucks engine	W 8433		
1926	Jowett Light Four	NM 8092	**STEAM ENGINE**	
1931	Austin Burnham 12hp	GT 1944	1914	Clayton and Shuttleworth compound
1934	Austin 7 open tourer	AGG 163		
1935	Austin 7 open tourer			
1937	Railton 8 cylinder 2 seat coupé	JNM 700	Plus a variety of bicycles and horsedrawn vehicles.	
1937	Fiat Topolino			

Admission: OAPs, students and 5-16 years old £3; others £6.00; family ticket, 2 adults and 2 paying children £15; group rates over twenty £4.00 each. Flying and 'special' events are subject to increased prices.

Some of the motorcycles on display at the Shuttleworth Collection, Shuttleworth, Bedfordshire.

One of David Burke's favourites! A superb 1937 Railton 8 cylinder 2 seater coupe at the, Shuttleworth Collection, Shuttleworth, Bedfordshire.

Stondon Museum and Garden Centre, Station Road, Lower Stondon, Henlow, Bedfordshire, SG16 6JN.

Tel. 01462 850339. Curator: Maureen Hird.

Stondon is 35 miles north of London. The Museum is located on the A600, 4 miles from Hitchin, Hertfordshire. There are brown tourist signs showing the way to the Museum.

One of the country's largest private collections of cars: a total of around 350 exhibits of motorcycles, fire engines, army vehicles from the early 1900s to the 1980s, even a Russian SAM missile! These are displayed in five separate halls: hall one, the old timers; hall two ,the forties and fifties; hall three ,the sixties and seventies; hall four,fire engines, tractors, military items, buses and American cars; hall five has an exclusive collection of Rolls-Royce and Bentley motor cars. There is also a replica of Captain Cook's ship, *The Endeavour.*

Open: 7 days a week from 10.00am to 5.00pm. Phone for opening times at Christmas/New Year. Admission: £3 adults; children £1; family ticket £7. Parking (coaches by appointment only). Coffee shop, toilets, picnic area. Special rates for groups. The Curator advises that the list opposite is incomplete, as at least another 100 vehicles have been added since the list was given to us! Lots to look forward to and there is a garden centre there as well.

MOTORCARS

Year	Make	Reg		Year	Make	Reg
1886	Mercedes-Benz replica	N562DNR		1959	Bristol	LXG 1
1913	Lagonda 1400cc	SV6677		1960	Berkeley	872KKM
1914	Ford Model T	YWH 85		1960	Hillman coupé	YYJ309
1923	Chevrolet	FU1391		1961	Austin Metro	TYJ834
1927	Ford Model T	SV4748		1961	Ford Anglia 105E	640NHT
????	Austin Seven	HY8075		1961	Sunbeam Rapier	VVS918
1928	Humber	VL525		1962	Rover P4 saloon	MLT765
1928	Raleigh	VW7461		1964	Bentley S3	3644RA
1929	Swift	VL1912		1964	Bond Minicar	997KO
1930	Rover Ten	GK5752		1964	Humber	EMT399B
1931	Peugeot 201	BSK142		1964	Jaguar Mark X	BDY98B
1932	Morris Minor	EV5568		1964	Sunbeam Rapier	748WCV
1933	Austin Seven	HY8075		1964	Vauxhall Viva	BXD797B
1934	Austin	AHY487		1965	Bentley S3	AHC128C
1934	Jowett	CPC34		1966	Ford Anglia 105E	FED176D
1934	Standard	BPJ956		1966	Ford Corsair	MPG893D
1934	Wolseley Nine	YSV294		1966	Singer Gazelle GFH436D	
1935	Armstrong-Siddeley	AAK233		1966	Sunbeam Alpine	HUA134D
1935	Morris Eight	AWE872		1966	Vanden Plas Princess	LBB349D
1937	Austin Chummy	BZ5314		1966	Wolseley Hornet	FAN930D
1937	Austin Ruby	COG280		1968	Austin Cambridge	WPF685G
1937	Morris Ten	DXO413		1968	Bristol	9888PJ
1938	Austin Cambridge	NSK380		1968	Daimler Limousine	NON682F
1938	Dodge	EXP206		1968	Daimler Jaguar	TAN710F
1938	Ford Model Y saloon	YYJ651		1968	Goggomobil	WUU61
1938	Jowett 10 Javelin	DXE142		1968	Jaguar 420 saloon	VJD214G
1938	Lanchester saloon	ABD676		1968	Morris Minor	SRM84G
1939	Morris Eight	NFF459		1968	Triumph 1300TC	UPG633F
1939	Vauxhall Fourteen	FXN280		1969	Bugatti replica	TKG531H
1949	Armstrong-Siddeley	NNU277		1969	Fiat 500	WML275G
1949	Lanchester Fourteen	SNW34		1969	Ford Cortina	VYX652G
1950	Lanchester	BJE951		1969	Jaguar E-type	RON4G
1951	Allard	MLW872		1969	Rover 3.5	RHP371H
1951	Lea Francis saloon	GBO415		1970	Daf	RAR837H
1951	Triumph Mayflower	JSK748		1971	Jensen Interceptor	WLJ375J
1953	Riley 2.5	NRR712		1971	Reliant	JLB153K
1954	Austin Somerset	GVS369		1971	Sunbeam Rapier	DLR998J
1954	New Hudson	NCE755		1971	Vanden Plas Princess	AAR390K
1954	Rolls-Royce Silver Dawn	OLB3		1971	Volkswagen Beetle	GRK570J
1955	Ford Prefect	UXB586		1971	Volkswagen Karmann Ghia	VXF828M
1955	MG Magnette	ONM526		1973	Citroën SM	YYY153M
1956	Bentley S1	TGO158		1973	Citroën SM, right hand drive	MLE187L
1957	Austin Healey	YPP874		1973	Hillman Hunter	WEH871L
1958	Austin A30	YTX430		1973	Hillman Imp	FJG466L
1958	Ford Fairlane	VSU508		1973	Jensen Interceptor	GYY401L
1958	MG Magnette	SFJ300		1973	Morris Marina	PBL756M
1958	Wolseley	TVS582		1973	Triumph Spitfire	VCH546M

An Austin Seven, one of the many exhibits at Stondon Museum and Garden Centre, Bedfordshire.
(Courtesy Ron Middleton)

A 1938 Lanchester saloon at Stondon Museum and Garden Centre, Bedfordshire.
(Courtesy Ron Middleton)

1974	Bond Bug	PGB409M
1974	Rover 2200	XNK789M
1974	Tatra	ABE9931
1974	Triumph 2000 estate car	NMJ345M
1975	Enfield electric car	YYX698N
1976	Citroën Maserati	OPW456P
1977	Triumph Stag	VDF66S
1978	Bristol 603	603EOW
1978	Oldsmobile	UCN940S
1978	Reliant Scimitar	ETA548T
1978	Triumph Dolomite	BYB14S
1979	Ferrari	TTW3V
1979	Ford Escort Ghia	DVS447T
1979	Peugeot 405	JNV89T
1979	Rolls-Royce Corniche	FJS22
1979	Rolls-Royce Silver Shadow II	MUM87
1980	Aston Martin Lagonda	GYV960W
1980	Lincoln Continental	VCG670V
1980	Triumph TR7	GOV680W
1981	Renault Five	XBH236X
1982	Maserati	GGH446X
1982	Maserati	GGH447X
1982	Panther J72	CRO598X
1982	Rolls-Royce Camargue	FJS32
1984	Chrysler (USA)	A14FJS
1984	Reliant Fox	A250PKP
1984	Trabant	A175ANK
1985	Citroën 2CV	B958KUF
1985	Cursor	C722CKP
1988	Bentley Eight	F160TLW

MOTORCYCLES

1914	Douglas	HB763
1919	ABC Scooter	BD4072
1920	ABC	BN4384
1922	Terrot	WE1
1924	AJS	KK9166
1925	Humber	SV5306
1928	Ariel motorcycle combination	DF5197
1930	Velocette	VK2966
1931	BSA	ESK359
1932	BSA Tricycle	RH4909
1934	Rudge	not registered
1934	BSA Tricycle	BKE89
1935	Sunbeam	AUR279
1939	Francis Barnett	LVS625
1947	BSA	MKX368
1947	Corgi	HSV823
1948	James	JRT977
1948	Scott	KTU879
1949	BSA Bantam	NVS279
1949	Sunbeam	BGR344
1950	Sunbeam	MSK342
1950	Triumph display motorcycle	not reg.
1952	Ariel	TFC2552
1953	Cyclemaster	

1953	James	HJY384
1954	Matchless Army	WDX515A
1954	Triumph	MSK167
1954	Vincent	TVK960
1955	Velocette LE	GVS369
1957	Douglas Dragonfly	698SC
1957	Excelsior	XRL579
1958	Ariel motorcycle combination	NAN856
1959	BSA	WXV101
1960	BSA	HVS 803
1961	AA m/b sidecar	949ARW
1965	AJS	HLE795C
1971	Cossack Ural	
1972	Jawa Scrambler	
1973	Solo Electra	ANC110M
1975	Gilera	JYC125N
1978	BMW	WDB476S
1981	Benelli	PEL938W
1985	Honda Stream	B710AGE
	Swiss Army motorcycle	

COMMERCIAL

1926	AEC single decker bus	VA5777
1937	Morris commercial van	No reg.
1948	Bradford van	NSK358
1968	Austin A35 van	PYO95F
	(Unique, experimental 4 w/d Metro size car)	
1971	Winchester taxi	EGW710J
1973	Reliant van	HOM779L
1973	Ford campervan	CTT479L

MISCELLANEOUS

1948	Ferguson tractor	LVF372
1953	Dennis fire engine	PYB781
1960	Mack pumper F' engine, USA	ESK716
1966	Merryweather fire engine	JUL57D
1968	Bedford flat lorry	ANK157G
1978	Wales and Edwards milk float	YVL255S
1982	Jeep pick up	RCF775Y
1985	Volvo Snowcat	Q516PFE
1990	Rover Scout original reg	H539NOA
????	Fordson tractor	DNG407
????	Wartburg	IH45-85
????	Titanic (donated by RAF)	
????	Sinclair C5 electric trike	
????	Bedford fire engine	
????	Tennant roadsweeper	
????	Saunders Roe helicopter	
????	Benson girocopter	
????	Russian SAM missile, tractor unit	
????	Abbot tank	
????	Russian aquacar	IYA3-55
????	Rickshaw	
????	Trabant 1	1150 89

Stockwood Craft Museum and Gardens, Farley Hill, Luton, Bedfordshire, LU1 4BH.
Tel. 01582 738714. Principal Keeper: Marian Nichols.

Stockwood Museum is located close to Junction 10 of the M1 and the Stockwood Park Pavilion and Golf Course. It is close to Luton rail and bus stations.

The Craft Museum and Gardens also house the Mossman Collection of horsedrawn vehicles, the largest of its kind on display in Britain, which tells the story of horsedrawn transport before the invention of the motorcar. The story of transport is brought into the 20th century with the Transport Gallery which includes displays of bicycles, a model of the Luton tram system and vintage cars. Stockwood country park is adjacent to the Museum. Free parking, toilets, facilities (including parking) for the disabled, tea room, gift shop, picnic area, horsedrawn vehicle rides. Special days throughout the year including transport events. Hamilton Finlay sculpture garden.

Exhibits include an early F-type Vauxhall Victor saloon and a Vauxhall Viva, plus several cars which are on loan from the Chiltern Vehicle Preservation Group. The Group organises an annual Transport Festival which normally takes place on the second Sunday in June. It includes a rare opportunity to see the Vauxhall Heritage collection at Luton. The Group operates a service to Luton from Stockwood using vintage buses. For details contact the Secretary, Mike Cain, on 01582 872587.

The Collection

1928	Austin Chummy tourer
1928	Morris Oxford tourer
1937	Vauxhall 14hp saloon
1945	Talbot Nine tourer
1950	Lanchester Twelve saloon
1959	MGA sports

In addition, the Group haa a unique Ariel Arrow twin two stroke sectional motorcycle which was rescued from the Ariel factory when it closed, plus a BSA Bantam 125cc and a TWN 199cc split single motorcycle. There is also a display of automobila centred around a 1950s replica garage, together with some interesting pedal cars.

Open in summer (April to October) Tuesday to Saturday between 10.00am and 5.00pm; Sundays 10.00am to 6.00pm. Winter (November to March) Saturday and Sunday 10.00am to 4.00pm. Owned by Luton Borough Council. Admission is free but the Museum does welcome donations.

Vauxhall Heritage Centre, F/1, Griffin House, Osborne Road, Luton, Bedfordshire, LU1 3YT.

Tel. 01582 426527. Curators: Bernard Ridgley and Ray Cooper.

Directions will be provided when viewing arrangements are made.

This is Vauxhall Motor Company's historic vehicle collection and is normally only open to organised clubs and groups. There is an annual public Open Day operated in conjunction with the Festival of Transport at Stockwood Craft Museum (see separate entry), run by the Chiltern Vehicle Preservation Group.

The Collection totals 58 vehicles, a few of which are kept at the company's Ellesmere Port factory.

The Collection includes:

1903	Vauxhall single cylinder, 5hp - the 45th car built by Vauxhall, chassis no. 0345, believed to be the oldest complete Vauxhall car in existence
1904	Vauxhall 6hp, built by Vauxhall Iron Works, the forerunner of Vauxhall Motors
1905	Vauxhall 3 cylinder, twin cam, 1558cc two seater
1909	Vauxhall 4 cylinder, B-type 2.3, two seater semi-sports
1911	Vauxhall Prince Henry C-type, 4 cylinder, 3 litre, four seater
1918	Vauxhall staff car D-type, 4 litre, four seater
1923	Vauxhall 23/60 OD-type, 4 cylinder, ohv, four seater Kington Tourer
1923	Vauxhall M-type 2.3 litre Princeton Tourer 14/40
1924	Vauxhall 24 M-type 2.3 litre Melton
1926	Vauxhall 30/98 OE-type 4.25 litre, ohv, four seater Velox tourer
1929	Vauxhall R-type 20.9hp, ohv, 6 cylinder Bedford Saloon
1930	Vauxhall 20/60 T-type 20.9hp, Melton Golfer's coupé
1932	Vauxhall Cadet 6 cylinder, 17hp, four seater saloon
1936	Vauxhall B-type 6 cylinder, 27hp, Grosvenor BXL Limousine
1938	Vauxhall H-type 10hp, 4 cylinder, four seater saloon (first British car of integral construction)
1953	Vauxhall E-type Wyvern 4 cylinder saloon
1959	Vauxhall PA Velox 6 cylinder saloon
1959	Vauxhall F-type Victor, 4 cylinder, 1503cc saloon
1961	Vauxhall Victor 1503cc saloon
1964	Vauxhall HA Viva, 4 cylinder, 1057cc saloon
1964	Vauxhall FB Victor GW estate car, 1594cc
1965	Vauxhall Victor 101, 1594cc, four door saloon
1965	Vauxhall PB Cresta four door saloon
1966	Vauxhall HB Viva SL saloon
1966	Vauxhall HB Viva ,1159cc saloon
1971	Vauxhall PC Viscount, 3294cc, 4 door saloon
1971	Vauxhall FD Victor Ventura, 3.3 litre, four door saloon
1975	Vauxhall FE Victor, 2003cc, four door saloon
1981	Vauxhall Series 1 Cavalier, 1596cc, four door saloon
1983	Vauxhall Series 2 Cavalier saloon
1993	Vauxhall Lotus Carlton saloon
1995	Vauxhall Series 3 Cavalier saloon

COMMERCIALS

1931	Bedford 26hp, 6 cylinder, dropside truck
1931	Bedford 14 seater bus

1959 Vauxhall Victor F-type 4 cylinder saloon. The famous Vauxhall 'flutes' were incorporated in the front side panels.

Admission: free

1905 Vauxhall 3 cylinder, twin cam two seater. A rare vehicle from the Vauxhall Heritage Collection.

History on Wheels Motor Museum, Longelose House, Little Common Road, Eton Wick, near Windsor, Berkshire. SL4 6QY.
Tel. 01753-862637.

Access is via junction 7 of the M4 onto A4 (west) at roundabout by Sainsburys, left on to B3026 (signed Eton Wick or Datchet) through Dorney and over the cattle grid. This takes you on to the common. Continue on this road across the common until you enter Eton Wick. Take the first left after the shops and follow the dead end road as far as it will go. At the fork in the road, take a right turn; the Museum is at the end of the lane.

Built up over the past 25 years, this private museum contains over a hundred vehicles. The military section alone is said to be one of the best displays of its type and includes display dummies dressed in militaria. Hot and cold snacks may be available from the NAAFI canteen adjoining the entrance area. Admission: adults £2.50, OAPs/children (5-16 years) £1.25.

The Museum is open by prior request. Toilets and parking available.

The Collection includes:

1920s Citroën taxi
1950s Post Office Van

Plus various vehicles that have been used in film and TV series such as:
The Battle of Britain
Bergerac
Raiders of the Lost Ark

Royal Electrical and Mechanical Engineers Museum of Technology, Regimental HQ, Isaac Newton Road, Arborfield, Berkshire, RG2 9NJ.

Tel. 01189 763567. Deputy Curator: B. S. Baxter. e-mail: reme-museum@gtnet.gov.uk

Location: from the A325 Farnham/ Petersfield road 8 miles south of Farnham, turn west to Bordon Camp. Reading, the nearest large town, is 39 miles west of London.

The REME museum at Arborfield is, at the time of writing, undergoing an extensive redevelopment programme. As a consequence, the transport collection, which is only a part of the Museum's exhibits, is housed at Bordon Camp. Visitors are welcome but prior booking must be made with Roger Jones on 01420 485544. By the time you read this copy, it is hoped that part of the Collection will have been returned to Arborfield.

Leyland 6x5 wheeled recovery vehicle, fitted with a 15 ton winch.

At Bordon Camp, opening hours are by arrangement. Admission is free. Catering for parties by arrangement. Disabled access. Parking free. At Arborfield, all of the usual facilities are available.

DOMESTIC & NON-SPECIALIST VEHICLES

Land Rover GS Series 2¾ ton truck	
Austin Champ CT ¼ ton truck	Q2500R
Austin Champ CT ¼ ton and ¾ ton trailer	
Bedford RL/GS, 3 ton truck	72FG99
Armoured Humber 1 ton truck	26BK80
Rover 1 ton cargo	54BT08
Ford E2, store binned 3 ton truck	
AEC 10 ton tractor	01CE06
Thornycroft 10 ton Big Ben tractor	Q521CPF
Alvis Stalwart 5 ton load carrier	07ER86
House-type semi trailer 10 ton	
BSA B40	
Canam motorcycle	33HG58
BSA M20 motorcycle	OAU 68F
Eager Beaver rough terrain fork lift	05FW61

OVERSAW VEHICLES

ST Snowtrac vehicle	56RN55
Volvo BV vehicle	41GJ29

TRACKED RECOVERY & REPAIR VEHICLES

Conqueror armoured recovery Mk20	1BB88
Centurion armoured recovery Mk 20	0ZR12
Centurion armoured recovery Mk 20	3ZR57
Chieftain armoured repair and recovery	00BB81
Challenger armoured repair and recovery	70KG64
Sherman M74 tracked. recovery vehicle	
Churchill armoured recovery Mk 25	1ZR94
Sherman beach recovery vehicle	
M578 armoured recovery vehicle	04ED82
Chinese armoured recovery vehicle	
Samson Combat recovery, tracked ARV	03SP38
T72 armoured recovery vehicle	
REME ½ track, ¾ ton truck	Q920 NTR
FV432 armoured personnel. carrier	08EA44
FV434 Carrier maintenance truck	01ED80

WHEELED RECOVERY VEHICLES

AEC wheeled medium recovery	TOR 95G
Volvo EKA wheeled recovery vehicle	TBK 113J
Chevrolet 3 ton light recovery	MSU 674
Leyland heavy recovery	Q566 OBD
Ward La France truck wrecker	ASJ 449
Austin 3 ton breakdown truck	GSU 679

Scammell Pioneer tractor heavy breakdown SV1S	Q9
Scammell Pioneer tractor heavy b'down SV2S USU	210
Scammell Pioneer tractor heavy b'down SV2S	36XZ08
Scammell Explorer GS tractor heavy recovery	34BC92
Ditto, with a diesel engine	Q71 FLF
Scammell Explorer heavy recovery tractor	Q921 NTR
Scammell EKA wheeled recovery vehicle	66GT50
Foden wheeled recovery vehicle	04HJ08
Bedford 3 ton light recovery vehicle	Q347 OBP
Bedford MJP light recovery vehicle	02HJ88
NTR 20 Western Star wheeled r/v	B523XOW
Thornycroft Hathi tractor	JPL 545
Land Rover 1 ton folding crane	F3FL42

WHEELED ARMED RECOVERY VEHICLES

Ferret wheeled ARV	
Saxon wheeled armoured recovery vehicle	00WA75

TANK TRANSPORTERS & TRAILERS

Thornycroft Antar 30 ton tractor	Q743 OCR
50 ton trailer tank transporter	40BR31
7 ton trailer light recovery	56YL50
10 ton trailer light recovery	24DE21
Scammell Pioneer 30 ton semi-trailer	JRV 240P

WORKSHOP & REPAIR VEHICLES

AEC 10 ton power repair platform	14EK06
Albion 10 ton machinery truck	Q922NTR
Albion 10 ton machinery truck	55BK79
Albion 10 ton machinery repair truck	Q924 NTR
Bedford QL 3 ton machinery truck	Q925 NTR
Bedford RL 3 ton repair truck	Q741 OCR
Commer Q4 3 ton telecomm truck	36BH41
Commer Q4 3 ton fuel inj repair truck	Q26 NTR
Alvis Stalwart high load carrier	91ET61
Austin K9 1 ton radio repair truck	81BG80
Land Rover 1 ton fwd drive repair crane	69FL11
Land Rover 1 ton electrical repair shop	54BT07

MISCELLANEOUS COMBAT VEHICLES

Chieftain main battle tank	01FD40
ZSU23/4 light anti-aircraft tank	
Rapier missile system, tracked	
Dummy Rapier missile launcher trailer	
Launcher Giant Viper trailer	

Commer 3 ton 4x4 fuel injection equipment repair truck. Contains test equipment and tools within a dust-free container body.

...ht Austin K6 3 ton 6x4 breakdown truck, fitted with a 5 ton winch.

Bedford RL 3 ton 4x4 light recovery tractor. Fitted with a 5 ton winch.

...dford QL 3 ton 4x4 type M machinery truck. Fitted with a lathe and other powered tools.

Aston Manor Transport Museum, Old Tram Depot, 208-216, Witton Lane, Birmingham, B6 6QE.

Tel. 0121 322 2298 (24-hour information line).
Chairman: Malcolm Cooper.

Location: approximately 1.5 miles from junction 6 of the M6, near Aston Villa F.C. ground. The Museum is at the far end of Witton Lane. Witton Rail station is a short walk and the Service 7 bus from Central Birmingham goes to Witton Square.

A registered charity, the Museum is open at weekends throughout the year. Opening hours: 11.00am until 5.00pm with last admission at 4.30pm. Usually open Saturdays and Sundays but phone first for special times during September and Christmas.

On special event days or Bank Holidays, admission charges may be altered. For group admission at other times prior booking is required. Disabled access (except shop). Free car and coach park. Shop and cafe.

Exhibits include:

BUSES & COACHES		LORRIES, VANS & MISCELLANEOUS	
1931 AEC Regal	JF2378	1923 Ford Model T	CJ5811
1946 Maudslay Marathon Mk III	DDM652	1928 Dennis 2.5 ton delivery van	PX7867
1949 BMMO C1	KHA311	1937 Scammell MH3 Mechanical Horse	CUV754
1950 Sentinel STC4	GUJ608	1948 Fordson 7V	HVP167
1950 Guy Wolf	SB8155	1950 Lister road sweeper	
1951 Daimler CVD6	JOJ707	1954 Austin A40 ice cream van	BJM567
1954 Leyland Royal Tiger PSU1/13	NLJ271	1959 Morrison milk float	XVP785
1954 Daimler CLG5	LOG302	1965 Ford Transit	EEA508D
1956 Sunbeam F4A trolleybus	XDH72	1965 Wales and Edwards milk float	DVP519C
1964 BMMO D9	6370HA	1969 Wales and Edwards milk float	ROL982G
1967 BMMO S21	LHA870F	1971 Wales and Edwards milk float	WOL877J
1971 Daimler Fleetline CRG6LX	XON41J		
1976 Bristol VR	JOV714P	There were 10 other vehicles undergoing restoration at
1979 Leyland Fleetline FE30AGR	WDA700T	the time of compilation.
1988 MCW Metrorider MF150/113	F685YOG		

Some of the bus and electric vehicle exhibits in Aston Manor Transport Museum, near Aston Villa football ground, Birmingham. (Courtesy Aston Manor Transport Museum)

Admission: adults £1; children 50p; family tickets, two adults and three children £2.75.

The Discovery Centre, Digbeth, Birmingham (opens September 2001)
Tel. Information Officer on 0121-303-2983.

The Discovery Centre is at Millennium Point, off the A47 at Jennens Lane, which is accessed from the M6 junction with the A38 (known as Spaghetti Junction). It is a 5 minute walk from Birmingham centre and New St. rail station.

The old Birmingham Museum of Science & Industry in Newhall Street, Birmingham, closed in October 1997. A superb new museum is now under construction, the Discovery Centre at Millenium Point, Birmingham.

At the Discovery Centre, transport will have a major place with "The Age of the Car" section leading to "Transport of the Future" and a nearby "Transport Systems" section. It is planned to open on September 29th 2001 and enquiries may be made to the Visitor Information Officer on the above number,

Transport exhibits which were formerly shown at Newhall Street should be on show at the new centre.

The Collection should include:

MOTORCARS

Year	Description	Reg
1898	Star, made by Star Motor Co., Wolverhampton	
1900	Benz Dogcart	RX997
1912	BSA Tourer, 65,000 miles from new	CH676
1920	Lanchester Petrol/electric car, wooden body & suspension	OP13
1923	Austin 7 Chummy soft top saloon	XO4133
1924	Ariel 10hp (Ariel made cars before motorcycles)	HU3012
1927	Bean 14hp coupé	
1932	MG Midget (J series) sports version of Morris Minor MG TC	7775MG
1932	Austin 7 saloon de luxe	KY2999
1934	Riley Imp Sports, competed in 1934 Le Mans race	WG3688
1935	Austin Lichfield saloon with 10hp engine	AOM470
1947	Railton Mobil Special, driven by John Cobb, holder of 394mph world land speed record	
1949	Austin A90 Atlantic convertible	HOM841
1958	Jaguar XK150	WWR352
1959	Morris Mini Minor	XEW583
1969	Riley Elf cutaway model.	
1971	Rover P5B	FYU450J
1976	Metro 6R4, 6 cylinder 4 wheel drive rally car	D222ERW

MOTORCYCLES

Year	Description	Year	Description
1902	Singer	1948	Velocette LE
1904	Rex	1951	Vincent Black Shadow
1920	Lewis	1951	BSA Bantam
1926	AJS	1955	Ariel Huntmaster
1931	Brough Superior Seagull	1958	BSA AA Patrol inc. sidecar
1936	Francis Barnett	1962	Velocette Viper
1937	Manx Norton	1982	Hesketh
1939	Royal Enfield	1982	Triumph TSX

Admission: there will be an admission charge, but details are not yet available.

Birmingham and Midland Museum of Transport, Chapel Lane, Wythall, Birmingham, West Midlands, B47 6JX.
Tel. 01564 826471. Curator and Trustee: Paul Gray. Web site: www.solnet.co.uk/bammot

The Museum is reached from the A435 dual carriageway, Redditch to Birmingham road. It is signposted from the nearest roundabout on that road.

A specialist collection of buses, coaches, commercial vehicles, fire engines and battery electric vehicles. Open from April to the end of October at weekends only, plus some Bank Holidays and other event days.

Bus rides of the collection are available at most times when the Museum is open. There's a miniature railway, coffee shop and picnic area, plus specialist publications are on sale at the gift shop. Limited parking is available nearby and a bus service from the Museum does a ferry run to the site.

The Museum started in its present form in 1977 when the Charity Commission agreed to award it Trust status. Since then, through several phases of development, additional land has been acquired and buildings constructed. The Museum now has two large halls and three and a half acres of land, which accommodates buses, fire engines, lorries and, unusually, a large collection of commercial electric vehicles. Manned entirely by volunteers from the outset, this quality collection and its buildings must be the envy of many.

In common with many museums, the visible collection is only a small part of the stock. Time, lack of funds and the sheer labour involved in restoration often dictates what is and isn't on show.

Admission: 13th April/ 7th June/31st August/ 31st October: adults £3.00; OAP/child/ unemployed £1.50; family (2 + 2) £6.00. 4 May/25 May/9 August: £2.00; £1.00 and £5.00. All other weekends: £1.25; £0.75 and £3.50. Admission charges vary with the day. Normal opening hours on open days are 11.00am until 4.00pm.

Exhibits include:

THE MIDLAND RED COLLECTION		
1913	Tilling-Stevens TTA2	O 9726
1925	Standard SOS	HA 3501
1927	SOS Q	CN 2870
1928	SOS QL	CC 7745
1935	SOS DON	AHA 582
1940	SOS SON	GHA 337
1946	BMMO S6	HHA 637
1950	BMMO S12	NHA 744
1951	BMMO D5B	NHA 795
1953	Leyland Titan PD2/20	SHA 431
1955	BMMO S14	UHA 255
1960	BMMO D10	943 KHA
1961	BMMO D9	3016 HA
1962	BMMO S15	5073 HA
1964	BMMO S16	6545 HA
1965	BMMO D9	BHA 399
1965	BMMO CM6T	BHA 656C
1966	BMMO S17	EHA 767D
1966	Daimler Fleetline CRG6	GHA 415D
1967	BMMO S21	JHA 868E
1969	Leyland Leopard PSU4A/4R	SHA 645G
1970	BMMO S23	UHA 956
1970	BMO 923	UHA 981H
1974	Ford R1014	PHA 370M
1976	Leyland National	NOE 544R

BIRMINGHAM CITY TRANSPORT COLLECTION

1931	Morris Commercial Dictator	OV 4090
1931	AEC Regent 1	OV 4486
1933	Morris Commercial Imperial	OC 527
1937	Daimler COG5	CVP 207
1948	Leyland Titan PD2/1	HOV 685
1950	Leyland Tiger PS2/1	JOJ 245
1950	Guy Arab IV	JOJ 533
1953	Guy Arab IV	JOJ 976
1957	Guy Arab IV	SUK 3
1965	Daimler Fleetline CRG6	BON 474C
1968	Daimler Fleetline CRG6	COX 780F

ALSO SERVING THE WEST MIDLANDS		
1948	Leyland Tiger PS1	GUE 247
1949	Sunbeam F4	FJW 616
1966	Leyland Titan PD2A/27	HBF 679D
1950	Leyland Tiger PS2/3	JUE 349
1953	Leyland Royal Tiger PSU1	PDH 808
1953	Walsall Leyland Titan PD2/12	RDH 505
1958	Bedford SB3	VVP 911
1966	Leyland Titan PD2A/27	HBF 679D
1967	Daimler Roadliner SRC6	NJW 719E
1968	Daimler CRC6-36	XDH 56G
1968	Daimler Fleetline CRG6	NEA 101F
1969	Daimler Fleetline CRG6	XDH516G
1963	Daimler CVG6/30	248 NEA
1974	Volvo Ailsa ABS	TOE 527N
1975	Daimler Fleetline CRG6	JOV 613P
1976	Leyland Fleetline FE30 ALR	KON 311P

BRISTOL FASHION

1950	Bristol L5G	KFM 775
1961	Bristol Lodekka FSF6G	802 MHW
1967	Bristol RELL6L	KHW 306E
1969	Bristol RELH6G	OTA 632G
1970	Bristol RELL6G	WNG 864H
1970	Bristol VRT/SL2	FRB 211H
1972	Bristol VRT/SL3	CBD 778K
1972	Bristol VRT/SL2	OWE271K
1973	Bristol RELH6G	TCH 274L

LONDON TRANSPORT

1948	AEC Regent III 0961	JXC 432
1952	AEC Regal IV 9821LT	MXX 23
1965	AEC Routemaster	CUV 219C

OTHER BUSES

1937	AEC Regal 0662	RC 4615
1947	Leyland Titan PD2/3	FFY 402
1948	Foden PVD6	FDM 724
1948	Leyland Titan PD1	JRR 404
1948	Daimler CVD6	KAL 579
1949	Albion Venturer CX19	HDG 448
1949	Guy Arab III	HWO 334
1955	Leyland Titan PD2/12	FRC 956
1957	Guy Otter NLLODP	UTU 596J
1958	Albion Victor FT39	HFO 742

1959	Leyland Tiger Cub PSUC1	WDF 569
1966	Leyland Titan PD3A/1	GRY 60D
1974	Leyland National	GNU 569N
1974	Leyland National	JMY 120N
1976	Den Oudsten	No reg.

COMMERCIAL VEHICLES

1935	Leyland Tigress	BOF 389
1936	Leyland Titan TD4	CKO 998
1952	Bedford SB Special	LYP 118
1956	Bedford A4SS	SYF 431
1956	Bedford A	TGJ 341
1961	Karrier	VPM 560
1966	BMC FFK 100	JBF 460 D

BATTERY ELECTRIC COLLECTION

1935	7 cwt CY2 Electricar, Airline	AOX 653
1947	10/14 cwt Bush Mk II, delivery	HYN 86
1950	15 cwt Standard milk truck	XMT 422
1953	20 cwt D1 M-E , bakery	NVP 144
1954	20 cwt D1 M-E ex milk	OOA 655
1954	15 cwt Partridge-Wilson, bakery	LBC136
1955	10 cwt Helecs milk truck	RLW610
1957	10/14 cwt SS milk truck	WOA 26
1958	15 cwt Intermediate milk truck	XOG847
1964	15 cwt D5 M-E milk	ERO620B

A 1937 AEC Regal coach, one of many exhibits at the Birmingham and Midland Transport Museum, Wythall, Birmingham.

The Black Country Living Museum, Tipton Road, Dudley, West Midlands, DY1 4SQ.

Tel. 01215 579643 for information.
Web site: http://www.bclm.co.uk
e-mail: Info@bclm.co.uk

Only 3 miles from junction 2 of the M5 motorway and 6 miles from junction 10 of the M6, the Museum is easily accessible from the Midlands motorway network. Located 1 mile north of Dudley town centre and 9 miles west of Birmingham city centre.

Reputed to be one of Britain's best open-air museums, the Black Country Living Museum is the perfect place to visit for a family day out, with a difference. Original buildings from around the Black Country, including shops, houses, a school, chapel and pub, have been dismantled brick by brick, reconstructed and furnished to create an old-fashioned canalside village, and much more, on a 26 acre site.

Museum visitors enjoy a warm welcome from the many costumed demonstrators and working craftsmen who bring the buildings to life. The whole day can be spent enjoying the Museum's many attractions and features. Wander around the shops and houses of the old-fashioned village, tour the underground coal mine, enjoy classic silent comedy in the Limelight Cinema, plus sweet making, glass-cutting and chain-making demonstrations. Take a ride on an electric tram, or on the trolleybus on its 1200 metre circuit of the site.

The Transport Collection features some fine, rare vehicles such as the 1926 REO 'Speedway' Charabanc which is in use around the site.

Most buildings are accessible to wheelchairs by ramp. Facilities include baby changing facilities, gift shops, Stables restaurant and fish and chip shop. Free car and coach parking.

Open: March to October every day 10.00am to 5.00pm. November to February, Wednesday to Sunday 10.00am to 4.00pm. Closed 21st-25th of December inclusive. Admission (1998): adults £6.95; senior citizens £5.95; children £4.50; family ticket (2 + 3) £19.50. Tunnel and fairground optional extras. Group rates for booked parties of ten or more.

Exhibits

1904 Turner steam car	1926 Bean 25 cwt 14hp flat bed truck
1911 Turner petrol car	1926 REO Speedwagon
1912 Turner 10hp 4 cylinder, 3 speed gearbox, petrol	1931 AJS saloon, 9hp car
1919/20 Wolverhampton train no. 34	1931 Star, 4 door coupé, 'Comet 18,'18/50hp 6 cyl
1920 Dudley/Stourbridge tram no. 5	1936 Stevens Brothers, 3 wheeled van
1925 Bean 14hp long tourer	1946 Wolverhampton trolleybus (433) Sunbeam W
	1951 'D' Contessa, 200cc, motorcycle
	1955 Walsall trolleybus (862) Sunbeam F4A

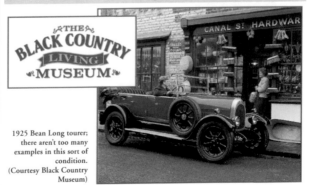

1925 Bean Long tourer; there aren't too many examples in this sort of condition. (Courtesy Black Country Museum)

National Motorcycle Museum, Coventry Road, Bickenhill, Solihull, West Midlands, B92 0EJ.

Tel. 01675 443311. Curator: Roy Richards.

Location: By car to the junction of the M42 and the A45, opposite the National Exhibition Centre (NEC). By train to the Birmingham international mainline station. By air, from Birmingham International Airport via the bus to the NEC.

Set on an eight and a half acre site, the purpose-built complex is at home in its landscaped surroundings. The short list of Museum motorcycles shown below is a small percentage of the 750 motorcycles displayed in four ground floor exhibition halls, each machine restored to original condition. This museum presents one of the finest opportunities for the enthusiast to view over ninety years of British motorcycles. A wealth of historic documentation and photographs enable the visitor to mentally recreate the past. Many of the exhibits have a history of racing, including 'Slippery Sam,' winner of five production races in the Isle of Man TT. There's too much to describe; you should visit!

There is a well stocked shop with books, gifts of all sorts, posters and souvenirs. The restaurant offers a range of food from snacks to a full meal. Disabled facilities, toilets and access to shops and exhibits. Free parking for cars and coaches.

Open: every day, except Christmas, Boxing and New Year's days 10am to 6pm. Admission: adults £4.50, OAPs and children (5 to 16) £3.25. Concessions for organised party visits of 20 or more.

MOTORCYCLES

1898	Royal Enfield 736cc Interceptor Mk 11
1906	Lloyd Thomas 3hp
1898	Royal Enfield 2¾hp quad
1898	Dennis 'Speed King' trike
1898	Beeston Humbler tricycle 400cc
1902	BAT 327cc
1902	Clement Victoria 145cc
1902	Century Forecar 3½hp
1903	Excelsior
1904	MMC 2¾hp
1904	Ormonde 1¾hp
1904	Riley 4½hp watercooled Forecar
1905	Rexette 5hp trike
1906	Imperial 500cc
1907	Fairy 2hp horizontal twin
1908	Norton V twin JAP 750cc
1909	Arno TT
1909	Premier V twin 548cc
1910	Auto Carrier delivery tricar
1910	Lincoln Elk 499cc
1911/2	Brough 3½hp
1912	Campion V twin Rex 5hp
1912	Humber 3½hp
1912	New Imperial JAP engine 500cc
1913	Rover 500cc and wickerwork sidecar
1913	Abingdon 696cc V twin
1914	Premier 499cc
1914	Invicta, Villiers, 269cc
1915	New Hudson 770cc s/c elec. lighting
1918	Rover 700cc JAP V twin
1919	Ixion 269cc
1920	Metro-Tyler 269cc two stroke
1920	Norton 500cc s/v Model 9
1920	Stafford Mobile Pup scooter 150cc
1921	68θcc V twin
1921	Kingsbury 170cc scooter
1921	Ariel 500cc
1922	Sunbeam 4½hp 599cc
1923	Grigg 343cc Villiers

1924	Diamond JAP 250cc
1925	Dunelt 250cc, sidecar, 2 stroke
1925	James 500cc V twin
1925	Chater Lea Blackburne 348cc
1926	Douglas 500cc Sports
1926	New Hudson 596cc ohv Super Vitesse
1926/7	Zenith 680cc s/valve JAP '680'
1927	Norton 500cc Model 21
1928	BSA 174cc 2 stroke
1929	Scott 298cc
1929	AJS 9hp, 2 seater
1930	Brough Superior ohv 680
1933	Rudge Radial four valve 350cc
1933	Rudge Whitworth 499cc, semi-radial valve, ex-works
1934	Sunbeam 500cc Model 95 racer
1934	New Imperial 250cc works racer
1934	Excelsior 500cc ohv racer
1934	Norton International 350cc
1934	Rudge 500cc semi-radial valve racer
1935	Rudge 500cc semi-radial valve racer
1936	Excelsior 250cc 4 valve radial 'Manxman'
1936	Excelsior 250 'Manxman'
1936	OEC 1000cc
1936	New Imperial 250cc works racer
1936	Excelsior Manxman 250cc Special
1937	Scott 596cc Flying Squirrel
1938	AJS 350cc ohc
1938	Excelsior Manxman ex-works racer 250cc
1938	Excelsior Manxman ex-works racer 350cc
1939	Brough Superior 1150 model/cruiser sidecar
1939	Brough Superior SC 100, 1000cc
1939	OK Supreme 250cc ohc
1947	International Norton 490cc ex-George Formby
1948	Velocette 348cc Model KSS
1949	Velocete KTT Mk VIII racer 348cc

1949	Scott Flying Squirrel 596cc	1959	BSA 250cc ohv Model C15 Star
1949	Corgi Runabout 98cc	1960	Meteor Minor Royal Enfield 496cc twin
1950	Ariel KG gwin 498cc	1962	Royal Enfield Crusader Sports 248cc
1952	Velocette 192cc Model LE	1965	DMW 250cc 'Hornet'
1952	P&M Panther 598cc	1965	Matchless CSR. 650cc twin
1953	DMW 125cc 'Hornet'	1966	Cotton Telstar 247cc
1955	Velocette Venom 499cc	1966	DMW 500cc 'Typhoon'
1956	Ariel Fieldmaster, sectioned twin engine 498cc	1966	Triumph TT Bonneville 650cc
1957	Ariel 500cc HS Mk 111	1970	Ariel 3 wheel moped 50cc
1958	Ariel 646c Twin 'Cyclone'	1985	Armstrong 500cc ex-military

An early Ariel outside the National Motorcycle Museum.

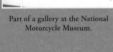

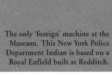

Part of a gallery at the National Motorcycle Museum.

The only 'foreign' machine at the Museum. This New York Police Department Indian is based on a Royal Enfield built at Redditch.

Patrick Motor Museum, 180, Lifford Lane, Kings Norton, Birmingham, B30 3NT.

Tel. 01527 857799. Curator: John Ward.
Address for correspondence - Priory Mill, Castle Road, Studley, Warwickshire, B80 7AA.

The Collection is located near Kings Norton rail station. By car, take junction 3 of the M42 and then travel towards Birmingham on the A435. Lifford Lane is off Wharf Road and Baldwin Road and the A441 Kings Norton to Birmingham Road.

Several years ago, Autoworld, as the Collection was then known, had to close for various reasons. Recently the remaining Collection has been made available for public viewing but only on a group basis; minimum group size is ten people. Guided tours can be arranged if required. The Collection comprises some 70 cars, 45 of which are on display. The vehicles are all of a high standard and include a number of rare models.

There is access for the disabled and also toilets. Parking is permitted and the facilities of The Mill House Hotel (Tel. 0121 459 5800), which is adjacent to the Museum, are available. Another major tourist attraction, the Cadbury World exhibition, is nearby.

Exhibits include:

MOTORCARS

Year	Model	Reg
1904	Wolseley 12hp	FF13
1905	Mass 8hp 2 seater	LC5670
1913	Austin 10hp Coquette	AJ2397
1931	Invicta 4.5 litre Model S	GP8096
1933	Austin 10 Patrick Special	AOA282
1937	Packard Super 8 Brewster Town	GSK932
1938	Jaguar SS 100 3.5 litre	FGC674
1939	Alvis Speed 25	FOB506
1948	Austin A40 Devon chassis	unreg.
1949	Land Rover 81" wheelbase	TAB767
1951	Cadillac Type 61	HSU896
1952	Austin Champ four wheel drive	EHV786D
1958	Ford Popular	WOH793
1959	Armstrong Siddeley Star Sapphire	YRM666
1959	Chevrolet Impala	XSV302
1959	BMW Isetta bubble car	VCJ147
1961	Morris Mini Minor	13 DOE
1962	Vauxhall Cresta	163FOV
1962	Austin A60 Farina	775FOB
1963	Daimler SP250 sports	1NOH
1965	Daimler Majestic Major	YOC1
1967	Daimler V8 250	TYY101E
1968	Daimler V8 250	LRU700F
1968	Triumph Vitesse	PAC714F
1969	Jaguar 420G	ROB662G
1970	Jensen FF	7777RE
1970	Volkswagen Beetle	ELM402J
1971	Triumph Herald 13/60 convertible	PFY399J
1973	Rover 3.5 litre P6	GAD777L
1974	MG MGB GT V8	MGB57
1974	Austin Vanden Plas Princess 1300	RRU305N
1977	Daimler Double Six Vanden Plas	VOP22S
1978	Triumph Stag sports	TOE1S
1978	Austin Mini 1275 GT	1918XJ
1980	Rover 3500 Patrick Motorsport	Unreg.
1981	Talbot Sunbeam Lotus	LOG81X
1981	Daimler Forte	2888AP
1982	Austin Metro Tickford	NUK1X
1982	Volkswagen Golf Gti	NOE567X
1982	Ford Cortina	POH82Y
1982	De Lorean right hand drive	SOA82Y
1982	Audi Quattro rally	MVV44Y
1983	Citroën 2CV Charleston	BRU2Y
1983	Mazda RX7 Turbo	TOF7Y
1983	Triumph Acclaim	A83HDU
1983	Jaguar Lynx Eventer	DOM12V
1984	Nissan Prairie	A50WDM
1984	Toyota Tercel 4 w/d	LOG1X
1984	Trabant 601S	3655MD
1984	BMW 635 Alpina M9	B935BOL
1985	Austin Maestro 700 Cityvan	6982PF
1985	Renault 5 Zandra Rhodes	C85HUK
1985	Porsche 928 S2	A928WJW
1985	Rolls-Royce Silver Spur Centenary	OO4160
1986	Toyota MR2 'T' Bar	DOM1V
1986	Vauxhall Cavalier Cabriolet	C867GOM
1987	Ford Capri 280i	D187MOV
1987	Lancia Delta S4 Group B	D86OOB
1987	Aston Martin Zagato	610 VZ
1987	Aston Martin Lagonda	JAP456
1987	Reliant Shetland	7828PF
1988	Jaguar XJS cabriolet	XJV12
1988	Lancia Thema	LOK1X
1989	Mercedes 190 2.5	9388AP
1989	Lancia Integrale 16V	G44FOM
1990	BMW Z1	EEL1Y
1990	Alfa Romeo SZ Zagato	558SZ
1991	Mazda 121	H391MOM
1991	Mazda MX5 Le Mans	J5LMX
1991	Honda NSX	H910NDA
1991	Daimler Limousine	1PMG
1991	Mercedes 500E	AP9484
1994	Mazda 323	M975KUK
1995	Mercedes E320 cabriolet	M300AMG

MOTORCYCLES

Year	Model	Reg
1954	Ariel motorcycle combination	PFD 135

COMMERCIAL

Year	Model	Reg
1923	De Dion fire engine	150 GMO
1926	Morris Minor van	PPR 369
1935	Ford box van	BUC 852
1979	Peugeot 304 goods van	TNP540V

Admission: £4.

The Patrick Collection of Motor Cars, Birmingham.
(Courtesy The Patrick Collection)

Bristol Industrial Museum, Princes Wharf, Wapping Road, City Docks, Bristol, Avon, BS1 4RN.

Tel. 0117 925 1470. Curator: Andy King.

The Museum is on Princes Wharf in the City Docks. It's easy to find - just look for the huge quayside cranes which stand outside the building near Prince Street swing bridge.

The Museum adjoins the River Avon at the Old Bristol dockside and covers the industrial, maritime and transport history of the Bristol region. The vehicle stock is small but reflects a past local industry. Steam trains run every fifteen minutes, past the Museum, from noon (on advertised dates) to the Maritime Heritage Centre and SS Great Britain.

The Museum is totally accessible to the disabled and staff are pleased to help if required. There's a sales point, and refreshment facilities near the Museum, plus pay and display parking at nearby Wapping Wharf car park. Coach parties may be dropped at Wapping Road.

Circa 1880 Grenville Steam carriage and the entrance to the Bristol Industrial Museum. (Courtesy Bristol Motor Museum)

MOTORCARS

1880c	Grenville steam carriage	
1898	Daimler	Y 99
1906	Bristol 16/20 tourer	AE 1061
1954	Bristol 403	OLV 90

MOTORCYCLES

1909	Douglas V4	BO 4655
1934	Douglas OW 600cc	LV 7194

1952	Douglas Vespa OL scooter	GSW101
1974	Quasar	TWS 632T

COMMERCIALS

1952	Bristol HG lorry	NEL 968
1966	Bristol Lodekka bus	FHW 158D
1926	Bristol 2 ton chassis	
1978	Bristol RE chassis	

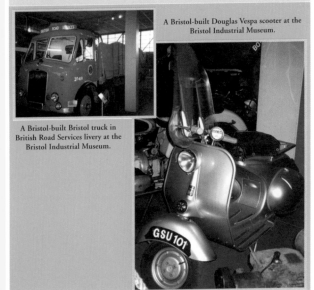

A Bristol-built Douglas Vespa scooter at the Bristol Industrial Museum.

A Bristol-built Bristol truck in British Road Services livery at the Bristol Industrial Museum.

Open: April to October, Saturday to Wednesday, 10.00am to 5.00pm. November to March, Saturday and Sunday only, 10.00am to 5.00pm. Admission: free.

Bletchley Park, The Mansion, Bletchley Park, Bletchley, Milton Keynes, MK3 6EF.

Tel. 01908 640404. Curator: Tony Sale.

Bletchley Park is a 200 yard walk from Bletchley rail station. Directions by road are: from the V7, Saxon Street, take the B4034 in Milton Keynes, continue across the old A5 into Buckingham Road, Church Green Road at the Eight Bells Pub, and then into Wilton Avenue.

Admission: adults £3.50; concessions £2.50 with accompanied children under 8 free.

Described as 'Britain's Best Kept Secret,' Bletchley Park houses a display of wartime vehicles belonging to the Military Vehicle Trust, and there is also a display of restored wartime fire engines. A museum of cryptology shows how extraordinary codebreaking saved many lives in World War II. Bletchley Park also features a rebuild of Colossus, the world's first electronic valve computer. Model boats and a model railway exhibition are further attractions.

Parking is free in the grounds and there's good wheelchair access. Cafe. Toilets. Bletchley Park is open every other weekend from 10.30am until 5.00pm, with last entry at 3.00pm. There are several special event weekends; phone for details.

The Collection

Over 50 vehicles - including motorcycles - are on display and additions are made all the time. Included are -

1930	Mercury truck and tractor
1940	Bedford OXC articulated vehicle
1942	Humber Light reconnaisance car
1944	Bedford QL mobile workshop
1944	Bren gun carrier
1944	Daimler Dingo car
1944	Fordson WOT6 recovery vehicle
1944	Humber heavy utility four wheel drive staff car
1948	Centurion tank
1954	Bedford Freen Goddess fire engine
1959	Saladin armoured car
1960	Thornycroft Antar tank transporter
1950	Moto Guzzi

Enquiries about this Collection should be made to Gordon Beale, c/o the above address.

Imperial War Museum, Duxford, Cambridgeshire, CB2 4QR.

Tel. 01223 835000. Curator: Edward Inman.

Location: 10 miles south of Cambridge, next to J10 of the M11, less than 50 miles from London and 30 mins. from the M25. By bus

Part of the Imperial War Museum of London, this Museum has fine army and other service vehicles displayed on a former RAF fighter airfield, which was used by the USAF during the Second World War. Originally, the Museum started life as a Royal Flying Corps training centre. There's a licensed restaurant, shop and mail order catalogue, plus a Museum Society.

The Museum makes every effort to maximise the enjoyment of visitors from Cambridge, ring Stagecoach on 01223 423554 or from London, National Express on 0990 808080. For rail travel ring 0345 484950.

with special needs and most of the Museum is accessible to wheelchair users. Ring for advice and further information. There's a self-service restaurant and gift shop and parking is free. In summer 1999, a new permanent display 'The Forgotten War,' which is about World War Two in the Far East, will be opened in the Land Warfare Hall.

In the following list, the number before each vehicle is the Duxford inventory number.

Open: daily except December 24th-26th inclusive: summer (14th March to 24th October inclusive): 10.00am to 6.00pm; winter: 10.00am to 4.00pm. Admission: adults (17+) £7.20; OAPs (60+) £5.00; students/ unemployed £3.50; children under 16 free. Groups of 20 or more at discounted prices. Pre-booked school parties £2.00. Disabled visitors and their carers at half the appropriate rate.

BRITISH

1	AEC-type B43
2	Matador medium artillery 4 x 4 tractor 0853
3	Matador armoured cd vehicle
4	AEC 0854 fuel bowser
5	Albion CX22S heavy articulated tractor
6	Armoured carrier FV 6109AO
7	Saracen armoured personnel. carrier Mk 1
8	Saladin armouredd car 6 x 6
9	K2 heavy ambulance
10	Austin K2 fire tender
12	K3, 3 ton truck, civil defence
13	K6, 3 ton balloon winch
15	K6, 3 ton crash rescue
16	Bedford general purpose truck
17	Bedford MWR wireless vehicle
18	Bedford 15cwt 4 x 2 MWC
19	Flat bed trailer, 4 x 2-2
21	GS-QLD, 3 ton truck 4 x 4
22	Bedford QLC bowser
23	Tasker 10 ton tractor and Queen Mary 40ft
31	Thornycroft 6 ton truck
32	FV 432 Mk 1 armoured personnel carrier
33	Abbot 105mm self propelled gun
34	Alvis Scorpion reconnaissance vehicle
35	Bedford RL 3 ton truck
36	Valentine Infantry tank Mk III
37	Vickers Mk VIA light tank
44	Land Rover ¾ ton 4 x 4
46	Centurion Mk III main battle tank
47	Centurion Mk 12 OP, main battle tank
48	Chieftain Mk 6/4C main battle tank
49	Churchill Mk VII infantry tank
51	Comet A34 Cruiser tank
52	Conqueror Mk II heavy tank
53	Daimler 4 x 4 armoured car Mk I
54	Ferret light scout/reconnaissance Mk IV car
55	Dingo Mk II scout car
59	Fordson tractor
65	4 x 2 light utility car
66	FV 1611, 4 X 4 armoured personnel carrier
70	Land Rover Mk I, Royal review
72	Royal Flying Corp, mobile workshop
74	Hippo, 10 ton truck
76	Lloyd tracked troop carrier towing Mk II
77	Light reconnaissance vehicle
78	Quad 4 x 4, field artillery tractor
80	GS truck 15cwt, 4 x 4
83	Map lorry
84	Mk V (male) tank
85	Matilda Mk II tank
87	Nash Ambassador ambulance
89	Wrecker SV/2S 6 x 4
90	Beaverette Mk 111 reconnaissance car
91	Sexton 25lb self prop. gun
97	Thompson refueller
98	Thornycroft J-type lorry
99	Nubian fire tender, 5 ton
100	Antar Mk 2 heavy tractor and trailer
101	Universal carrier, combat vehicle
102	Windsor carrier
103	Willys MB, AGPV
106	Motorcycle M20 500cc
107	Motorcycle (Jap) KE125
109	Motorcycle Triumph Mdl H solo
110	1918 motorcycle and sidecar, Vickers-Clyno
111	GPV Welbike
119	25Pdr Ammo limber
121	Field kitchen
130	Humber Super Snipe
132	Crusader cruiser tank
138	Morris Commercial 12-15cwt truck
141	Austin Champ 4 x 4
144	Flat bed truck, 3 ton, K6
147	Centaur Mk I cruiser tank
148	FV 1611 armoured personnel carrier 'Pig'
155	Churchill armoured vehicle. Royal Engineering
156	AEC 850, articulated tractor, 6 x 6
157	Ferret scout 4 x 4 reconnaissance

AMERICAN

24	Chevrolet YP-G-4
29	General Grant medium tank
45	Cletrac M2, high speed tractor
56	Federal 6 x 6, 604 C-2 wrecker
58	Ford GPW ¼ ton reconnaissance vehicle.
64	DUKW 2.5 ton 6 x 6
86	M40 self propelled gun
92	Sherman medium tank M4
112	1.5 ton truck 94 Stuart gun tractor
123	Jeep bantam trailer
127	Electrical flat truck
131	Jeep
145	CCKW-353, 2.5 ton truck
146	Jeep ¼ ton 4 x 4
151	M5 half truck, personnel carrier
154	Sherman M4 medium tank

CHINESE

25	Type 69-II main battle tank

RUSSIAN

26	BMP-1 mechanical infantry combat vehicle
27	152mm self-propelled gun/howitzer
28	ZSU-23-4 anti-aircraft gun
30	Guidline missile tractor and trailer
38	T34/85 medium tank
39	T72 M main battle tank
40	T55 A main battle tank
41	PT-76 light amphibian tank
42	BTR 60 armoured personnel. carrier
43	BRDM-2 amphibian scout car
69	Joseph Stalin heavy tank
95	SU-100 self-propelled assault gun
96	T34/85 medium tank
122	Field kitchen
129	T62 main battle tank
142	Gaz 69, 4 x 4 field car
143	Gaz 66, 4 x 4 truck

CANADIAN

57	3 ton general purpose GS F60L truck
135	Grizzly I, cruiser tank
150	Bombardier motorcycle

GERMAN

67	Jagdpanzer 38(t) tank destroyer
68	Jagdpanther (sd Kfz 267) tank destroyer

104	Self-propelled gun, Heuschrecke 10
105	Motorcycle and sidecar R750cc
136	Sd Kfz 303 Goliath demolition vehicle
137	Kubelwagon light car
160	Zundapp K800-W, motorcycle

RHODESIAN
71   Leopard security vehicle.

CZECHOSLOVAKIAN
88   V35, 3 ton 6 x 6 cargo truck

ARGENTINIAN
120   Field kitchen

ITALIAN
139   Fiat 1.5 ton truck

SWEDISH
158   Full truck. Artillery carrier

One of the US Army trucks in the World War Two display at the Imperial Science Museum, Duxford, Cambridgeshire.

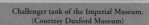

Challenger tank of the Imperial Museum. (Courtesy Duxford Museum)

A World War Two tank, part of the Military vehicle display at the Imperial War Museum, Duxford, Cambridgeshire.

British Comet A34 Cruiser tank owned by the Duxford Museum and presently loaned to the Muckleburgh Collection. (Courtesy Duxford Museum)

25

Hooton Park Griffin Trust, North Road, Ellesmere Port, Cheshire, L65 1BQ.

Tel. 0151 350 2598. Enquiries: Christine Thomas.

Hooton Park can be reached from junction 6 (Eastham Oil Terminal exit) of the M53 mid-Wirral motorway. Hooton Park is 27 miles west of Manchester.

The Griffin Trust, Hooton Park, adjacent to the Ellesmere Port Vauxhall factory, is a museum of historic aircraft and vehicles of all types, many of which are privately owned and loaned for extended periods to the Trust. The collection is housed in four 1917 listed Belfast aircraft hangars, which, having a catalogued history, are worth the visit. Plans and applications for a large grant have been made which, if successful, will add to the present facility and provide an improved, all-weather family attraction.

The Museum is open every Sunday from 10.00am to 4.00pm, Easter to October. Some special events take place on Bank Holidays.

MOTORCARS

	Sectionalised Vauxhall Astra	
1961	Ford Thunderbird	XSV 768
1963	Vauxhall Cresta	ONW 352B

COMMERCIAL/EX-MILITARY

AEC Matador 4 x 4 recovery vehicle	Q894 RCA
Austin K9 radio repair	KOD 30
Bedford Angus fire tender	STU 918J
Bedford 32 ton articulated tractor unit	WRO 681X
Bedford TM articulated trailer unit	GBH 455N
Bedford TM articulated trailer unit	B923 UBM
Commer Q4 ex-Auxiliary Fire Service	486 ELM
Ford Trader artic & Carrimore car t'sporter	JAK 875B
Leyland Retriever chassis with Coles crane	No reg.
Morris Commercial 3 ton 4 x 2 office truck	SKD 17
Queen Mary aircraft transport trailer	G3 AW 74
Volvo F88 articulated tractor unit	NAW 500G

BUSES

AEC Routemaster double-decker bus	321 CLT
AEC Routemaster double-decker bus	WTS 418A

TRACTORS

Fordson Major tractor	No reg. (two-off)

STORED

Bristol passenger coach	EFM 163H
Hyster 27 ton crane	No reg.
Bedford TM arcticulated	WRO 616X
Scammell 6 x 6 recovery vehicle	WSU 865
Tolman Thames Trader Carrimore	JMK 975B

AIRCRAFT
1950ish Antonov AN-2 Russian Transport biplane

MISCELLANEOUS
World War 1 horsedrawn ambulance
2 childrens' bicycles

Admission: adults £2.50; child/concession £1.50. The entrance fee includes an optional guided tour of the centre. Group visits may be arranged in advance by contacting the curator. Car and coach parking adjacent to the Museum. Toilets and refreshments are available. No facilities are yet provided for the disabled; however, all services and exhibits are on the ground floor.

Hooton Park Museum logo.

Part of Hooton Park's internal display; from left to right: Morris Commercial 3 ton 4x2 Office truck; Austin K6 6x4 recovery vehicle, and AEC Routemaster double-decker bus. Note also the intricate wooden roof structure of the listed Belfast hangar.

When Tom Price visited Hooton Park, this 1950s Antonov AN2, previously a workhorse of Russian military aviation, was undergoing renovation. The aircraft is now complete, and more ambitious individuals are looking to obtain a Certificate of Airworthiness for it!

Mouldsworth Motor Museum, Smithy Lane, Mouldsworth, Cheshire, CH3 8AR.

Tel. 01928 731981. Curator: James Peacop.

Mouldsworth is 19 miles west of Manchester and 6 miles east of Chester, near to Delamere Forest. By road, leave the M6 motorway at junction 18 and take the A54 to Chester. Continue on the A54 through Middlewich and Winsford. Turn right onto the B5393 signposted Helsby, and continue until you enter the village of Mouldsworth. Take the left turn, Smithy Lane, and follow the brown tourist signs; the Museum is approximately half a mile down on the right.

Open: March to September, Sunday to Wednesday and all Bank Holidays 12.00pm to 5.00pm. Arrangements may be made for educational and club visits through the Curator. Admission 1998/9: adults £2.50; children £1.00; OAPs £2.00; concessions, family ticket and group rates by arrangement.

Close to Delamere Forest, Mouldsworth Motor Museum is housed in an amazing 1930s Art Deco building, set in its own grounds and safe for children. The splendid collection comprises over sixty vintage, classic and sports cars, motorcycles and early bicycles. There are organised activities for children with prizes; also old toys and pedal cars to see.

Automobilia is on sale and there is a 'vehicle sale' board. There are no catering facilities but a nearby cafe is recommended. Disabled access. Toilets. Parking.

MOTORCARS				
1922	Wolseley 4 seat cabriolet		1936	Rover Streamline coupé chassis
1922	Wolseley 2 seat/2 cylinder		1950	Dellow trials car
1923	Morris Bullnose 2 stroke with 'dickie'		1951	Austin A40 Sports
1924	Austin 7 Chummy		1956	Hillman Minx saloon
1925	Triumph SD 500cc		1958	Austin Healey Frogeye Sprite
1928	Chevrolet 6 cylinder coupé		1958	Heinkel bubble car
1930	Austin 7 Mulliner bodied 2 stroke		1959	MG twin cam
1930	Morris Minor 2 door		1962	Jaguar E-type, 4.2 litre
1930	MG Double 12, 848cc		1962	Triumph Vitesse saloon
1930	Sunbeam Doctor's coupé		1965	Wolseley 16/60
1931	Alfa Romeo 8C		1968	Austin 1800S saloon works rally car
1932	Morris Minor McEvoy special		1969	Jaguar E-type 4.5 litre
1933	MG F-type sports		1970	Morris 1000 Traveller
1933	MG J2 sports		1973	Ferrari Dino
1935	Austin Ashley bodied special		1975	NSU Ro 8, Wankel engine
1936	Armstrong Siddeley saloon		1980	Triumph TR8
			1989	Austin Mini, 30th anniversary

Jim Peacop not only owns and runs Mouldsworth Museum, but also practises and teaches art. This cartoon was prepared by him for the Citroën Car Club in 1994.

MOULDSWORTH MOTOR MUSEUM
6 MILES EAST OF CHESTER

"Welcome to Cheshire (Deva), behold tis a fine restoredus Chariot you bring, and frontus wheel drivous too!"

Entry to the Mouldsworth Motor Museum, Cheshire.

Interior of Mouldsworth Museum, which was originally a pumping station owned by the the local water board until purchased by Jim Peacop. (All photos this page courtesy Mouldsworth Museum)

The Mouldsworth Motors Garage scene at the Mouldsworth Motor Museum, Cheshire.

A 1930 Morris Minor at the Mouldsworth Motor Museum, Cheshire.

Pacific Road Transport Museum and Tramway, Pacific Road, Birkenhead, Cheshire, L41 5HN.

Tel. 0151 6664010. Principal Museum Officer: David Hillhouse.

The Museum is 200 metres from the Woodside Ferry at the Birkenhead end of the A41. Birkenhead is 31 miles west of Manchester.

The Museum is subject to continued development at present. There are approximately 35 vehicles on display plus a variety of motoring accessories. Due to this work, it's advisable to phone first before a visit to check what vehicles will be on display. A working tramway is in operation which, by the Millenium, should be serving the Twelve Quays development area and a complete service loop of city streets, Open Tuesday to Sunday, 1.00pm to 5.00pm during school holidays, and at weekends the rest of the year. Ample street parking. Disabled access, level site but a little rough.

MOTORCARS

1929	Lancia Lambda
1936	Austin 6 Ascot
1949	AC 2 litre
1951	Ferrari 212, 2.6 litre
1961	Ford Popular 100E
1964	Jaguar S-type, 3.4 litre
1965	Ford Anglia 105E
1972	Ford Escort 1300XL
1980	BMW M I 3.4 litre
	Volvo 1800E

COMMERCIAL/MILITARY

1944	Austin K4 Merryweather fire engine
1945	Bedford QL army lorry
1946	Guy Vixen tower wagon
1949	Leyland bus (Wallasey)
1950	Scammell Explorer recovery vehicle
1951	Leyland Titan bus (Wallasey)
1958	Leyland Titan bus (Birkenhead)
1967	Leyland bus (Birkenhead)
	Leyland open top bus
	Alvis Saracen armoured personnel carrier

MOTORCYCLES

1923	Diamond 147cc
1923	Scott 486cc
1925	Excelsior autocycle
1929	Panther 250cc
1929	Scott 500cc
1929	Scott Squirrel 500cc
1933	Velocette KTT 350cc
1938	Norton 16H 500cc
1938	Norton International 500cc
1946	BSA C11 250cc
1948	Scott 600cc
1949	Triumph T100
1955	Maserati 50cc
1956	AJS 7R 350cc
1979	Ariel BSA 50cc tricycle

TRAMS

1890	Liverpool horsedrawn
1900	Birkenhead
1928	Wallasey
1931	Liverpool
1993	Hong Kong built trams (in operation)

Admission: during refurbishment a transfer ticket, which allows entry to the Museum and a tram ride, is priced at £1.30 for adults; £0.80 OAPs/ children and £4.50 family.

Automobilia, The Old Mill, St. Stephen, St. Austell, Cornwall, TR6 7RX.

Tel. 01726 823092. Owner/curator: Colin Vincent.

Automobilia is located just off the A30, 2 miles west of Indian Queens on the A3058 Newquay/ St. Austell road.

This is the owner's personal collection, gathered and restored over many years. Over 50 working-condition vehicles, dating from 1901, are on display over three floors. Automobilia and motor accessories are also on show, plus period signs and advertisements relating to the 'good old days.' Video presentations illustrate many facets of motoring.

Opening hours are: April, May and October, 10.00am to 4.00pm; June to September, 10.00am to 6.00pm. Students and organised groups are welcome. Parts and automobilia auto jumble on the third floor. Vintage and classic cars bought and sold. There's a cafe with homemade food, plus picnic and childrens' play area. Limited free parking for cars; coaches by arrangement. No disabled toilets and access is limited to the ground and first floors.

Admission: adults £3.30; OAPs £2.75; children £1.60; family ticket (2 + 2) £8.20. Limited free parking for cars, coaches by arrangement. No disabled toilets and access is to ground and first floors only.

MOTORCARS

Year	Model	Reg.	Year	Model	Reg.
1903/4	Belsize 16/20 3 cylinder	K 76	1958	FMR Messerschmitt	HHJ 362
1904	Peugeot 9hp	AD 1904	1959	MG twin cam	RSF 26
1935	Austin 10hp	DTA 743	1960	Austin Healey 3000	3015 UE
1906	Sunbeam 16/20	AF178	1960	Wolseley 1500	937 JUO
1924	Bean 14hp tourer	MR 2459	1961	Aston Martin DB4	6963 PP
1926	Morris Cowley Chummy	CV 313	1964	Austin Mini	ACV 726B
1927	Austin 7 Chummy	FU 7017	1964	Daimler Dart SP250	392 EYP
1928	Bean lorry	CV 1650	1964	Daimler Jaguar	ACV 576
1929	Bentley 4.5 litre VDP	GU 7242	1964	Ford Anglia 123E	AXC 903B
1929	Swift 10hp	FC 6473	1964	Renault 8	CPF 912B
1930	Lagonda 2.0 litre	G0 5479	1965	Riley 1.5	BRL 85C
1930	Morris Cowley flatnose	PL 3454	1965	Riley 1.5	HPE 167C
1932	Sunbeam	CV 5860	1966	Jaguar E-type	244 XKE
1933	Aston Martin le Mans	AGY 530	1967	Lotus Elan (chassis no. 1)	LPW 120E
1934	MG PA	AHH 911	1971	Hillman Avenger	UBP 789K
1935	Morris 8 series 1	DCV 347	1974	BMW coupé 3.0 csi	SCV 560M
1936	Maendaz Special 15/90	No reg.	1983	BMW coupé 635 csi	UAF 5
1936	Austin taxi	CYH 973			
1936	Talbot 105 VDP tourer	DYY 789			
1937	Frazer Nash/BMW 328	KME 327	**MOTORCYCLES**		
1937	Lancia	TL 6898	1916	Douglas flat twin	BC 3351
1937	Riley Lynx Sprite	CWK 816	1923	Sunbeam	HC 4168
1938	Morgan Aero Sports	MY 12	1929	AJS	VE 2111
1938	Riley Falcon Continental	AJY 283	1934	Sunbeam	JW 2950
1948	MG TC	KAE 629	1935	SU	WD 9532
1950	Jaguar Mk. V	AHC 413	1949	Vincent HRD Rapide & Steib s'car	LTA 528
1951	Lea Francis Coventry	KOM 31	1954	Vespa	UPE 730
1952	MGA YB	HFJ 631	1958	Triumph TR 3A	PDR 483
1952	Riley 2.5 litre RM series	SRL 486	1971	Ariel 3 trike	ACV 760K
1954	Jaguar XK 120	No reg.		NSU	No reg.
1956/7	Aston Martin DB 214 Mk11	ULC 423		Sinclair C5	No reg.

Automobilia logo, Cornwall's largest motor museum.

Cornwall's **Motor Museum**

Automobilia entrance and delivery vehicle. The Collection is displayed over several floors in the main building and several surrounding stores. It's the result of many years of collection and restoration by the owner and his wife. (Courtesy Automobilia)

Dairyland and Country Life Museum, Tressillian Manor, Summercourt, Newquay, Cornwall, TR8 5AA.
Tel. 01872 510246. Contact: Rex Davey.

The Museum is on the A3058 St. Austell Road, 4 miles from Newquay.

A premier family farm attraction with entertainment for all, which includes a Nature Trail. The site extends to 75 acres, on which is housed a Tractor House (which contains four restored World War One tractors), Heritage Centre, Milking Parlour and childrens' playground. Many of the attractions for children involve active participation.

Parking is free. There are toilets for the disabled, wide doors and ramps where necessary and a special viewing gallery in the Milking Parlour. Wheelchairs are available. Country gift shop with fresh dairy produce, plus coffee shop serving light meals and cream teas. Picnic garden.

Open daily 10.30am to 5.00pm, April to October. Admission: adults £4.95; OAPs £4.75; children £3.95; family ticket £14.95. Party rates on application.

TRACTORS		
1915	International Mogul single cylinder	No reg.
1917	International Titan twin cylinder	No reg.
1917	Ford 4 cylinder	AF 1918
1919	Austin 4 cylinder	No reg.

'Maggie,' a 1915 International Mogul, one of a small collection which was originally owned and used on a local farm.

Dairyland logo.

1917 Ford 4 cylinder at the Tractor Gallery. (Courtesy Dairyland)

Flambards Village, Culdrose Manor, Helston, Cornwall, TRI3 OGA.
Tel. 01326 573404. Director of Marketing: David Edwards.

To get to the Museum from Helston take the A3083 towards RNAS Culdrose. Flambards is well signposted half a mile along on the left hand side.

The Flambards logo.

Principally offering family entertainment, Flambards may be considered the West Country's leading all-weather attraction. Amongst the forty or so award-winning set pieces are many that include vehicles as props. Most of the exhibitions - the Victorian Village, Britain in the Blitz, the Chemist's Shop, Time Capsule, Transports of Delight, The War Galleries, Cornwall's Secret Navies, Luftwaffe's Target for Tonight, The Evacuees - and so on, are undercover. There is much for all the family inside and in the grounds, from rollercoaster to log flume ride and Exploratorium, to toddlers' play zone, pets paradise and prize-winning gardens.

There are shops of all types, and a wide variety of catering with hot and cold dishes. Toilets plus disabled toilet facilities on level ground near the entrance; free wheelchair loan and route guide available. Free parking.

MOTORCARS					
1896	Columbia	BS 8024	1919	Rhone 125cc	Unregistered
1927	Austin 7	Z 3544	1921	Sun 293cc	BP 5702
	Willys Jeep (US)	290511-5	1922	Raleigh 348cc	NR 1260
				Sinclair C5	
			1924	Royal Enfield 225cc	YB 206
MOTORCYCLES			1925	Triumph Baby 249cc	NN 9758
The Ivan Kessel Vintage Collection			1925	Raleigh 800cc 'V'	KH 241
1914	Swift 490cc	AF 1423	1929	Velocette 248cc	CU 333
1915	Triumph Model H	AF 2368	1938	Scott Flying Squirrel 596cc	EAF 432

Open (1998 hours): 3rd April to 3rd November 10.00am to 5.00pm; 22nd July to 5th September 10.00am to 7.00 pm. Admission: standard ticket (ages 12-59) £7.50; juniors (4-11) £6.50; seniors (60 - 79) £5.00. Family Saver £25.00. Under 4s and over 80s free. Afternoon only tickets available. Discounted Return Card scheme and reductions for groups of over fifteen.

1896 Columbia and James Kingford Hale, MD of Flambards, and his dog, Barney. Flambards is probably Cornwall's largest undercover tourist attraction.

Land's End is 32 miles west of Truro.

Land's End and John O' Groats Company, The Custom House, Sennen, Penzance, Cornwall, TR19 7AA.

Tel. 01736 871501. Exhibitions Manager: Paul Johnson.

Early motorcycles are included in the 'End to End' display room, which charts the history of the many records set by various challengers for the best or 'most different' time from John O' Groats to Land's End. Apart from the history and scenic beauty of the area, the site has many family attractions, with much to offer for all ages, including many which are biased towards children. Regular car and motorcycle rallies are also held on the site.

Car and coach charges include the entrance fee. There are disabled and baby changing facilities and a first-aid post (a nurse is on site during the holiday season). There are many gift shops, plus an hotel, restaurant and fast food outlets.

MOTOR VEHICLE			MOTORCYCLES		
1927	Austin Seven	RL 6545	1927	New Imperial 346cc	HN 5366
1947	VW Beetle	JLT 420	1937	New Imperial Model 36	DAR 769
1950s	Austin FX3 station wagon	TSK 652	1937	Royal Enfield	JSU 361
1950s	A30/35	TVS 753	1939	Royal Enfield 'Flying Flea' 125cc	JYV 448
1964	Scootercar	HMF 729B	1949	LE Velocette 150cc	ERD 641
1972	MGB GT	GOF 120L	1950	LE Velocette 200cc	NKR 593
1978	Rolls-Royce Silver Shadow	VPG 676S	1957	Lambretta	NTY 396
1988	Bar Stool (kit car)	Q685 HCP	1975	'Dorset' Ambassador diesel 3.5hp	893 GBF
1998	Skoda	R148 NNV			

Admission: car park and entrance to site: £3.00. 'Miles of Memory' (vehicle hall): adults £2.00; OAPs/unemployed/children £1.00. Admission to site and all halls: adults £7.00; OAPs/unemployed/ children £3.50. All prices are lower off-season. Open daily from 10.00am, except Christmas Eve and Boxing Day. Closing time varies.

Land's End logo; one of two used by the company.

Land's End hotel and Cornish coastline, used in the Land's End advertising.

The Cockermouth Motor Museum, Aspects of Motoring, The Maltings, Brewery Lane, Cockermouth, Cumbria, CA13 9NE.

Tel. 01900 824448. Museum Manager: Andrew Saggerson.

The Museum is located at the Castle in Cockermouth Town, about 20 miles west of Carlisle.

The Museum is housed on two floors within the Maltings of Jennings Castle Brewery. Every effort has been made to reflect, as the name 'Aspects' suggests, the many varied faces of motoring, from the earliest vehicles to the present day. There are examples from the worlds of veteran and vintage motoring - leisure and sporting - classic saloons and sports, world famous rallying, formula racing, speedway, scrambling, trials, classic motorcycling, karting and military. Many vehicles are displayed in tableaux settings. There are audiovisual displays and a large slide projection booth featuring local motoring events. The 'Bill Gray' model collection is made up of some 400 detailed model vehicles, with a further 100 models of military motoring. For the children there's a computer showing presentations, a quiz and a four-lane slot racing set.

Open: 10.00am to 4.00pm (last admission), March 15th to November 1st, seven days a week. November 2nd to December 31st weekends only, same hours. Closed throughout January and February; open weekends and half-term. Group visits at any time, including evenings, by appointment.

The 'Pit Stop' coffee shop has light refreshments, gifts and souvenirs. Baby changing facilities available. Wheelchair users catered for, including toilet. Car parking nearby.

Admission: adults £3.00; OAPs £2.00; children £1.50; under-fives free; family ticket (2 + 2) £7.50.

MOTORCARS

Year	Model	Reg.	Year	Model	Reg.
1912	Overland	DS 7996	1972	Ford RS 2000 safari winner	RWC 455K
1925	Ford Model T Doctor's coupé	DS 9706	1975	Lotus Europa	KUG 84N
1926	Renault NN1 saloon	SV 4772	1975	Formula Ford Royale RP21	No reg.
1928	Austin 7 Chummy	SV 4620	1977	March PDS Formula 3	No reg.
1929	Morris Flatnose Cowley	YT 3834	1978	Panther Lima	AAO 398T
1930	Austin 7 Ulster	KJ 2158	1980	Jaguar D-type replica	KRE 900B
1930	Austin 7 Tourer	KR 9644	1990	RS 500	TIA 500
1932	Wolseley 9hp	ARM 310		Can-Am promotional car	KKM 350L
1934	Morris 12/4 saloon	AKD 847		Ferrari 246 Dino replica	YKE 847J
1934	Singer 9hp	HH 7933		Sporting trials car	No reg.
1935	Riley Merlin Special	AKV 655			
1935	Riley Brooklands Special	DRO 684			
1936	Austin 10hp saloon	VFF 896	**MOTORCYCLES**		
1936	MG SA cabriolet	MG 5026	1921	Ariel 350cc	AO 6484
1936	Morgan 4/4 Flat Rad.	MYP 802	1930	RMW 200	HH 7934
1938	Fraser Nash BMW	DMK 190	1949	BSA M20	MVK 560
1938	Austin 8hp saloon	EAO 26	1953	Ariel 500cc	XKA 922
1946	Morris van, Z-type	HGW 438	1954	Ambassador	LRM 30
1953	Ford Anglia	MAO 983	1955	BSA B33	RAO 11
1960	TVR Grantura	No reg.	1959	Greeves Scottish trials bike	No reg.
1963	Daimler SP250 Dart	9666 UK	1964	BSA B40 trials	No reg.
1964	Fasta Kart (go kart)	Not reg.	1974	Ducati 250cc	VEC 83V
1965	Ford Cortina Lotus Mk 1	DTP 966C	1975	Montessa 414 Cappra motocross	No reg.
1966	Triumph Spitfire Sprint special	RTW 450D	1975	Bultaco Sherpa 250 trials	No reg.
1967	Mini Cooper S	PRM 536F	1976	Ossa 250cc trials	No reg.
1968	California GP Dune Buggy	GHP 326T	1990	CZ motocross	No reg.
1969	Ford Cortina Lotus Mk 2	SRY 249G			
1971	Lotus 7 (No. 1) series 4	KVX 189J	Plus a selection of speedway bikes from 1949 to 1980		

Cockermouth
Motor
Museum logo.

...is interior photograph of the Cockermouth Museum illustrates the interests
of two generations of the Saggerson family. Father, son and their wives are all
involved in the Museum and have been interested in motorsport for many
years. On the right is a 1912 Overland ...

**COCKERMOUTH
MOTOR MUSEUM**

Aspects of Motoring

... on the
left, a 1980
Jaguar D-
type
replica.

Cars of the Stars Motor Museum, Standish Street, Keswick, Cumbria, CA12 5LS.

Tel. 01768 773757. Curator: Peter Nelson.

Cars of the Stars Motor Museum is in Keswick town centre between Victoria Street and Market Square. Standish Street is accessed from Station Street or Pack Horse Court. Keswick is 48 miles north of Lancaster.

This Museum is open daily from 10.00am until 4.45pm from just before Easter until 31st December; during December it's open weekends only. The Museum is also open during February half-term holidays.

There's a shop, refreshments and toilets. The Museum houses many cars that have been featured in films and TV series and, because of this, some vehicles may be out on location or at other shows. Phone to check before travelling if you wish to see a specific car. Each vehicle is displayed in its individual film set setting.

The Collection

1902 Oldsmobile Curved Dash: one of the first vehicles to appear in films	
1923 Ford Model T tourer: as used by Laurel and Hardy	
1935 Morris 8 Tourer: appeared in *All Creatures Great and Small*	BAF892
Triumph Roadster tourer: appeared in *Bergerac*	
Fiat Gamini: appeared in *Noddy* series	
Reliant 3 wheeler van: appeared in *Only Fools and Horses*	
Postman Pat van	
1965 Lotus Super Seven: appeared in *The Prisoner*	KAR120C
Austin Mini Moke: as used in *The Prisoner*	
De Lorean sports car: appeared in *Back to the Future*	
Volvo P1800 sports saloon: appeared in *The Saint*	77GYL
Lotus Elan sports car: appeared in *The Avengers*	
Aston Martin DB5: as used in *Goldfinger*	JB007
Lotus Esprit Turbo: appeared in *For Your Eyes Only*	
BSA Lightning motorcycle: appeared in *Thunderball*	
KITT car: appeared in *Knightrider*	
VW Beetle: appeared in *The Love Bug*	
Chitty Chitty Bang Bang: appeared in film of the same name	
Batmobile: appeared in *Batman*	
FAB1: appeared in *Thunderbirds*	
Chevrolet van: appeared in *The A Team*	
1942 Willys Jeep: appeared in *Mash*	
The Flintstone's car	
The Munster's Koach	

Admission: adults £3.00; children £2.00. Reduced rates for groups.

The star of the film *Chitty Chitty Bang Bang* at the Cars of the Stars Museum, Keswick, Cumbria. (Courtesy Cars of the Stars Museum)

Lakeland Motor Museum, Holker Hall, Cark-in-Cartmell, Grange-over-Sands, Cumbria, LA11 7PL.

Tel. 015395 58328.
Commercial Manager: E. L. Maher.

Holker Hall is 15 minutes south of Newby Bridge on the B5278, and is signposted from the M6 at junction 36 on the A590. The associated display of a replica of Bluebird is at Lakeside, Windermere. Cark-in-Cartmell is 55 miles northwest of Manchester.

Situated in the idyllic surroundings of Holker Hall and Gardens, the Lakeland Motor Museum, with exhibits spanning over a hundred years of transport heritage, is an additional and complementary attraction that conjures up nostalgic motoring memories.

This ever-changing collection comprises vintage vehicles, classic and curious cars, authentic automobilia, scooters, tractors, motorbikes and mechanical marvels, plus a 1930s garage re-creation, timeless toys and collectables with hands-on activity items. The Campbell Legend Bluebird Exhibition features the lives and careers of Sir Malcolm Campbell and son Donald who captured 21 land and water speed records for Great Britain.

Open: Sunday to Friday (closed Saturdays), 10.30am to 4.45pm, April to October.

Since some of the loaned vehicles in this collection take part in rallies and races during the year, it may be advisable to ring and check availability of particular vehicles you may wish to see before planning your trip.

Admission: discounted tickets (including a family option) are available which allow entry to the Motor Museum, Holker Hall, gardens and grounds. Please phone for details.

MOTORCARS

1922	Citroën-type C Shooting Brake
1923	Wolseley 2 seater
1923	Jowett 7/17 coupé
1927	Model T Ford
1929	Dodge Senior Six Landau saloon
1929	Essex Super Six
1929	Fiat 509A
1929	Ford Model A
1930	Royal Ruby
1931	MG M-type
1932	Morris Eight saloon
1933	Buick Eight Series
1933	Buick Eight Special
1936	Morris 10/4 saloon
1937	Cadillac Fleetwood limousine
1938	Lagonda V12 DHC
1939	Packard Six
1939	Hanomag-type 13
1950	Healey Silverstone
1951	Lotus Mark III
1959	Scootercar
1960	Messerschmitt Cabin Cruiser
1964	Alfa Romeo Guilia Spider 1
1965	Volga Mk. 21
1965	DMW Amphicar
1971	Trabant
1973	Pontiac Trans-Am 'Celestial'
1981	MGB Roadster (limited edition)
1981	De Lorean
1983	Bamby
1982	Pelland steam car Mk II
1990	Limited edition Mini Cooper

MOTORCYCLES

1922	Rudge Multi
1923	Raleigh
1925	AJS G5 230cc
1925	Velocette 350cc
1926	Triumph model P
1928	Levis Model H 247cc
1929	Ariel 350cc
1930	Excelsior 123cc
1935	Triumph Recumbant
1946	LFS Special
1950	James 125cc
1952	LE Velocette
1953	BSA Bantam Major 150cc, sectioned
1954	Sunbeam SS 500cc
1956	Bantam D3
1959	Moto Guzzi
1960	Matchless G12 650cc
1962	Manx Norton 500cc
1972	Ural M63 650cc

MOTORSCOOTERS

1920	Grigg
1923	ADC Scootermota
1950	Corgi
1956	New Hudson
1963	Vespa Sportique
1983	Italjet
1991	Scooter

COMMERCIAL

1914	Dennis fire engine
1920	Ford Model T van
1940	Lister auto truck
194?	Ex-US army jeep
1952	Nipper milk delivery truck
1978	Africar pick-up truck

TRACTORS

c1924	Austin		1947	Ford-Ferguson Model 8N
1936	Ferguson-Brown Model A		1957	Massey Ferguson Model 35
1940	Ford-Ferguson Model 9N		1944	US airfield tractor
1941	Fordson			

One of the wooden Peugeot Africars, a project that never got off the ground, at the Lakeland Motor Museum, Holker Hall, Cumbria.

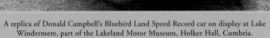

A replica of Donald Campbell's Bluebird Land Speed Record car on display at Lake Windermere, part of the Lakeland Motor Museum, Holker Hall, Cumbria.

1954 Sunbeam S8 at the centre of an array of Lakeland bikes.

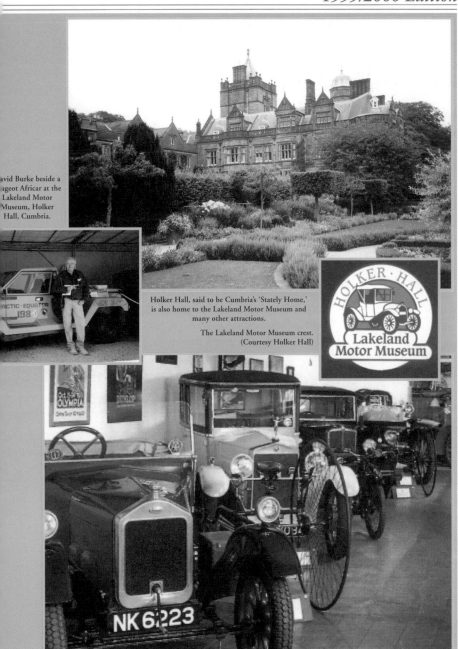

...avid Burke beside a ...ageot Africar at the Lakeland Motor Museum, Holker Hall, Cumbria.

Holker Hall, said to be Cumbria's 'Stately Home,' is also home to the Lakeland Motor Museum and many other attractions.

The Lakeland Motor Museum crest. (Courtesy Holker Hall)

A selection of Lakeland Motor Museum's many cars. (Courtesy Lakeland Motor Museum)

Westmoreland Motor Museum, Rellandsgate, Kings Meaburn, Penrith, Cumbria, CA10 3BT.
Tel. 01931 714624. Owner: Gideon Booth.

Visits only by prior arrangement. Kings Meaburn is 50 miles southwest of Newcastle.

Admission: free but donations welcome.

Probably the largest private collection of Morris motorcars (80) in the country. The models run from 1913 to 1963, with the favourite year being 1934. The Museum restores cars and all forms of motoring memorabilia, such as signs, petrol pumps, globes, etc. Gideon Booth has a special building to house his collection. The Museum is open by prior arrangement.

National Tramway Museum, Crich, Matlock, Derbyshire, DE4 5DP.
Tel. 01773 852565. Marketing Manager: Lesley Wyld.
web site: http://www.tramway.co.uk

The Museum is situated 15 miles north of Derby, 6 miles from Matlock and 8 miles west of junction 28 on the M1. Crich is 42 miles southeast of Manchester.

This is claimed to be the finest transport museum of its type, with over 50 vintage steam, electric and horsedrawn trams. Gathered from all over the UK and abroad, they are painstakingly restored for enthusiasts to admire. Trams run every few minutes through a period street, beneath the elegant Bowes Lyon bridge and on to stunning views of the Derwent Valley. Visitors may get on and off at will. 30,000 square feet of indoor attractions give an insight into the beginning of this century. Excellent for all the family.

Open: March and November, Sundays only, 10.30am to 5pm; April, May, September and October daily, except Friday, 10.00am to 5.30pm. June, July and August, 10.00am to 5.30pm. 6.30pm closing all Saturdays, Sundays and Monday Bank Holidays. Special holiday opening 5th and 12th of April, 31st of May, 1st and 2nd of November

Free parking for cars and coaches. Owners of classic vehicles registered before 1st January 1968 enter without charge, provided that they park in Museum St. for a minimum of two hours. Unlimited tram rides and entry to the Video Theatre is also included in the ticket price. Dogs (on leads) are welcome to enjoy the visit with you! There are shops - the Forge and the Emporium - tea rooms and refreshment kiosk, and picnic areas. Toilets are located around the site which have baby changing facilities. For the disabled there are toilets, ramps, Braille guide books and hearing assistance as required.

Note: in winter whilst all Museum attractions will be open, limited demonstration vintage tram rides only are available. No trams will run when the ground temperature is 5 or below degrees C .

The National Tramway Museum at Crich, Derbyshire. (Courtesy The National Tramway Museum)

PASSENGER CARS

1873	Oporto mule car
1874	Sheffield horse car
1885	Blackpool Tramways Co
1885	New South Wales Government (locomotive)
1894	Dundee and District steam trailer
1896	Douglas Head Marine Drive
1898	Blackpool and Fleetwood
1899	Chesterfield
1899	Sheffield
1900	Glasgow
1900	Sheffield
1901	Newcastle
1902	Blackpool
1902	Hill Of Howth
1903	London County Council
1903	Southampton
1904	Chesterfield
1904	Derby
1904	Leicester
1905	Johannesburg
1908	Prague
1912	London Transport
1915	Grimsby and Immingham
1919	Paisley and District
1921	Leeds (2)
1922	Gateshead and Blackpool
1922	Glasgow
1926	Blackpool
1926	Blackpool
1926	Leeds
1927	Blackpool
1927	Gateshead and District
1927	Oporto
1928	Blackpool
1928	Glasgow

1929	Glasgow
1930	Metropolitan Electrical Tramway
1931	Leeds
1932	London Transport
1934	Sheffield
1936	Liverpool
1937	Blackpool
1937	Sheffield
1931/54	Leeds
1939	New York Third Avenue Transit
1940	Glasgow
1948	Edinburgh
1948	Glasgow
1950	Sheffield
1953	Leeds
1957	Hague
1969	Berlin

WORKS VEHICLES

	Manchester horse tower wagon
	Derby horse tower wagon
	P.W. flat truck
	Leeds tram recovery vehicle
1903	Glasgow welders tool van
1905	Cardiff water car
1905	Glasgow cable laying car
1905	Welding trailer
1906	Brussels snow broom
1919	Sheffield railgrinder
1932	Leeds tower car
1935	Blackpool mobile generator
1937	Sheffield tower wagon
1979	Modern tower wagon
1980	Crane wagon (crane ex-Sheffield)

Unlimited rides around the two mile circuit take the tram passenger from cobbled streets ...

Admission: April to October inclusive, adults £6.50; children £3.20; OAPs £5.60. Family (2 + 3) £17.60; group rates on application. Please phone for winter admission charges.

... to the beautiful panorama of the Derwent Valley. (Courtesy the National Tramway Museum)

Cobbaton Combat Collection, Chittlehampton, Umberleigh, Devon, EX37 9SD.
Tel. 01769 540414/ 540740. Contact/owner: Preston Isaac.

Chittlehampton is 46 miles north of Plymouth. From Barnstaple take the A377 (signposted Tourist Route Exeter). Take the first left after Bishops Tawton filling station and follow the signposts

Described by the owner as 'an undercover attraction for the whole family,' over 50 ex-military vehicles are displayed in the 1500 square metres of covered exhibition area. This includes vehicles from the 1939/45 war, Warsaw Pact countries, Falklands and Gulf wars. There are set piece scenes depicting military and civilian life during the 1939/45 war.

Open: Easter to 31st October, 10.00am to 6.00pm, seven days a week. The Museum is open during the winter months, but please phone for times.

The Quartermaster's store offers a range of surplus uniforms, militaria, deactivated guns and books for sale. Light refreshments are available from the NAAFI wagon. There's also a picnic area and a childrens' play area with tanks and guns. Parking is free.

MILITARY VEHICLES		
1936	Ford Y 8hp saloon	WFO 666
1938	DH Leyland Lynx	JTT 724
1939	GMC 3 ton, converted to LRDG CHEV	Not reg.
1939	15cm SFH 18 Howitzer, German	
1939	Morris C8 FAT Mk2, Quad	
1940	Bofors gun 40mm, Sweden, Mod 36	
1940c	122mm Mod 1938 (M-30) Howitzer, Russian	
1940c	Thorneycroft Tartar WOF/DC/4	Not reg.
1941	Austin K2 ATV + Den./Gwynne pumps	GXH 171
1941	Ford F15A, No. 12 cab	Not reg.
1941	Lloyd Carrier	Not reg.
1942	Daimler AC Mk I 'The Dame'	JFO 505
1942	GM Fox, unrestored	Not reg.
1942	Light recovery trailer, 6 wheel, 7 ton	
1942	Sherman V M4A4, ex-range target	No reg.
1943	3.72 Med AA gun	
1943	5.5" Gun, ex-range target	
1941	Standard Beaverette Mk3	
1942	Bofors 40mm Mk2 Ottis Fenson Elev.	Not reg.
1942	Daimler Dingo Mk2	Not reg.
1942	Ford Mk 6 AFV, Eire	ZD 1760
1943	Austin K6, 3 ton crane	143 UYC
1943	Daimler AC Mk 1, 'Clyde'	RSY 953
1943	Bofors 40mm Mk2 c. Ottis Fenson Elev.	
1943	Fordson 7V. Converted, NAAFI to HPU	Not reg.
1943	25Pdr Limber Mk2	No reg.
1943	Morris Light Recon' Mk2 unrestored	Not reg.
1943	Morris C9B, SP Bofors	JFO 700
1943	Scammell TRMU 30	HJJ 716
1943	Sexton Mk2 25Pdr SP	FYU 582
1943	Univ. Carrier, No 3, MKII, Canada	Not reg.
1944	Centaur Mk4 Cruiser Tank	Not reg.
1944	Churchill Mk7, Crocodile	Not reg.
1944	Cranemobile crane	Not reg.
1944	C15TA, APC	Not reg.
1944	DH Diamond T 981	PTT 425W
1944	Farmall Model H tractor, USA	Not reg.
1944	2Omm Flak 38	
1944	Ford F60S LAAT, Canada	JUO 52
1944	Morris 08 FAT Quad, No. 5 body	JUO 245P
1944	Standard Light Utility	
1944	T34/85	No reg.
1944/5	T16 Universal unrestored	Not reg.
1944	Windsor Carrier, Ford Canada	Not reg.
1945	Comet Cruiser tank, unrestored	No reg.
1945	Leyland Hippo, Mk2	YDV 530X
1945	Morris C8 GS	TG 9332
1947	David Brown VAK1	JDV 295
1949	Centurion AVRE	No reg.
1950c	87mm Recoiless, Czech	No reg.
1950	Tatra OT810 ¾ track	Not reg.
1954	T54 MBT, Czech	No reg.
1960	Daimler Ferret Mk 2/3	RSY 904
1966	FV434 Q348 JTA	Not reg.
1976	Land Rover 101	ODV 339P
1987	Seddon Atkinson D411 and trailer	D895 UTA
MOTORCYCLE		
1943	BSA M20	
BICYCLE		
1940	Mercury WD cycle	
1940	BSA folding parabike	

Admission (1998): adults £4.00; school children £2.25; OAPs £3.50.

The childrens' play area has a number of climb on/in military vehicles; this Sherman tank and the T16 US Ford personnel carrier are particularly popular. (Courtesy Cobbaton Combat Collection)

This ex-MoD BSA M20 motorbike and Churchill tank are part of the display in one of the Cobbaton exhibition halls. (Courtesy Cobbaton Combat Collection)

The Combe Martin Motorcycle Collection, Cross Street, Combe Martin, North Devon, EX34 ODH.

Tel. 01271 882346. Owner: Terry McCulley.

The Collection is located by the beach, adjacent to the main car park in Combe Martin, which is 8 miles north of Barnstable.

This collection of around sixty British motorcycles reflects the owner's enthusiasm for them. The Collection - which is set against a background of period pumps, signs and garage memorabilia - varies as loaned motorcycles are returned to owners and replaced with new exhibits. The owner runs an interesting annual raffle; the first and second tickets out of the hat each take away a classic British motorcycle!

Open daily 10.00am to 5.00pm from the end of May to the end of October. There is a shop which sells a range of motorcycle-related gifts and books. No food facilities on the premises but there are many cafes nearby. Public car park and and toilets also nearby.

MOTORCYCLES

1920	ABC 398cc
1921	Sun 275cc
1923	Atlas 13/4hp
1923	Excelsior 147cc
1924	BSA 250cc
1924	Triumph DI and sidecar 799cc
1924	Triumph SD 550cc
1926	AJS G8 498cc
1928	Norton Model 18, 500cc
1931	Coventry Eagle 196cc
1931	Norton International 490cc
1933	Sunbeam long stroke sports 246cc
1936	BSA Racer 250cc
1937	Royal Enfield 248cc
1946	Ariel 350cc
1946	Royal Enfield WD/C 350cc
1947	James ML 125cc
1948	Excelsior 197cc
1948	New Hudson Autocycle 98cc
1950	Excelsior Corgi 98cc
1953	BSA Cl1 250cc
1954	Cyclemaster 32cc
1954	Francis Barnet 125cc
1954	Trojan Minimotor. 49cc
1955	New Hudson 98cc
1955	Velocette MSS 500cc
1956	BSA M33 500cc
1957	BSA Dandy 70cc
1957	Douglas Dragonfly 350cc
1957	Mercury Hermes 98cc
1958	Velocette Valient 200cc
1959	James 150cc
1959	Norman Nippy 49cc
1960	BSA Gold Star DBD34 500cc
1960	Royal Enfield Meteor Minor 500cc
1960	Velocette Viper 350cc
1961	Douglas Vespa 125cc
1961	Greeves Sports 250cc
1961	James Scooter 150cc
1961	Norton Jubilee 249cc
1962	Ariel Sports Arrow 250cc
1962	Raleigh Supermatic 50cc
1962	Triumph Tiger Cub T20 200cc
1962	Triumph Tina 100cc
1963	James 199cc
1963	Raleigh Roma 78cc
1964	Ariel Pixie 49cc
1964	Butler Greeves and sidecar 246cc
1964	Raleigh Runabout 49cc
1965	BSA B40, 350cc
1965	Triumph Trophy TR6 650cc
1967	Raleigh Wisp 49cc
1967	LE Velocette 200cc
1968	BSA Starfire 250cc
1971	BSA Victor 500cc
1973	BSA Ariel 349cc
1985	Sinclair C5, electric

INVALID CARRIAGES

1939	Carter Trycycle, electric	
1955	RA Harding, 3GV, electric	
1963	AC (Acedes) 199cc	MOH 57
1965	Reselco Solocar 36v, electric	
1969	Frank Tippen Ltd. 197cc	MOH 49
1971	AC (Acedes) 197cc	DHSS 57
1971	Invercar (Mk 12) 197cc	MOH 62

Admission: adults £2.50; children and OAPs £1.50; children under 10 accompanied by an adult free.

Combe Martin Motorcycle Museum advertising literature.

This type of motorcycle, a 1967 water-cooled 200cc LE Velocette, was once popular with many County Constabularies. (Courtesy Combe Martin Motorcycle Collection)

1965 Reselco Solocar electric invalid carriage, part of the owner's collection of similar vehicles. (Courtesy Combe Martin Motorcycle Collection)

West of England Transport Collection, Winkleigh Airfield, Winkleigh, North Devon. EX19 8DW.

Tel. 01769 580811. Curator: Colin Shears.
Address for correspondence: 15 Land Park Road, Chumleigh, Devon EX18 7BH.

Located at Winkleigh Old Airfield, west of the A347 on the B3220, 40 miles northeast of Plymouth. On the annual Open Day there is a free bus service from Winkleigh Village and also from nearby Eggesford rail station.

As yet, the Collection has no permanent visitor facility, although an annual Open Day is held on the first Sunday of October: a charge is made but there's free parking. The Collection comprises some 60 single and double-decker buses with a West Country flavour from the late twenties to the mid-sixties, and there are some commercial vehicles, too. Individual visits may be arranged with the Curator in return for a donation towards the upkeep of the Collection. The first bus bought was one on which the Curator used to travel to school in Exeter in the 1940s. The Collection is associated with the Scottish Vintage Bus Society.

BUSES		
1927	Austin 20 coach	UO 2331
1932	Tilling-Stevens B10 A2	JY 124
1933	Leyland Lion LT/5	OD 5868
1934	AEC Regent I	OD 7497
1934	AEC Regent I	OD 7500
1935	Bristol JJW	ATT 922
1935	Bristol J-type	ADV 128
1935	Leyland Lion,	AUO 744
1936	Leyland TD4C	No reg.
1937	Leyland Lion	No reg.
1938	Leyland Tiger	EFJ 666
1938	Leyland Titan	EFJ 241
1940	AEC Regal I	DOD 474
1941	Bristol K5G/ECW	FTA 634
1941	Bristol LL5G/BBW	GTA 395
1943	Guy Arab II	JTA 314
1947	AEC Regal II	HUO 510
1948	Crossley DD42/5	DYJ 965
1949	Bristol K6B ECW	KUO 972
1949	Daimler CVD6	JFJ 606
1949	Leyland PD1 ECW	GLJ 957
1950	AEC Regal III	LUO 595
1952	AEC Regent III	NTT 661
1953	AEC Regal rebuild	ETT 995
1953	Leyland PD2/12	HJY 296
1956	Guy Arab Mk IV	TFJ 808
1957	AEC Regent V	VDV 817
1958	Leyland PD2/40	OCO 502
1960	Guy Arab Mk IV	974 AFJ
1964	AEC Reliance/Harrington	No reg.
1965	AEC Regent	CTT 513C

BUSES (unrestored)		
1927	Leyland Lion PLSC3	VW 203

1949	Mann Egerton coach	MAF 544
	Leyland TD5	EUF 204
	Leyland TD5	FCD 506

CARS		
1939	Austin Eight, unrestored	FFJ 262
1939	Austin 10hp saloon	BBX 57
1956	Morris Minor saloon 800cc	PSP 619

OTHER COMMERCIAL VEHICLES		
1940	Std Fordson tractor	JTA 396
1943c	Crossley WWII 4 X 4 transporter	CTA 72
1948	Bedford 30cwt tower wagon	FJY 336
1960c	Guy Vixen pantechnicon	717 NYB
1963	SD 10 ton fork lift	No reg.
1968	Foden 6 wheel flat lorry	SOY 147F
1968	BMC LD, parcels van	MUO 656F
1969	Ford Transit van	PCR 261G
1970	Leyland Retriever tipper lorry	UAF 756H
1971	AEC box van	TUO 288J
1971	BMC ex-library van	TUO 575J
1981	Bedford 500, pantechnicon	NJP 549W
1982	Bedford 'KM' pantechnicon	OMO 212X
1983	Sherpa ex-BT van	ETT 998Y
1983	Ital 440 ex-BT van	ETT 999Y
1985	Ford Transit minibus	C748 FFJ
	Leyland turntable fire engine, unrestored	EDV 499
	Stephens/Ford 2 ton ex-RN truck	15 RN 25
	Bristol L5G towing lorry	BOW 169

The Tank Museum, Bovington, Wareham, Dorset BH20 6JG.

Tel. 01929 405096. Curator: David Fletcher. Accessions Officer: Elizabeth Wallis.

To get to the Museum turn south off the A3 or A35 at Bere Regis onto the Bovington Camp/ Wool road. The Museum is signposted off to the right.

The Tank Museum extends to a total of six halls, with some 150 vehicles on show, displayed chronologically and by area of conflict. The Museum has a further 200 in store or elsewhere. A popular and explosive free display, 'Tanks in Action,' is staged every Thursday during July, August and September. Other special events are staged throughout the year. There are displays of uniforms, weapons, engines and memorabilia, plus an extensive library/photographic library, video theatres, amusement arcade, remote-controlled cars, simulators and astro-jet simulator.

Open: 10.00am to 5.00pm, seven days a week. Closed over Christmas, re-open by the New Year. There's a gift shop, restaurant, excellent free parking, disabled access and toilet facilities, Braille and audio tours.

Admission: adults £6.50; children (5 to 15) £4.50; OAPs and disabled £5.50. Family ticket (2 + 3) £17.50. Concessions for ten or more people; ring for details.

Vehicle list

Due to temporary exhibitions, some of the listed vehicles may not be on display. Similarly, vehicles not mentioned may be on display in the Museum. If a specific vehicle is sought, check first with the Museum to avoid disappointment.

UK
ARMOURED CARS
AEC II Charioteer
Coventry 1
1923 Crossley on Chevrolet chassis
Daimler II
Guy I
Humber I
Lanchester Mk II
1919 Peerless
1920 Rolls-Royce, Silver Ghost
Saladin 1
Shorland Mk 3
Bison (Thorncroft)

SCOUT CARS
Daimler I (Dingo)
Daimler II
Ferret 4
Ferret 2/5
Ferret 1
Ferret 5 'Swingfire'
Humber

CARRIERS
Carden Lloyd Mk VI
FV402 Cambridge AOP
Humber one ton 'Pig'
Oxford Carrier
Saracen ACV
Saracen Mk1
Universal Carrier Mk II

TRACTOR/CAR
1909 Hornsby chain track tractor
1904 Wilson-Pilcher car

TANKS
Mark IX
Challenger
CDL Matilda
Praying Mantis
Tetrach
Centurion bridge layer Mk 5. FV4002
Centurion Mk 1
Centurion Mk 3
Centurion sectionalized, 2 pieces
Tog 2
Amphibious light tank no. 3
Valentine, Mk I
A1E1 Independent Valentine bridge layer
A33 Assault Tank
A 38 Valiant
A43 Black Prince
Vickers-Carden-Loyd light tank
Vickers 6 tonner-type
BD1E1 Vickers wheel-cum-track
Vickers medium Mk II
Medium A 'Whippet'
Mark I Male
Mark II Hermaphrodite
Mark IV Male
Mark V Female
Mark V Male
Chieftain 10 (Stillbrew)
Chieftain Prototype G2
Chieftain (Aluminum)
Churchill Crocodile flamethrower trailer
Churchill Mk VII
Churchill Mk VI
Comet
Conqueror Mark 1
Light tank Mk II

The Tank Museum's modern entrance, flanked by two examples of the modern fighting vehicle. (Courtesy Bovington Tank Museum)

FV4004 Conway
Covenanter Mk III
Centurion Mk 13
Centurion FV4202, 40 ton
Chieftain 900
Cromwell Mk IV
Centaur Dozer
A 13 Cruiser Mk III
A 10 Cruiser Mk I CS
A 9 Cruiser M I
Crusader Mk III
Harry Hopkins
A 11 infantry tank Mk I (Matilda I)
A 12 infantry tank Mk II (Matilda II)
Little Willie (the first recognized tank)
Light tank Mk VIB
Light tank M IV
Mark VIII 'International'

REMOTE-CONTROLLED DEMOLITION VEHICLES
SdKfz 304 Springer
SdKfz 303 Goliath

SELF-PROPELLED GUNS
Contentious
Tortoise
Valentine Archer

CVRs (T and W)
Fox
Scorpion
Vixen

MISSILE VEHICLES
Humber Hornet Malkara
FV438 Swingfire
Striker

HELICOPTERS
Skeeter

TRAIN
Armoured train gun truck

France
ARMOURED CARS
Panhard AML 245
Panhard AML 90 (ex-Argentina)

CARRIER
Renault UE Chenilette

TANKS
AMX 13
Char B 1
AMX 30
Renault FT 17
Somua S35

Germany
ARMOURED CARS
Sd Kfz 234/3
Spadhpanzer Luchs
HS-30 and HS-30 Mortar Carrier

ARMOURED PERSONNEL CARRIERS
Sd Kfz 251 'Hanomag'
Kleines Kettenkrad

RECONNAISSANCE VEHICLE
Schultzenpanzer Kurz, Hotchkiss Sp 11 A

TANKS
Leopard 1
Panther G
Panzer I Befehlswagen
Panzer IIF
Panzer II Luchs (Lynx)
Panzer IIIL
Panzer IIIN
Panzer IVD/H
Tiger IE
King Tiger
Porsche Turret

SELF-PROPELLED GUNS
Jagdpanzer 38T 'Hetzer'
Jagdtiger
Sturmgeschutz III
M5A1 Stuart Mk 6
M5A1 Stuart Mk 2

US
ARMOURED CARS
T18E2 Boarhound
M8 Greyhound
M6 Staghound
White scout car
Armoured personnel carriers
LVT 4 Buffalo
M9 (International Harvester) half-track
M29 Weasel amphibious carrier
M59
M113

TANKS AND TANK DESTROYERS
M10 Achilles
T14 assault tank
M24 Chaffee
M3 Grant
M22 Locust
M2595 Ha Go
M46 Patton 1
M47 Patton 2
M48A1 Patton 3
M60A1 Patton
M26 Pershing
M4E8 Sherman I BY (105mm howitzer)
M4A1 Sherman II Michael
M4A2E8 Sherman III with 76mm gun
M4A4 Sherman V Firefly
M74 Sherman ARV
M4A2 Sherman III Duplex Drive
M4A4 Sherman V Crab Flail

Sweden
TANK
Stridsvagen M40/L

USSR
TANKS AND SELF-PROPELLED GUNS
T34/85 2
T34/85 ex-target incomplete
T54 M
T62
T72
KV1B
SU76M
SU100

ARMOURED PERSONNEL CARRIERS
BTR 60

orld War Two Sherman Tank at the Bovington
Museum, Dorset. (Courtesy Bovington Tank
Museum)

Tank Museum has display days when this, and
y other types of armoured vehicle, may be seen
a similar setting. This photograph shows a
Chieftain tank at speed on a dusty day.
(Courtesy Bovington Tank Museum)

BTR 50
BW1
MTLB
ACRV

ARMOURED CARS
BRDM 1
BRDM 2

China
TANKS
Type 59 ARV
Type 69 Mk2
Type 59, Iraqi modified
Type 69 command tank
APC
YW503 armoured command vehicle
WZ751 armoured ambulance

Poland
TANK
T55 Iraqi modified

Hungary
ARMOURED CAR
FUG (OT-65)BRDM 2

Finland
TANK
T26

Brazil
ARMOURED CAR
Engasa EE9 Casvacel Mk 5

Switzerland
TANK
PZ 61

ARMOURED CAR
Leyland armoured car

South Africa
ARMOURED CARS
Marmon Herrington Mk 4
Marmon Herrington Mk 6

Canada
ARMOURED PERSONNEL CARRIER
Ram Kangaroo

Czechoslovakia
SMALL SELF-PROPELLED GUN
Hetzer

New Zealand
EX-AMERICAN TANK
M 41

Australia
TANK
Australian Cruiser Mk 1, Sentinel

Italy
TANKS
CV3/33 flamethrower
M13/40

Holland
EIGHT-WHEELED PERSONNEL CARRIER
YP 408

Belgium
EX-GERMAN SELF-PROPELLED GUN
Jag Pauzer KannoneN

A German Panzer tank performing at an Open Day. (Courtesy Bovington Tank Museum)

Christchurch Motor Museum, Matchams Lane, Hurn, Christchurch, Dorset, BH23 6AW.

Tel. 01202 488100.
Administrator: Miss N. J. Singleton

The Museum is located at the Christchurch Ski Centre, near Bournemouth airport at Hurn, just off the A338 Bournemouth Spur Road.

The Christchurch Motor Museum has a collection of rare and exciting cars, as well as memorabilia, and there are regular Formula One exhibits. The Museum shop has a wide range of Formula One merchandise for the enthusiast. There's also a display of household memorabilia and press cuttings dating from the 1920s. You can even treat yourself or a friend to a vintage car ride (prior booking only). Refreshments and toilets are available at the neighbouring Ski Centre. Coach parties and car clubs welcome by arrangement: free parking. Open daily from 10.00am until 5.00pm during the summer months, and 10.00am until 4.00pm in the winter months. Closed Christmas Day and Boxing Day.

Exhibits include:

1921	Auto Red Bug	(USA origin)
1926	Hispano Suiza	PG3830
1928	Austin Dixi	SV4288
1930	Austin Ulster	VJ1410
1935	Daimler	EJ4231
1937	Austin Seven Ruby	RFF529
1947	Rolls-Royce Silver Wraith	SMG720
1957	MGA Roadster	PWV506
1962	Trojan 200 van	OYM666A

Admission: adults £2; concessions £1.75; children £1.

Stapehill Abbey, Crafts and Gardens, Wimborne Road West, Stapehill, Ferndown, Dorset, BH21 2EB.

Tel. 01202 861686. Curator: Jim Robinson.

Stapehill is 18 miles west of Southampton via the A31.

An exhibition - 'Power to the Land' - displays various tractors. Historic tractors and agricultural machinery are also on display in the Hunday Museum, which is housed at Stapehill. In Stapehill Abbey, 14 different crafts are demonstrated in the craft centre. There are also gardens and a farm yard. The Abbey has a shop, cafe, toilets (also for disabled) and free parking.

Open: Easter to September, 7 days a week from 10.00am to 5.00pm. October 1st to December 24th, and February 1st to Easter, Wednesday to Sunday, 10.00am to 4.00pm.

Admission: adult £5.00; OAPs £4.50; children £3.50.

Beamish, North of England Open Air Museum, County Durham, DH9 ORG.
Tel. 01207 231811. Keeper of Industry: Jim Rees.

The Museum is four miles along the A693 towards Stanley, reached from junction 63 of the A1(M). Service buses operate from Durham/Newcastle and the main railway stations.

A working example of what life in the north of England was like in the early 1900s. Set in 300 acres of woodland and rolling countryside are many different exhibits, such as Home Farm, the Town Railway Station and engine shed, chapel, school, Co-op, sweet shop, newspaper office, pub and the colliery village. The Transport Collection includes steam engines, electric tram cars, motor buses, commercial vehicles and fire engines. Free rides are given on the trams and buses. At the Motor and Cycle Works is a typical Edwardian town garage complete with a Model T Ford under repair, and other period exhibits. Definitely a family attraction.

Open: 27th March to 31st October, 10.00am to 5.00pm, 7 days a week; 1st November to 26th March, 10.00am to 5.00pm, closed Mondays and Fridays. Closed 16th of December to 1st of January inclusive. Winter visits centre on the town and tramway only.

On site are several shops that have a variety of gifts for sale; there's also a tea room and pub. Beamish is not ideal for the disabled, although a helper is admitted free and toilets are provided. Free parking.

MOTORCARS		COMMERCIAL	
1903	De Dion Bouton 6hp	1914	Daimler lorry
1910	Armstrong Whitworth 25/30hp	1913	Daimler replica open top bus
1913	Ford T saloon		
1916	Ford T saloon		
1913	Armstrong Whitworth replica	**TRAMS**	
		1900	Sunderland, to be restored
		1901	Blackpool double deck, open top
MOTORCYCLES		1901	Newcastle double deck, open top
1916	Royal Enfield V twin 425cc	1907	Sheffield double deck
1918c	Dene 980cc Jap twin	1925	Gateshead single deck
1919	Triumph 500cc	1935	Oporto single deck
		1952	Sheffield double deck

Admission (including tram rides) high season (from April 1st): adults £10.00; OAPs £7.00; children (5-16) £6.00. Please phone for details of low season prices.

Lord Montagu of Beaulieu on a tour of Beamish in a 1913 Armstrong Whitworth replica. (Courtesy Beamish Museum)

1913 Daimler replica bus, of the period when 'old money' was the accepted currency. (Courtesy Beamish Museum)

The Beamish period garage and replica Armstrong Whitworth. (Courtesy Beamish Museum)

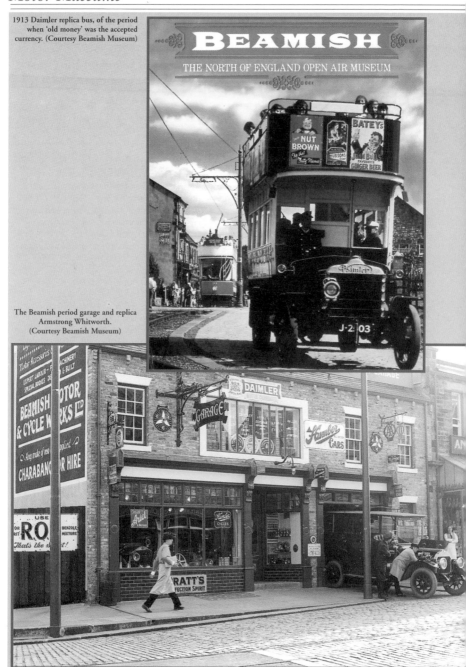

Ford Heritage Centre, 3/001, Thames Avenue, Dagenham, Essex, RM9 6SA.
Tel. 0181 526 4216. Curator: Ron Staughton.

Ford's Heritage Centre can be found adjacent to the main production factory at Dagenham. It's well signposted and is 12 miles east of London.

Ford's first ever Heritage Centre opened in 1996 and houses historic and significant vehicles from as far back as the Quadricycle and Model T right up to the Mondeo. The 40-plus exhibits, including working and motorsport vehicles, are displayed in air-conditioned buildings. Formerly a works canteen in the now demolished Thames Foundry, the Centre has a small conference centre and houses the Reception Centre for factory tours which welcomes more than 30,000 visitors annually. Although a private collection not generally open to the public, groups which make prior arrangement with the Curator are able to visit the Centre.

Exhibits include:

1896	Ford Quadricycle replica (actual vehicle is in the Ford Museum, Dearborn, USA)	
1910	Model T Runabout	
1936	Fordson Tug	
1953	Zephyr Mark I	
1965	Transit Van, believed to be the oldest of the marque in Britain	
1970	Escort RS Mexico	FEV1H
	Lotus Cortina	
	Capri, last built	
	Sierra Cosworth, last built	
	Escort RS2000, last built	
	Cortina 1600, last built	
	Cortina Mk II 1600E	
	Capri Ferguson four wheel drive	
1993	Mondeo used on the Overland Challenge - London to New York	
1995	Escort Mexico	

Model Y Ford car at the Ford Heritage Centre, Dagenham, Essex.

Ford Cortina MkI at the Ford Heritage Centre, Dagenham, Essex.

Castle Point Transport Museum Society, The Old Bus Garage, 105, Point Road, Canvey Island, Essex, SS8 7TD.

Tel. 01268 684272 (ansafone Monday-Friday).
Hon. Secretary: Glynis Webster.

Castle Point is 38 miles east of London. The nearest railway station is Benfleet on the London, Tilbury and Southend line. Thamesway buses stop outside the Museum in Point Road. Note: Arriva buses do not go to Point Road. Road access to Canvey island is via the A130 and brown tourist signs will direct you once on the island.

The Castle Point Transport Museum building was originally constructed in 1934 for the Canvey and District Motor Transport Co. Ltd. After several different operators, commercial operations ceased in 1978. At the same time, part of the building was being used to house a collection of vehicles owned by the Eastern National Preservation Group. The Castle Point Transport Museum Society was formed to purchase the building, establish a transport museum and attract vehicles owned by other preservation groups and individuals. ENPG is an autonomous organisation which continues to provide a valuable part of the display. CPTMS was granted charitable status in 1979 and secured the freehold to the building in 1983.

The building is recognised by the local council as being of architectural interest, and much work has been necessary to improve its safety and appearance. Approximately five years ago an annexe was built at the rear of the building to house five single deck vehicles. The Society has a plan of action to develop public facilities at the Museum.

Around 35 vehicles are on show, spanning the years 1929 to 1972, and they include some notable 'milestone' vehicles - consult the Society for details. Visitors can always see buses being worked on, with at least six vehicles undergoing major restoration and a number of others being progressively improved.

Special opening arrangements can be made at other times during the season for schools and other organised group visits. The annual Open Day and Rally is on the second Sunday in October and there is a charge for this day only. No special facilities for the disabled at present, although all public areas are on ground level. There is a hot drinks machine and car parking is available in the Museum grounds.

Open: Sundays, 10.00am to 5.00pm, April to October. Admission: free; donations welcome.

COMMERCIAL VEHICLES

Year	Vehicle	Reg	Year	Vehicle	Reg
1928/39	Leyland Tiger	KD 5296	1958	Ford Thames 4D	SXF 233
1935	Dennis Lancet 1 (chassis)	BTW 488	1958	Leyland PD3/6	PHJ 954
1944	Bristol K5G	JVW 430	1959	Bedford C4Z2	UHJ 842
1944	Daimler CWA6	FOP 429	1959	Bristol MW6G DP	217 MHK
1947	Leyland PD1A	MPU 52	1959	Bristol LDLX6G	236 LNO
1948	Bedford OB	CFV 851	1960	Leyland PD3/2	SGD 407
1949	AEC RT3/8	KGU 413	1961	Guy Arab V	373 WPU
1949	AEC RT3/3	LYR 997	1962	AEC Reliance	28 TKR
1949	Bristol K6B	LHY 937	1963	AEC Regent V	918 NRT
1949	Leyland OPD2/1	NEH 453	1963	AEC Regent V	SDX 57
1950	Bristol L5G	ONO 49	1963	Ford Trader	581 EYU
1950	Bristol L6B	PTW 110	1965	AEC Routemaster	CUV 223C
1950	Scammell Discovery	35 BC 74	1965	Bristol FLF6G	NTW 942C
1951	AEC Turntable Ladder	JFS 372	1965	Leyland PD3	CFJ 68C
1953	Bristol KSW5G	WNO 478	1966	Bedford RL	13 RK 13
1953	Maudslay Mogul	MYF 974	1967	Ford Transit	KHJ 215E
1954	AEC RT3/8	OLD 717	1968	Bristol FLF6LX	AVX 975G
1954	Bristol LD5G	XVX 19	1968	Bristol VRT	CPU 979G
1954	Harrington Contender	JAP 698	1972	Dennis D series FF	POO 464K

London Ambulance Museum, Ilford Ambulance Station, London Ambulance Service, Aldborough Road South, Newbury Park, Ilford, Essex, IG3 8HQ.

Tel. 0181 557 1767 or 1711.
Curator: Terry Spurr, MBE.
email: Terence.Spurr@lond-amb.sthames.nhs.uk
LAS website: http//www.lond-amb.sthames.nhs.uk

The nearest rail station is Seven Kings on the Liverpool Street line; across the road from the Ambulance station is Newbury Park London underground station on the Central line.

A fascinating collection of ambulances, vintage radio equipment, photographic records and memorabilia is displayed at Ilford Ambulance Station, which is open to the public Mondays to Fridays between 9.00am and 5.00pm, and at weekends by prior arrangement, subject to outside events that have been arranged. Facilities include souvenir shop, disabled access, toilets (including disabled) and parking. No refreshment facilities. Groups are welcome by prior appointment with a maximum number of 12.

Exhibits include:

1870	Horsedrawn ambulance	
1926	W. G. du Cros ambulance (one of only 10 made by the founder of Australian road trains)	YT9792
1962	Austin Wandsworth ambulance	394BXA
1965	Morris Wandsworth ambulance	CYH540C
1966	Land Rover emergency control vehicle	KGY597D
1973	Sovam Reeves ambulance (prototype, cost £38,000) on Citroën chassis with a wheel at each corner	MMF447L
1973	Bedford Dormobile swb CF ambulance	MLM922L
1975	Morris Wadham Stringer ambulance (first built)	PYP516E
1984	Citroën, French model with limousine style ambulance body	
1987	Bedford Mountain Range ambulance	E322DPK
1989	Leyland Daf Ambulance towing vehicle	G454BPJ
1991	Norton Commando paramedic motorcycle	H536GPD
1993	LDV Bernard Collett ambulance	L738FPG

In addition, Daimler, Talbot and Dennis ambulances from the Collection are kept at the LAS Hillingdon ambulance station for use at public events. There are also small Metropolitan Police and London Fire Brigade sections of the Museum with some Police BMW motorcycles on display.

London County Council 1935 Talbot ambulance with spare wheel stowed alongside the bonnet. (Courtesy London Ambulance Museum)

Admission is free but donations are welcome.

Museum of Transport in Essex (in formation)

Tel. 01621 819858. Campaign Officer: Michael Ryan.

Address for correspondence: c/o Tudwick Farm Bungalow, Tudwick Road, Tiptree, Essex, CO5 0SG.

A group of some twenty people has been working for two years towards the establishment of a transport museum in mid-Essex. For further details contact the Campaign Officer on the number above.

The Bugatti Trust, Prescott Hill, Gotherington, Cheltenham, Glos, GL52 4RD.

Tel. 01242 677201. Curator: Richard Day.

The Bugatti Trust is accessed from junction 9 of the M5 and then the A435. From the Cheltenham A40 take the Evesham Road (A435), leave this road at Bishops Cleeve and follow the signs for Gotherington. Prescott Hill Climb is about 2 miles past Gotherington.

Open weekdays only from 9.30am to 3.30pm. When weekend hill climbs take place, the Trust is open at certain times.

The Bugatti Trust houses various memorabilia about the Bugatti family, the cars they designed, some engineering exhibits, and many illustrations about this famous marque. There's also a study centre about Bugatti cars. There are normally one or two Bugatti cars on display and details can be obtained by phoning the Curator.

There are toilets and disabled access and facilities. A booklet about the Trust is on sale at the reception desk. Limited free parking.

Admission is free but donations are welcome.

A 1935 replica Bugatti Type 35B, 2.3 litre.

Cotswold Motor Museum, The Old Mill, Bourton-on-the-Water, Glos, GL54 2BY.

Tel. 01451 821255. Curator: Mike Cavanagh.

Bourton-on-the-Water is just off the A429 (Fosse Way), some 8 miles off the A40 London to Cheltenham road. The Museum has no parking but Bourton has several large public car parks.

Famous as the home of 'Brum,' the lovable little car that features in the childrens' TV series shown throughout the world, the Museum has a definite air of the golden days of motoring. in the car collection which is displayed amidst motoring memorabilia and other items of interest from days gone by. Children can take one of the Museum's push-along dogs round to keep them interested and many model cars are on display. The Museum's collection of pedal cars is one of the largest in the country. A 1926 Bertram Hutchings Caravan is one of the rarer exhibits to be found.

The admission price also allows entry to the Village Life exhibition, opened in 1984, which adjoins the Motor Museum. Open: 10.00am-6.00pm, daily from March to November. Disabled access upon request. Refreshments are available at various nearby tearooms.

NB The Museum was for sale at the time of writing so please check by phone before planning a visit.

A glimpse of motoring in the forties at the Cotswold Motor Museum, Bourton-on-the-Water, Gloucestershire.

Vehicles displayed:

Year	Vehicle	Reg	Year	Vehicle	Reg
1929	Austin 7 Chummy	CA95354	1938	BMW 6 cylinder, 2 litre cabriolet	
1929	Brooklands Riley	CB129	1938	Riley 2.5 Big Four	
1929	Maclure Baby Brooklands Riley		1946	Standard Eight drophead	
1931	Austin 7 Swallow	GP7171	1950	Jaguar Mark V drophead	MGW31
1931	Austin 7 Ulster		1950	MG Y saloon	JDG560
1932	Invicta 6 cylinder, 4 door saloon	OJI306	1950	MG TD	5399DG
1932	MG J2	AKE207	1950	Riley 2.5 drophead coupé	
1933	Alvis Speed Twenty		1950	Sunbeam Alpine convertible	
1933	Morris Minor	JW3118	1956	Jaguar XK140 hardtop	CB3140
1934	Riley Kestrel	BLE792	1922	Rover 8hp van	EP2027
1935	Austin taxi		1921	Sunbeam motorcycle	YA8853
1936	Austin 7 Nippy	AOX172	1915	Indian motorcycle	PW2777
1936	Morgan Super Sports 3 wheeler	CWL588	1913	BSA motorcycle	

A 1922 Rover 8hp OXO van at the Cotswold Motor Museum, Bourton-on-the-Water, Gloucestershire.

Admission: £2.00 (adults); £1.00 (children). Family ticket and group discounts available.

Gloucester Transport Museum, The Old Fire Station, Longsmith Street, Gloucester. GL1 2HT.
01452 526467. Curator: Nigel Cox.

The Museum is best approached from the Westgate Street outdoor car park, which is adjacent to the inner ring road leading to Gloucester Docks and signposted to Gloucester Cathedral.

This is a very small museum housed in a former Fire Station (next to the Police Station). Admission is by appointment with the Gloucester Folk Museum, 99-103, Westgate Street, Gloucester, GL1 2PG. Tel. 01452 526467. Curator: Nigel Cox. Folk Museum hours of opening are 10.00am to 5.00pm, Monday to Friday. Bank Holidays and Sundays (July to September) 10.00am to 4.00pm.

No parking on site but there is a large public car park nearby.

A Cotton motorcycle rally, held at the rear of the Folk Museum, is organised annually by the Museum and takes place in August; usually about 30 Cottons are involved.

Exhibits include:

1922	Cotton motorcycle, made in Gloucester	DD512
1926	Morris 1 ton commercial (used in London-Brighton run in 1969)	DD9061
1933	JES motorcycle	
	1 ton Arthur Trotter steam roller (used at outside events)	

The Museum also has two Cotton Sturdy 3 wheel mechanical horses, one of which has been restored. One has a Briggs and Stratton engine and the other a Villiers engine. At times, a loan car is also exhibited which is a c1939 Humber 16/60 coupé with wooden bodywork by Mulliner.

Admission is £2 to non-residents of Gloucester or £4 for a season ticket. All children are admitted free and there are concessions.

One of a pair of Cotton (better known for motorcycles) Sturdy mechanical horses from the Gloucester Transport Museum. (Courtesy Nigel Cox)

Breamore House and Countryside Museum, Breamore, Nr. Fordingbridge, Hants. SP6 2DB.

Telephone 01725 512468. Curator: J. Forshaw.

Fordingbridge is 18 miles southwest of Southampton. The Museum is located on the A388 Ringwood to Salisbury road. Travelling north, turn left at Breamore and follow the signs for the Museum.

Breamore House, a red brick Elizabethan Manor, and its Countryside Museum are well worth a visit. Apart from the imposing interior of the Manor, the tractors of the transport collection are, to an enthusiast, collector's items. The Museum, which was opened in 1972, has a large collection of hand tools, initially gathered by Sir Edward Hulse as a hobby, but later forming the foundation of the Museum. Five buildings contain many special exhibits from agriculture and rural life, which are displayed in re-creations of workshops and buildings to form a village.

Open: April (Tuesday, Wednesday, Sunday and Easter Holidays). May, June, July and September (Tuesday, Wednesday, Thursday, Saturday and Sunday). August, every day. Hours: Countryside Museum 1.00pm to 5.30pm. Tea Barn from 12pm. House 2.00pm to 5.30pm.

Facilities include homemade teas and souvenir shop. No dogs admitted except for guide dogs, and there are facilities for the disabled. Parking is free.

TRACTORS

1917	International Mogul 8/16
1917	Overtime 24hp
1918	International Titan 10/20
1919	International Junior 8/16
1919	Saunderson Universal 23hp
1922	Fordson Model F
1924	Austin, French-built
1929	Rushton 14/20
1929	Wallis and Stevens motor roller
1930	Case Model L
1930	Oliver Hart Parr 18/28
1932	International harvester W14
1932	McCormick International F12
1935	Case Model R
1935	McCormick Decring W30
1935	Fordson Standard
1938	Marshall Model M
1939/43	Fordson Standard Rowcrop tractor
1941	John Deere Model B. Orchard tractor
1944	Fordson Standard on Spadelugs
1948	David Brown VAK
1948	Ransomes crawler

STEAM

1926	Burrell 7hp GP agricultural traction engine TD 8047

CAR

1925	Morris Cowley

Plus horsedrawn vehicles include a Pickering Float and several farm wagons.

Admission (for the House and Museum): adults £5.00; OAPs £4.50; children £3.50; family ticket (2 + 2) £12.00.

D-Day Museum, Clarence Esplanade, Portsmouth, Hampshire. PO5 3NT.

Tel.01705 827261. Military History Officer: Stephen Brooks.

The Museum is sited at Clarence Esplanade, near South Parade Pier in Portsmouth.

Opened in 1984, this specially designed and constructed building records the D-Day landings. There are many displays which recount the story of the landings with, perhaps, the Overlord Embroidery being the highlight. A collection of maps, diagrams, models and military equipment, together with an audio visual show, help to breathe reality into this exhibition. Some of the equipment, which actually took part in the D-Day landings, is also on display, including a rare beach armoured recovery vehicle.

Open: daily from April to October, 10.00am to 5.30pm. November to March, Tuesday to Sunday, 10.00am to 5.00pm. Closed 24th to 26th December inclusive.

There's a shop selling memorabilia and souvenirs and light refreshments are available. Parking for the disabled only, plus adjacent on-street parking. Toilets are available for the disabled and access is good throughout the Museum.

D-Day Museum vehicles:

Sherman Grizzly tank
Churchill Crocodile (flame-throwing) tank
Amphibious DUKW
Beach armoured recovery vehicle
Daimler Dingo scout car
German DKW NZ350 motorcycle
Willys Jeep
Enfield 125cc Flying Flea motorcycle
BSA folding bicycle

Admission (to 31st March 1999): adults £4.75; OAPs £3.60; children/student £2.85. Children under 5 free. Family ticket £12.35 (2 + 2), group rates available. Free admission on Monday afternoons 1.00pm to 5.00pm, November to March (not group bookings).

A 1939/45 Beach Armoured Recovery Vehicle setting off for a test run.
(Courtesy the D-Day Museum, Portsmouth)

Milestones (in formation), Hampshire's Living History Museum, Leisure Park, Basingstoke, Hants, RG21 6YR.

Web site: www.basingstoke.gov.uk
Progress news: Jo Bailey, Hampshire County Council Museums Service. Tel. 01962 846315.

Milestones will be located at the Leisure Park, Basingtoke, which is about 50 miles southwest of London. The motorway exit is junction 6 of the M3.

This is a major new museum in formation which is scheduled to open in 2000 with an exhibition area of around 5700 square metres. It is a joint development by Hampshire County Council, Basingstoke and Deane Borough Council and the Heritage Lottery Fund. Milestones will show how lives were affected by developments in transport and technology through a network of realistic 19th and 20th century street scenes. There will be toilets, free parking, refreshments, disabled access and toilets and a gift shop.

Hampshire County Council will be able to exhibit its extensive transport collection, which includes 18 Thornycroft cars and trucks as well as Tasker steam engines and a Gordon-Keeble car made in the county.

Exhibits will include:

1903	Thornycroft car	BS8239
1916	Thornycroft J-type military 3 ton general service	NB6684
1930	Thornycroft cattle float	OU6028
1931	Thornycroft Bulldog delivery lorry in Boots livery	TV5530
1935	Thornycroft handy BE/FB4	AAA469
1940	Thornycroft road sweeper	
1949	Thornycroft Nippy HF/ER4	DFK98
1960	Thornycroft Swiftsure HL/UR6 dropside truck	5474DT
1963	Gordon-Keeble car	472LKX

1903 Thornycroft 10hp 2 cylinder car. The earliest known production car manufacturer in Hampshire. (Courtesy Hampshire County Council Museums Service)

Artist's impression of the proposed Milestones undercover complex at Basingstoke.

The National Motor Museum, Beaulieu, Brockenhurst, Hants, SO42 7YL.

Tel. 01590 612345. Curator: Andrea Bishop.
24-hour information line: 01590 612123

Beaulieu is 5 miles southwest of Southampton and the Museum is between Bournemouth and Southampton, 7 miles from Lyndhurst. Access is via the M3 and M27 (from junction 2) and the main routes from Guildford, Newbury, Swindon and Bristol.

Beaulieu is a day out for all the family. In 1952, Lord Montagu displayed five cars in the Front Hall of Palace House, and this was the beginning of Britain's National Motor Museum. With approximately 400 historic vehicles and motorcycles from all periods of motoring history, it is now the largest and deservedly the best known car museum in Britain.

There are many transport displays including 'Wheels,' an automated exhibition which pictorially reviews a hundred years of motoring history. Without doubt, this is an enthusiast's museum and should be high on your to-visit list. The old Palace House, (1538), home to Lord Montagu, and the adjacent Beaulieu Abbey (1204) are well worth seeing. Although much of the Abbey was destroyed during the reign of King Henry the VIII, fortunately, some of the buildings survived.

Open daily from April to September, 10.00am to 6.00pm; October to March 10.00am to 5.00pm. Closed Christmas Day and New Year's Day. Parking is free and there are a multiplicity of services for the disabled, although access is not possible to all buildings. The Brabazon Food Court provide a full range of food and drink, or you may picnic in the grounds. There are gift shops and an information centre.

Admission: adults £9.00; children (4-16) £6.50; family ticket (2 + 3) £29.00. Reduced rates for OAPs and groups.

MOTORCARS

Year	Car	Reg	Year	Car	Reg
1895	Knight	P 2917	1909	Rover 6hp	UJ 7652
1886	Benz Replica	No reg.	1910	Bugatti type-15	BJ 2305
1896	Arnold	NIT 906	1912	Hispano Suisa Alfonso XIII	IK 1085
1896	Pennington Autocar	No reg.	1912	Sunbeam 3 litre.coupé de L'Auto	XE 9869
1897	Bersey Electric Car	No reg.	1913	Argyll 15/30hp	V 2821
1898	Benz 3hp	BW 37	1913	Thames Coach	W 215
1898	Daimler (Cannstatt) 4hp	AR 2	1913	Fiat Tipo Zero	AR 4965
1899	Daimler 12hp	AA 16	1913	Newton Bennett	N 1
1899	Renault Voiturette	Q 810	1914	Ford model T	BE 2789
1899	Fiat 3.5hp	AF 579	1914	Ford Model T baker's van	PO 326
1900	Royal Enfield Quadricycle	WOT 891	1914	R-R 40/50 Alpine Eagle	AA 43
1901	Columbia Electric	MPA 3	1914	Sunbeam 12/16hp tourer	LM 7339
1902	Arrol Johnston Dog Cart	NSP 25	1914	Albion	NA 1433
1903	Napier Gordon Bennett	DW 214	1914	Vauxhall Prince Henry	DL 821
1903	Cadillac 9hp	YU 1974	1915	Vauxhall Prince Henry	V 2948
1903	Daimler 22hp	AA 11	1920	Leyland Fire Engine	On loan
1903	De Dietrich	3 JOT	1921	AEC RT double decker bus	KYY 663
1903	Marenghi fairground organ		1922	Aston Martin 1.5 litre Strasbourg	XP 3037
1903	De Dion Bouton Model Q 6hp	AA 20	1922	Maxwell Chara	CJ 5052
1903	Mercedes 60hp	A 740	1923	Aveling and Porter steam roller	PR 678
1904	Knight Trike	No reg.	1923	Austin Seven	VA 7103
1904	Pope Tribune	EL 411	1923	Calcott 11.9hp	CK 650
1904	De Dion Bouton Model Q 6hp	A 8790	1923	Citroën Cloverleaf	ND 8106
	Edwardian childrens pedal cars	No reg.	1924	Bugatti type-35	No reg.
1905	Gregoire	EL 412	1924	Sunbeam Cub Model	DA 8667
1906	Renault 14/20hp	CC 6500	1924	Morris Cowley	OR 5885
1907	Gobron Brillie 40/60hp fire engine	AA 608	1924	Trojan PB	CJ 6672
1907	Itala 120hp	No reg.	1924	Daimler TL 30 Bottle	XT 5195
1907	Napier 60hp	A 8976	1924	Sunbeam 2 litre 'The Cub'	No reg.
1908	Unic 12/14hp taxicab	No reg.	1925	R-R 40/50 Phantom I	AA 19
1909	Humber 8hp	M 7371	1925	Austro Daimler	MH 338
1909	R-R 40/50 Silver Ghost	R 1909	1926	Citroën Kegresse	SM 7802

An 1899 Fiat 3.5hp at the National Motor Museum, Beaulieu, Hampshire. (Courtesy National Motor Museum)

1926	Eccles caravan	No reg.
1927	Morgan Aero Sports	YT 1920
1927	Jowett Long Four	RU 5649
1927	Sunbeam 1000hp	DA 8667
1927	Dennis fire engine 17.9hp	WK 603
1928	Bayliss Thomas	UR 1291
1928	Mercedes-Benz 36/220	YX 5964
1928	Bean	KD 1443
1928	Lancia Lambda 8th Series	YX 3125
1928	Austin Seven	DF 6352
1928	Austin Clifton	No reg.
1929	Bolster Bloody Mary	No reg.
1929	Golden Arrow Irvino Napier Special	No reg.
1930	MG Midget M-type	VG 2910
1930	Bentley 4.5 litre supercharged	GY 3905
1931	Morris Minor	OG 8580
1931	Austin Seven Swallow saloon	RV 423
1932	Austin Seven Swallow	NG 3576
1932	Dixon Bate Trailer	No reg.
1933	Duesenberg	648 HJX
1934	Crossley Burney Streamline	BJU 217
1934	Riley Falcon	CPB 461
1934	Talbot 105	BGT 112
1934	Fowler Showman's Supreme	EU 5313
1934	Lancia Augusta	BLP 999
1935	Hutchings Winchester Caravan	No reg.
1935	Austin Lichfield	JA 5797
1935	Auburn 851 Speedster	BZY 525
1935	Rolls-Royce 20/25	CYX 530
1935	Datsun	No reg.
1935	Riley 1.5 TT Sprite chassis	No reg.
1935	Morris commercial tipper	AAB 330
1935	MG PA-type	CPJ 5041935
1937	Cord Westchester sedan	TSM 1937
1937	Wolsey 25hp	DM 642
1937	Ford Model Y	ETA 808
1937	Alvis Speed 25	EGJ 186
1937	Ford V8 Utility	AV 9621
1938	Hillman Minx	EYX 108
1938	Austin Pearl cabriolet	DYD 80
1938	Morris 8hp	ARV 963
1938	Rover 14hp	GEY 322
1938	Rolls-Royce Phantom III	AFU 209
1939	Harrod's one ton electric	FYR 689
1939	Scammell mechanical horse	HNK 960
1939	Vauxhall 10/4 H-type saloon	BPO 31
1939	Atco Trnr 98cc	CAS 3
1943	Fordson Tractor	EP 8560
1944	Willys Jeep	EPR 241
1946	Standard 8/10hp chassis	No reg.
1947	Healey 2.4 litre	HUE 994
1947	Reliant van, three wheeler	FFU 446
1947	Brush Pony milk float (electrical)	No reg.
1948	Land Rover Prototype	HNX 950
1949	Morris Minor	NPL 409
1949	Cooper Mk III	No reg.
1949	Ford Anglia	FDL 968
1950	Allard J2	LLP 798
1950	BRM 1.5 litre V16 Mk 1	No reg.
1951	Standard Vanguard I	LCD 923
1952	Austin Atlantic	MRU 77
1952	Citroën Light 15	PCV 265
1953	Reliant Regal Mk I	NYY 162
1953	Triumph Mayflower	RKL 146
1953	VW Export-type I Beetle	KRY 724
1953	Austin A40 Somerset	LCE 479
1953	Champion 400H	MNM 451
1954	Jaguar D-type	OKV 1
1954	Triumph TR 2	RTT 417
1955	BMA Hazcar (electric)	JPN 149
1955	Ford Consul convertible	PLE 999
1956	Austin Healey 100rn	WWC 517
1957	Mercedes SL G/w	SYN 126P
1959	Austin Mini Seven	XAA 274
1960	Jaguar XK 150	44 JHY
1960	Triumph Herald	YYT 397
1961	Allard Dragster 5.8 litre	No reg.
1961	Bluebird CN7/62	No reg.
1962	Jaguar E-type Roadster	3800 R
1962	BMW Isetta	518 ELT

1962	Ford Consul Cortina Mk 1	7968 DP
1962	Lotus Elite	1329 PL
1963	Hillman Imp	1400 SC
1963	Morris Oxford	4777 ET
1964	Peel PSO	FMP 621
1964	Commer Autosleeper	ABL 293B
1965	AC Cobra	OTM 70OF
1966	Ford GT40 Mk III	YPE 798G
1967	Lotus 49 R3	No reg.
1967	Rover 2000	GNE 143E
1970	Morris 1000 Post Office van	DPB 195
1970	R. R. Phantom VI Limo.	BML 77H
1970	TVR Vixen Series III	HLU 894K
1971	Ford Capri 1600L	XEL 421K
1972	Mini Outspan orange	HOB 446L
1972	Ferrari Dino 246 GT	AYA 44K
1977	Lotus 78 JPS 16	No reg.
1981	Ford Escort rally car	No reg.
1983	Audi Quattro A2 rally car	No reg.
1985	Sinclair C5	No reg.
1985	Cummins Engine	No reg.
1986	Ford Cosworth Turbo F1 engine	No reg.
1988	Marlboro McL. Honda MP4/4	No reg.
1990	Citroën 2CV	No reg.
1993	Jaguar XJ 220	LT TWT
1993	Williams FW 15c	No reg.

MOTORCYCLES

1898	Ariel tricycle	No reg.
1899	Perks Birch Autowheel	AA 92
1900	De Dion Bouton tricycle	P 350
1900	James pedalcycle	No reg.
1900	Lady's attachment to motorised tricycle	No reg.
1903	Madison Clipon	EL 153
1903	Triumph 2.5hp	AO 135
1903	Werner 2hp	A 2201
1904	Phoenix 2hp	S 613
1905	Matchless	GC 5895
1905	Montgomery trailer	No reg.
1906	NSU 3hp	RSK 494
1906	Rex with sidecar	SO 97
1907	Deronziere Autocycle 282cc	VGC 441
1910	Bradbury 3.5hp	UF 586
1912	Zenith Gradua	LH815
1912	Matchless 8hp	H 8669
1912	Norton BS Old Miracle	AOK 200
1913	BAT 5/6hp with sidecar	AL 508
1913	Douglas Model R2hp	LMK 77
1913	Motosacoche 2.5hp	Y 2009
1914	Royal Enfield 346cc	XOT 4
1914	Triumph 4hp	B 6656
1914	Wall auto wheel fixed to cycle	No reg.
1915	Harley-Davidson llhp	CR 4732
1915	Triumph Junior	EO 1871
1919	Mobil Pup Scooter	HO 4319
1919	Royal Enfield Exp. 4 cylinder	AB 5704
1920	Douglas 600cc and sidecar	No reg.
1920	Wooler 2hp	KE 3001
1921	Autoglider 2.5hp	OH 3793
1921	Ner- A-Car	EH 3708
1923	Douglas 600cc with Dixon sidecar	8717 MN
1924	Henderson 11.9hp	XY 575
1924	Peters	PE 6478
1924	Sunbeam Model 3	H 5074
1925	Zenith 1000cc	
1926	Coventry Eagle B33, 300cc	TP 1934
1926	Rex Acme TT Z	EL 1060
1926	Triumph Model Q, 494cc	YP 1086
1927	Scott Squirrel	VE 4151
1927	Triumph P7 Combination AA	YF 3454
1928	BMW R63, 750cc	507 MMU
1928	BSA S280 HV, 493cc	No reg.
1928	Rudge Whitworth 499cc	KMG 734
1930	Ascot Pullin	GHB 358
1931	Ariel Square Four	OV 6427
1931	Matchless SilverHawk	OV 1480
1932	Norton International	No reg.
1936	Brough Superior Combination	CYE 945
1936	Norton RAC Combination	RGO 433

1940	Francis Barnett Cruiser K39, 249cc	DOU 871	1958	Ariel Square Four chopper	56 ETD
1940	Triumph 3TW	No reg.	1958	AJS 7R	No reg.
1942	Harley-Davidson Model 42 WLC	HUR 420	1958	NSU Quickly	82 SW
1942	Norton 16H, 490cc	GOR 251	1958	Royal Enfield 250cc	No reg.
1945	Royal Enfield	No reg.	1959	Ariel Leader 249cc	No reg.
1948	Lambretta Model B	DPR 872	1959	BSA Goldflash and Busmar sidecar	211 WMK
1948	Triumph 5T Speed Twin	No reg.	1960	Norton Manx Model 30	No reg.
1949	BSA Bantam DI 123cc	GCR 113	1960	BSA M21 combination	YUC 593
1949	Brockhouse Corgi Scooter	KLT 785	1961	Greeves motocross special	No reg.
1949	Excelsior AutoBike	JOK 351	1963	BSA Bantam D1 175cc	302 BLJ
1949	Matchless G3L	LWB 968	1971	Ariel tricycle	No reg.
1949	Triumph 6T Thunderbird	JAC 769	1972	Triumph T150 Trident	
1949	Vincent Series C Rapide	LKN 806	1972	Yamaha 195cc	YH 913L
1950	Rotax JAP Speedway	No reg.	1975	Kawasaki 500cc	No reg.
1952	Ariel HT5	GOV 132	1975	Norton Commando	
1952	Velocette LE200	No reg.	1976	Suzuki 500cc	LW 661P
1955	Ariel Square Four G	UKM 638	1978	Benelli 750cc	
1956	BSA Goldstar	VTA 40	1980	Rickman Kawasaki Metisse frame	No reg.
1956	Douglas Dragonfly	647 KMT	1987	Vespa model TS scooter	
1957	BMW with Steib sidecar		1990	Honda Dominator	No reg.
1957	Lambretta LD 150 scooter	STR 921	1995	BMW K 1100 LT	No reg.

An interior shot of the main floor display showing, in the forefront, ex-racing cars. (Courtesy National Motor Museum)

Interior shot of racing cars at the Museum. (Courtesy National Motor Museum)

Palace House, home of the Montagu family since 1538. (Courtesy National Motor Museum)

City of Portsmouth Preserved Transport Depot, 48-54, Broad Street, Old Portsmouth, Hampshire. PO1 2JE.
Tel. 01705 363478. Secretary: Clive Wilkin. Address for correspondence: 42, White Hart Lane, Portchester, Fareham, Hants. PO16 9BH.

Located within 'Old' Portsmouth, as the address. Portsmouth is 16 miles southeast of Southampton.

1964 Leyland Atlantean PDR1/1 with Metro Cammell Weymann 76-seat bodywork, ex-City of Portsmouth, No. 236. (Courtesy Portsmouth Vintage & Bus Museum

In the autumn of 1992 the City of Portsmouth Preserved Transport Depot, (part of the Working Omnibus Museum Project) was successful in its attempt to rent the Old Portsmouth Depot until the summer of 1999. Efforts continue for a permanent Transport Museum in Portsmouth, where vehicles can be displayed to best advantage. In view of this, it might be wise to ring before setting off to visit.

Main Open Days are held on the second Sunday of every month throughout the year, when visitors can see restoration work in progress, take vintage bus rides and often watch a colour slide or video show, all completely free of charge. On these days there is also a free connecting vintage bus service from Portsmouth Hard Interchange (stand K), hourly from 11.00am. There are also more modest Open Days on the last Sunday of each month, plus a number of other special event days.

A number of members of the Vintage Transport Association own vintage buses, which are stored in various premises all over the south. However, only vehicles which are usually present are listed. Some of the vehicles have been restored, whilst others are the subject of long-term preservation projects. Some may be away attending rallies, operating vintage bus services or being temporarily housed elsewhere.

If visitors prefer their donation to go to a specific vehicle, they can make their wishes known to one of the members. The Museum has disabled access, adjacent cafes and on-street parking.

COMMERCIAL VEHICLES				
1876	Horsedrawn coach	No reg.	1947	Leyland Titan PDI	DTP 823
1902	British Electric Car Co. open-top tram	No reg.	1951	A.E.C. Regent III	AHC 442
1903	British Electric Car Co. open-top tram	No reg.	1951	Bedford OB	EHV 65
1919	Thornycroft J	BK 2986	1956	Leyland Titan PD2/12	LRV 996
1933	Leyland Titan TD2 tower wagon	RV 3411	1958	Leyland Titan PD2/40	ORV 989
1934	A.E.C. 661T trolleybus	RV 4649	1964	Leyland Atlantean PDRI/1	BBK 236B
1935	Leyland Titan TD4	RV 6368	1964	Leyland Titan PD3/4	PRX 206B
1937	Leyland Cub KPZ2	ECD 524	1964	A.E.C. Regent V	BTR 361B
1942	Guy Arab I	EHO 228	1967	Morris LD 16 cwt van	KFX 33F
1944	Bedford OWB	CTP 200	1971	Leyland Atlantean PDR2/1	TBK 190K
			1975	Leyland Atlantean AN68	HOR 313N

1951 Bedford OB with Duple 29-seat bodywork, ex-East Ham Borough Council, but restored as Hants & Sussex No. 31. (Courtesy Portsmouth Vintage & Bus Museum)

Admission: free but donations welcome.

1942 Guy Arab I with 1955 Reading 56-seat bodywork, ex-Gosport & Fareham No. 55. (Courtesy Portsmouth Vintage & Bus Museum)

1919 Thornycroft J. with c1910 Dodson 34-seat open top bodywork, ex-City of Portsmouth No. 1. (Courtesy Portsmouth Vintage & Bus Museum)

Sammy Miller Museum, Bashley Manor, Bashley Cross Roads, New Milton, Hants, BH25 5SJ.
Tel. 01425 620777.
Marketing Manager: Mrs Rosemary Miller.
Curator: Norman Webster.

To find the Museum turn southeast off the A35 (Lyndhurst/ Christchurch road) at Hinton towards Lymington, from where you will find the Museum signposted.

The new Sammy Miller Motorcycle Museum, housed on two floors, is a must for any motorcycle enthusiast. Nearly 200 impeccably renovated, hand-picked motorcycles - many of which are prototypes - are displayed against mirrored walls which allow all-round inspection. Sammy Miller, eleven times World Trials Champion, who won over 1200 trophies, prepares all the exhibits himself in the Museum workshop, and is usually somewhere to be found in the building. He demonstrates Museum exhibits at classic meetings and still rides in competition. Open daily 10.00am to 4.30pm.

The Museum offers parking, tea rooms, picnic area and childrens' play area, plus gift and craft shops and disabled facilities.

Admission: adults £3.50; children £1.50.

MOTORCYCLES

Year	Model	Year	Model
1905	Norton (world's oldest!)	1931	Matchless Silver/Hawk 593cc
1914	Rudge 'Multi' 499cc	1933	Sunbeam Model 95, 493cc
1916	Ariel 4hp 498cc	1934	Excelsior Mechanical Marvel
1919	BSA and sidecar 559cc	1934	Rudge 250 Sports, 249cc
1920	Brough 692cc	1934	Velocette Mark IV KTT, 348cc
1921	Indian Powerplus 998cc	1935	Excelsior 'Manxman' 247cc
1923	Ner-A-Car 285cc	1936	Sunbeam 'Lion' 492cc
1923	Martinsyde 676cc	1935	Vincent HRD 500cc
1923	Velocette Model G3 249cc	1937	DKW 250cc
1924	Excelsior 2/s. 247cc	1947	Triumph 'Grand Prix' 499cc
1926	Triumph Model P 494cc	1947	AJS 'Porcupine' twin 498cc
1929	Brough Superior SS100	1948	Sunbeam S7 485cc
1929	Sunbeam Model 90 493cc	1949	Vincent HRD Rapide S.C. 998cc
1930	Brough Superior 680cc	1950	Earles-BSA 497cc
1931	AJS S3 498cc	1951	Douglas '90 Plus' 348cc
1930	Matchless Silver/Arrow 400cc	1951	Vincent 'Black Shadow' 998cc
		1953	Ariel 'Square 4' 998cc

Sammy Miller, in 1998, with the ex-works 750cc MV Augusta with Imola Daytona motor of 16 valves and 5-speed gearbox, being interviewed for a local TV appearance.

1953	BSA MCI 249cc
1953	MV production racer 125cc
1953	Norton Kneeler
1953	Royal Enfield 'Bullet' 346cc
1954	Arrow Ariel
1954	AJS Supercharged V4 500cc
1954	NSU 'Max' 250cc
1957	Ariel Leader
1958	BSA B34 'Gold Star' 499cc
1958	Motor Parilla 250cc
1958	Triumph T100 490cc
1958	Velocette LE 200 192cc
1959	Ariel 'Square 4' 995cc
1961	Ariel (trials) 500cc
1961	BSA A7SS 'Shooting Star' 497cc
1961	BSA 'Rocket Gold Star' 646cc
1962	Triumph 3TA 349cc
1963	Aermacchi 250cc
1963	Greeves 24TES 249cc
1963	Honda Four 250cc RC 162
1949	Velocette KTT Mark VIII 348cc

1964	Bultaco 'Sherpa' 244cc
1963	Suzuki Twin TR63 125cc
1964	AJS 16C 348cc
1965	Cotton 'Telstar' 250cc
1966	DMW 'Hornet' 250cc
1966	Royal Enfield GP5 250cc
1967	Suzuki V4 RS67 125cc
1967	Yamaha TDIC 250cc
1968	Greeves 24RES 'Silverstone' 250cc
1969	Kawasaki, HIR 500cc
1969	Yamaha TD2 250cc
1972	Yamaha TR2 350cc
1977	Honda TL 305cc
1978	Miller prototype 310cc
1980	Suzuki RG500 Mark IV 500cc
1980	Yamaha TZ 500cc

MOTORCARS

1929	Morgan Blackburn 1000
1934	James delivery van 680cc

The entrance to the recently built Sammy Miller Motorcycle Museum, showing the workshops and stores on the left and restaurant and shop on the right. (Courtesy Sammy Miller Motorcycle Museum)

1953 Norton Kneeler Motorcycle at the Sammy Miller Museum at New Milton, Hampshire. (Courtesy Sammy Miller Museum)

Designed in 1954 by Joe Craig, this horizontal-engined 499cc Norton was to be used by the 1956 works team. It never was completed. (Courtesy Sammy Miller Motorcycle Museum)

C. M. Booth Collection of Historic Vehicles, Falstaff Antiques, 63, High Street, Rolvenden, Kent. TN17 4LP.
Tel. 01580 241234. Owner: Chris Booth.

The Museum is situated three miles from Tenterden on the A28 Hastings Road. It cannot be seen from the road and access is via the Falstaff antique shop.

The display includes a unique collection of Morgan cars dating from 1913 to 1935, also a 1904 Morris van and other historic cars, motorcycles and bicycles, with toy and model cars and other memorabilia.

Open all year, Monday to Saturday, 10.00am to 6.00pm. Closed most Sundays. An antique/gift shop sells some automobilia. Toilets on the premises and unrestricted roadside parking.

MOTORCARS

1904	Humber Tri-car
1929	Morris van
1929	Ford Model A
	Morgan three wheelers - 11 are displayed

MOTORCYCLES

1911	Premier
1911	P and M and sidecar
1923	Levis
1938	Excelsior
1941	New Hudson

1949	Corgi

CYCLES

1880	Penny Farthing
1890	Quadrant
1898	Quadrant
1914	Sunbeam
1920	Sunbeam
1923	Dayton
1936	Raleigh
1938	Hercules tandem

Admission: adults £1.50; children £0.75p.

A 1934 Matchless-engined Morgan Super Sports. (Courtesy C. M. Booth Collection of Historic Vehicles)

Dover Transport Museum, Old Park, Whitfield, Dover, Kent. CT16 2HQ.

Tel. 01304 204612. Curator: Colin Smith.

Dover is 65 miles southeast of London. The Museum is to be found in the Old Park, Whitfield, off the A2, 2 miles north of Dover.

The Dover Transport Museum, after previous difficulties with accommodation, is now permanently housed in a former army barracks at Old Park. On display are vehicles ranging from bicycles to buses, a working model tramway in one-sixth scale and model railway, plus Kent coalfield items and, awaiting restoration, the unique Maidstone demi-tram. The Museum also features a Maritime Room, Railway Room, 'East Kent Road Car Co.' room, 'Bygone' shops and a 1930s garage.

Open: Sundays from Easter to the end of September, 10.30am to 5.00pm. In July, August and the first week in September, open Thursday and Friday 2.00pm to 5.00pm. Facilities on offer include a souvenir shop, tea room (open Sundays for the sale of soft drinks, tea and coffee), toilets, disabled access and parking.

Some vehicles are operational whilst others are on static display or awaiting restoration. Several are on loan, so it may be wise to ring in advance of a visit if you want to see a particular vehicle.

MOTORCARS

Year	Model	Reg.	Year	Model	Reg.
1932	Austin 7 Ruby	ELM 373	1961	AEC Reliance	WFN 513
1932	Rolls-Royce	JJ 7214	1961	Daimler CVG6	NSK 871
1934	Austin Lichfield	NJ 4422	1963	AEC Regent V	AFN 780B
1934	Triumph Super 7	KJ 8653	1966	AEC Regent V	GJG 751D
1954	Austin A30	OYM 795	1967	Leyland PD 2/40	JRJ 268E
1954	Ford Popular	7914 F			
1960	Austin Healey Sprite	8084 ME			
c1970	Rover 2000 TC	BPK 973H	**COMMERCIAL VEHICLES**		
			1929	Ford AA lorry	KX 6227
			c1943	Bedford lorry	640 UKK
BUSES AND COACHES			1949	Morris Y series van	MKE 515
1929	Dennis G	CC 9305	1959	Austin LC30 truck	SJG 501
1948	Bristol L6B	KHY 383	1953	Commer K1/HCB F/E	PKT 977
1950	AEC Regent III	KXW 488	1956	Lewis electric float	RGU 464
1952	Leyland TD5	GFN 273	1957	Bedford RL 4x4	SXF 283
1958	Leyland PD3	PHJ 953	1965	Commer K2/HCB fire engine	FKE 108C
1960	AEC Reliance	569 KKK	1967	Dennis fire engine	TOO 928E

Admission : adults £2.00; OAPs £1.50; children £1.00; family ticket £5.00. Pre-booked groups welcome.

Brattle Farm Museum, Five Oak Lane, Staplehurst, Tonbridge, Kent, TN12 0HE.

Tel. 01580 891222. Owner: Brian Thompson.

Staplehurst is 30 miles southeast of London and the Museum is located 10 miles south of Maidstone on the A229. It is signposted.

This country museum houses the personal collection of Brian and Anita Thompson, who are also working farmers. The Collection, which is housed in an oast house and purpose-built barn, consists principally of agricultural bygones illustrating country life, skills and tools from rural trades and crafts of the last two centuries. There is a section on vintage cars and other vehicles which includes the 'Wee Three.' This car was home-built in the 1950s and is a three-wheeler with three seats. It continued in use until the owner died in 1985.

For 1999, only pre-arranged group visits are accepted. There is wheelchair access to 85 per cent of the Museum.

MOTORCARS

Year	Model	Reg.
1920	Arrol Johnson	HS 1671
1921	Rolls-Royce 40/50	XH 6538
1923	Rolls-Royce 20hp	OK 9329
1924	Fiat 501	KU 3802
1924	Talbot 10/23	XR 2872
1927	Delage DI	YU 3108
1928	Austin 12/4	HC 9145
1931	Fiat 514	GP 8523
1936	Rolls-Royce 20/25	CLL 185
1955	'Wee Three'	UKT 619

Year	Model	Reg.
1916	Overtime	No reg.
1917	Titan 10/20	No reg.
1918	Weeks Dungey	KT 8525
1919	International Junior 8/16	No reg.
1920	Austin	No reg.
1922	Ford Model T Eros conversion	No reg.
1924	Ford Model F	No reg.
1927	Renault	No reg.
1928	Westbrook	No reg.
1930	Barford 2 ton roller	No reg.
1933	Fordson Standard	No reg.
1934	Bristol	No reg.
1936	Ransomes MG II	No reg.
1939	Standard Fordson	No reg.
1940	Case LA	No reg.
1946	Bristol	No reg.
1946	Ransomes MG	No reg.
1947	David Brown	No reg.
1947	Fordson Major	No reg.
1948	Grey Ferguson	No reg.
1948	Field Marshall	No reg.
1950	Ferguson TE 20, wood gas burner	No reg.
1950	Crawley	No reg.
1950	OTA	No reg.
1952	Ferguson 3 cylinder diesel	No reg.
1952	British Anzani Iron Horse	No reg.
1953	Trusty 4 wheel	No reg.
1954	BMB Ploughmate	No reg.
1957	Fiat Crawler	No reg.

MOTORCYCLES

Year	Model	Reg.
1917	Sunbeam combo	LT 728
1923	Sunbeam	UK 3943
1924	BSA, round tank	XT 4615
1927	Sunbeam	DC 4558
1930	BSA combo	ABH 653

COMMERCIALS

Year	Model	Reg.
1915	Ford T van	FN 2502
1928	Halley lorry	UU 9762
1934	Dennis bus	YD 9533
1935	Austin 10 van	BKT 73
1938	Bedford bus	PFX 932
1958	Commer Carrier fire engine	PRV 59

TRACTORS

Year	Model	Reg.
1914	Weeks Dungey	No reg.

Admission: adults £1.50; OAPs/children £1.00.

Canterbury Motor Museum, 11, Cogans Terrace, Canterbury, Kent, CT1 3SJ.

Tel. 01227 451718. Curator: Cyril May.

Location: off the A28 on the Canterbury to Ashford Road.

An interesting collection of veteran and vintage cars and motorcycles. There are also many items of motoring memorabilia, stationary engines, a 1920s general store, Post Office, haberdashery, hardware and toy shops.

Open Monday to Friday, 9.00am to 5.00pm, and weekends by appointment only. Disabled facilities are limited, with a public toilet nearby. On-street parking available.

MOTORCARS	
1904	Humberette
1904	Humber Olympia tandem
1908	Adler
1913	A C Sociable
1915	Bianchi
1921	Wolseley E3
1924	BSA saloon
1924	Austin 7 Standard Sports
1929	Austin 7 works coupé

1929	Humber Sportsman coupé
1932	Morris light van
MOTORCYCLES	
1918	Sunbeam and sidecar
1924	Fayor (French)
1927	Triumph model W
1949	Norton ES2 and sidecar

Admission: adults £1.00; concessions for children under 14 and OAPs.

Ramsgate Motor Museum, Westcliff Hall, The Paragon, Ramsgate, Kent. CT11 9JX.

Tel. 01843 581948. Curator: Edward Sharp.

Located in Ramsgate, on the clifftop above the Sally Line Harbour.

Ramsgate Motor Museum was founded in 1982 for the purpose of displaying motoring history, and every car and motorcycle is set against a backdrop from the past. The Museum endeavours to explore transport through the ages, from the early bone shakers and Penny Farthings to exotic vintage models and sleek sports cars of the 60s. There's an exhibition of memorabilia to back-up the main event.

Open: April to November, 10.30am to 5.30pm. Winter, Sunday only, 10.00am to 5.00pm.

Public car parks nearby. A shop sells postcards, model cars, books, posters and many other items of interest. Toilets provided for the disabled.

MOTORCARS

1900	Benz
1904	Pope
1904	Tribune
1904	De Dion Bouton
1904	Arrol
1904	Johnston
1904	Humberette
1905	Carre
1907	Rover
1907	De Dion Bouton
1909	Belic
1909	Zedel
1909	Renault AX
1910	Phoenix
1910	Renault
1911	Swift
1911	Austin
1912	Humberette
1913	Ford T
1913	Calcott
1915	Singer
1915	Overland Roadster
1915	Ford T delivery van
1918	Buick
1921	Rover
1921	Lagonda
1921	Packard Roadster
1921	Citroën Cloverleaf
1921	Wolseley
1924	Bentley 3 litre
1924	Humber
1925	MG Bullnose
1925	Morris Oxford
1925	Morgan
1925	Ford T
1927	Austin Seven
1928	Ford A
1936	Rytercraft scooter car
1936	Vauxhall
1937	Packard convertible
1938	MG TA
1939	Standard
1939	Ford V8 3 door coupé
1939	Ford V8 91A convertible
1951	Ford Zephyr Mk 1
1953	Ford Consul Mk 1
1958	Messerschmitt
1959	Heinkel
1959	Trojan
1962	Hillman Minx
1964	Ford Zephyr Mk 3
1964	Vauxhall Cresta
1964	Bond
1965	Vauxhall VX 490
1965	Hillman Super Minx
1967	Jaguar E-type
1972	Triumph TR6
1973	Charly
1973	Formulae Ford (Merlin)

MOTORCYCLES

1905	Rex
1912	Wall Autocycle
1915	Harley-Davidson
1919	James
1919	New Hudson
1920	Triumph
1921	BSA combination
1921	Royal Enfield
1921	Excelsior
1924	Triumph combination
1926	Douglas
1927	Douglas
1927	Le-Grimper
1929	Douglas
1930	Cotton
1930	Calthorpe
1935	Coventry Eagle
1939	BSA 1920
1944	Corgi
1947	Douglas Dragonfly
1948	New Hudson
1951	Moto Guzzi
1951	Vincent
1953	Sunbeam
1957	Francis Barnet (Cruiser)
1957	Velocette LE
1958	BSA
1959	Royal Enfield
1959	Triumph
1962	BSA
1963	AJS
1963	Royal Enfield
1966	Raleigh Runabouts
1968	Triumph
1973	Triumph Daytona
1973	BSA Bantam
1973	Ariel 3
1974	Norton Commando
1976	Harley-Davidson Electroglide
1977	Honda
1977	Triumph 'Silver Jubilee' Bonneville
1978	MZ
1984	Sinclair C5

SCOOTERS

Triumph
Lambretta
Capri
Dicome
Bella
DKM
Vespa
Hienkiel

BICYCLES

2 bone shakers
3 Penny Farthings
Durdsley-Penderson

Admission: adults £2.50; OAPs £2.00; students £1.50; children £0.50.

Bury Transport Museum, Bolton Street Station, Bury, Lancashire, BL9 0EY.
Tel. 0161 764 7790. Secretary: Graham Vevers.

The East Lancashire Railway, based near the Transport Museum, runs train services through the Irwell Valley to Summerseat, Ramsbottom, Irwell Vale and Rawtenstall.

Bury is reached from the A58 Bolton to Rochdale road. The Transport Museum is opposite the Leisure Centre in Bolton Street, adjacent to Castlecroft Road, off Peel Way.

The Collection includes historic buses and other vehicles, and steam and diesel locomotives, and operates as a joint venture between the East Lancashire Railway and the Greater Manchester Museum of Transport.

Facilities include disabled access, buffet, shop, toilets. Open: 10.00am to 4.00pm on Sundays between Easter until the end of September. The Museum is open for some special event weekends and also Bank Holiday Mondays, possibly with varying admission prices.

Exhibits include:

Bedford HA van
Atkinson truck
Foden truck

Plus a selection of vintage and classic buses, coaches and commercial vehicles.

Admission: £1; concessions £0.50. Fares are charged on railway trips.

British Commercial Vehicle Museum, King Street, Leyland, Preston, Lancashire, PP5 1LE.

Tel. 01772 451011. General Manager: Andrew Buchan. Museum Archives: Gordon Baron.

The Museum is in the centre of Leyland, a mile from junction 28 on the M6, or a five minute walk from the railway station. Leyland is 25 miles northwest of Manchester.

Housed in part of the former Leyland Motors South Works factory, the Museum, the largest of its kind in Europe, is devoted to the history of British commercial vehicles, from the close of the nineteenth century up to the present day. Efforts are made to ensure the exhibits include representations of all significant commercial vehicle manufacturers. The 60 exhibits range from the horsedrawn era through to steam wagons, and from early petrol vehicles to the present day. The latest sound and light technology has been introduced to give realism to a number of displays. The evolution of road vehicles can be traced as they developed to meet the vast growth in demand for passenger, goods and delivery services.

Special events during the season include, rallies, the Steaming of Vehicles, and rides on historic vehicles, which includes provision for disabled visitors. Open: 10.00am to 5.00pm, Tuesday, Wednesday and Sunday, 5th April to 30th September. October, Sundays only. Open Bank Holidays. Groups by arrangement; guided tours cost £6.00. Group visit discounts. Conference facilities available.

The Museum has a souvenir shop, facilities for the disabled and parking for cars and coaches. There is limited catering.

The Collection:

Year	Vehicle	Reg.	Year	Vehicle	Reg.
1896	Thornycroft steam van	Not reg.	1929	Albion LB41 van	UH 6939
1896	Horsedrawn bus	Not reg.	1929	Scammell 100 ton tractor	KD 9168
1902	Thornycroft steam lorry	EL 3908	1931	Beardmore Cobra tractor	PJ 3934
1905	Fowler signalman's engine	Not reg.	1932	Bedford WLG	EG 568
1905	Yorkshire steam wagon	CA 170	1934	Scammell mechanical horse	Not reg.
1908	Leyland X type	LC 6695	1936	ERF	AMR 461
1909	Thornycroft gun tractor	Not reg.	1937	Latil tractor	JD 8350
1913	Leyland open top bus	LF 9967	1938	30cwt horsedrawn van	Not reg.
1917	Leyland RAF type lorry	HOE 241	1938	Merryweather fire engine	JEV 802
1918	Leyland F5 steam lorry	Not reg.	1942	Morris Z van	GUW 24
1919	Bean van	WA 2974	1946	Bedford OLAD lorry	DAP 17
1919	Leyland RAF type van	CE 6065	1948	AEC Regal III coach	IF-14-62
1919	McCurd 5 ton van	BC 2345	1953	AEC RT 2 deck bus	KYY 653
1921	Ford van	XB 7758	1954	AEC Mammoth Major 8 Mk III	MMJ 410
1921	Leyland fire engine	TB 2597	1956	Leyland Tiger Cub PSUC1/2T	JRN 29
1922	Foden 6 ton steam lorry	AU 6695	1956	Foden 2 deck bus	OED 217
1922	Guy J	OU 3466	1957	Leyland Comet ECOS 2/6R	72 MTC
1924	Morris T lorry	HA 2064	1962	Sunbeam MF2b 2 deck bus	301 LJ
1924	Morris van	EN 4304	1982	Popemobile	SCW 533X
1924	Leyland LB5 2 deck bus	Not reg.	1986	Leyland Ajax 0400	TX 450
1929	Bean coach, 14 seat	UL 1771			

Admission: adults £4.00; OAPs/children £2.00. Family ticket (2 + 3) £10.00.

This 1918 Leyland F5 steam lorry once worked in Queensland in the 1960s. It was restored to its present condition by Leyland apprentices. (Courtesy British Commercial Vehicle Museum, Leyland, Lancashire)

Logo of the British Commercial Vehicle Museum, Leyland, Lancashire.

1919 Leyland RAF Type. Originally supplied to Chivers, the jam manufacturer, it was used in the Cambridge area until 1934. It was then restored by Chivers and attended the first London-Brighton run in 1962. (Courtesy British Commercial Vehicle Museum, Leyland, Lancashire)

The Ray Tomkinson Taxicab Collection, Salop Street Garage, Shakespeare Works, Bolton, Lancashire, BL2 1DZ.
Tel. 01204 533447. Owner: Ray Tomkinson.

Bolton is approximately 5 miles west from junction 5 of the M61 motorway.

A fascinating collection of ancient and modern taxicabs located at a site near to the contact address above. Ray Tomkinson will be pleased to arrange visits to his collection by prior appointment. His fleet of taxis has featured in various films and TV productions, such as *The Darling Buds of May* and *Carry on Cabby*. The taxis are available for hire for weddings as well as other occasions, and Ray says that if someone wants a cab that he hasn't got, then he'll find it!

The Collection includes:

1906	Renault De La Marne taxi with Laundaulette coachwork
1926	Citroën Rosalie Taxi
1933	Austin Highlot TT Laundaulette taxicab, Goode and Cooper body
1935	Austin LL Laundaulette taxicab, Jones Bros. body
1935	Austin LL Laundaulette taxicab, Jones Bros. body
1936	Austin LL Laundaulette taxicab, Strachan body
1937	Austin LL Laundaulette taxicab, Strachan body
1938	Austin LL Laundaulette taxicab, Jones Fishtail body
1938	Beardmore Ace taxicab
1938	Chevrolet Sedan Yellow Cab
1939	Austin LL Laundaulette taxicab, Jones Flashlot body
1949	Wolseley Oxford taxicab
1958	Austin FX3 taxicab
1959	Austin FX4 taxicab
1960	Beardmore Mk 7 Paramount taxicab
1965	Beardmore Mk7 Paramount, fitted fourth door
1966	Austin FX4 taxicab
1976	US Checker Yellow Cab, plus other examples up to 1982
1980	Austin FX4 taxicab
1987	Metrocab taxi
1990	Caprice New York cab
1992	Toyota Crown propane taxi from Tokyo

Plus a selection of more recent FX4s and Metrocabs from 1974 to the present day.

Admission: free, by prior arrangement only.

St. Helens Transport Museum, Old Bus Depot, 51, Hall Street, St. Helens, Lancashire, WA10 1DU.
Tel. 01744 451681.

St. Helens is 22 miles west of Manchester. Leave the M6 at junction 23; St. Helens is off the A580.

The Museum has mainly buses and some fire engines. Unfortunately, further information about this Collection has been unavailable.

Abbey Pumping Station, Corporation Rd., Leicester, LF4 5PX.
Tel. 0116 2995111.
Managing Curator: Stuart Warburton.

The Museum is located 32 miles northeast of Birmingham, off junction 21 of the M1 motorway.

The seven acre site, sitting alongside the river Soar on the northern outskirts of the city of Leicester, incorporates the 1891 Sewage Steam Driven Pumping Station, which has four of the largest Rotary Steam Beam Engines in the country, one of which is in operation on steam event days throughout the year. Exhibitions include, 'Flushed with pride, with interactive toilet,' 'Perception of vision,' deception of your eyesight, and 'Bright Spark,' the forces of electricity and magnetism. The Museum stores and displays the industrial heritage of Leicester City, including a variety of motorised transport vehicles.

Open: daily 10.00am to 5.30pm, Monday to Saturday, 2.00pm to 5.30pm on Sunday. Closed 25th and 26th of December. Wheelchairs are available and the Museum offers baby changing facilities and free car parking. The main gallery is on the ground floor and the Beam engines are on the first floor, which is accessed by stairways. Most transport vehicles are in the main store on site at ground level and can be viewed by prior arrangement. They include the following miscellaneous vehicles:

COMMERCIAL

1938	Bedford fish and chip van	CBC 707
1939	Dennis Merryweather fire engine	DRY 198
1943	Austin K2 Auxiliary fire engine	GXH 472
1945	Brush battery milk float	KPB 362
1947	Austin K2 Lorry	ERY 998
1947	Mords 5 ton diesel/electric crane	EJU 213
1950	Leyland PSI Coach	GAY 171
1954	Crompton Leyland electric tractor unit	OLU 366
1956	Dennis/Rolls fire engine	PRY 677
1958	Leyland Tiger Cub Coach	MTL 750
1958	Leyland PD3 Bus	TBC 164
1965	BL Mini Traveller electrical car	DAE 137C
1966	Wilson Major electrical van	FJF 647D
1984	Rootes/Ford Fox Cub Mini Bus	B401 NJF

MOTORCYCLES

1912	Coventry Premier Ltd 225cc	DU 6471
1923	BSA combination 557cc	BD 7423
1970	Triumph Daytona 500cc	UUT 381H
1951	Bond 125cc	JJU 631

Admission is free except on event days, when charges are: adults £2.50p; over 60s and concessions £1.00; family ticket £5.00 (2 + 2).

STEAM

1893	Aveling and Porter 10 ton roller	HR 6013
1929	Barford Perkins 2.5 ton petrol roller	FL 8427
1938	Aveling Barford 8 ton diesel roller	CCT 128
1956	Eddimatic 0.8 ton diesel roller	LCT 650
1961	Aveling Barford 1.5 ton petrol roller	XJU 359

1938 Morris Merryweather Fire Engine.
(Courtesy Leicestershire Museums, Arts & Record Service)

Donington Grand Prix Collection, Donington Park, Castle Donington, Leicestershire, DE74 2RP.
Tel. 01332 811027. Manageress: Rachael Brown.

Derby is 35 miles northeast of Birmingham, and close to Nottingham, Derby and Leicester, two miles from the M1 junction 23/ A24 and M42/A42. East Midlands International Airport is 2 miles away. The Museum adjoins the Donington race circuit.

The Donington Grand Prix Collection, which is located at Donington Park Race Circuit, is the largest assembly of Grand Prix racing cars in the world. It is the work of Tom Wheatcroft, who, for forty years, has acquired cars which reflect his love of the sport. Over 120 cars tell the history of motorcar racing from the turn of the century to the present day. Many of the cars on display have been raced to victory by the world's most famous drivers.

The display includes a reconstruction of 'The Crick,' a 1920s garage from Northampton, plus trophies and many other associated transport items. The 4500 square metres of ground level covered space is surrounded by 600 acres of parkland.

Open: all year Monday to Sunday inclusive, 10.00am to 5.00pm, last admission 4.00pm (open later on race days). Closed Christmas Day, Boxing Day and New Year's Day. Facilities include souvenir shop, restaurant, picnic area, conference facilities and school education trail. There are facilities for the disabled although no dedicated toilets. Extensive free parking for cars and coaches.

Admission (1998): adults £7.00; OAPs and students £5.00; children (6 to 16) £2.50; family ticket (2 + 3) £14.00. Special rates for schools, coach and private parties by arrangement.

RACING CARS

Brabham				
1962	Brabham Climax BT3		1952	Ferrari 500
1966	Brabham-Repco BT20		1952	Ferrari 375 GP 'Thinwall Special'
1967	Brabham-Repco BT24		1970	Ferrari 312B
1969	Brabham Ford BT26			
1975	Brabham Ford BT44B		**Lotus**	
1978	Brabham Alfa Romeo ST45		1957	Lotus Climax 12
1978	Brabham Alfa Romeo BT46		1958	Lotus Climax 16
1980	Brabham Ford ST49		1960	Lotus Climax 18
1981	Brabham Ford ST49C		1961	Lotus Climax 21
????	Brabham BMW BT54A		1963	Lotus Climax 25
1986	Brabham BMW BT55		1968	Lotus Ford 49B
1987	Brabham BMW RT56		1968	Lotus Ford 49B
			1973	Lotus Cosworth 72
BRM				
1949	BRM V16 Mark 1		**McLaren**	
1954	BRM V16 Mark 2		1968	McLaren Cosworth M7A
1959	BRM P25		1969	McLaren Cosworth M9A
1962	BRM P56		1972	McLaren M21
1964	BRM P67 four-wheel-drive		1973	McLaren Ford M23-002
1964	BRM P261		????	McLaren M16E Indycar
1966	BRM P83		1977	McLaren Ford M26-02
1969	BRM P139		1979	McLaren Ford M28
1970	BRM P153		1979	McLaren Alfa Romeo
1972	BRM P180		1980	McLaren Ford M29-5
1973	BRM P160		1982	McLaren MP4/1-1
			1983	McLaren Ford MP4
Ferrari			1984	McLaren TAG MP4
1949	Ferrari 125		1985	McLaren TAG MP4

1939 Merryweather fire appliance at Donington Park, Leicestershire.

1986	McLaren TAG MP4/2C-5
1987	McLaren TAG MP4/3-4
1988	McLaren Honda MP4/4-2
1989	Mclaren MP4/5-7
1990	McLaren Honda MP4
1991	McLaren Honda MP4/6-8
1992	McLaren Honda MP4/7A-8
1993	McLaren Ford MP4/8
1994	McLaren Peugeot MP4/9A
1995	McLaren Mercedes MP4/1OB-05
1996	McLaren Mercedes MP4/11A-04
1997	McLaren Mercedes MP4/12-5

Vanwall
1950	Thinwall
1957	Vanwall Streamliner
1958	2.5 litre Vanwall
1961	Vanwall VW14

Williams
1984	Williams Honda FW9
1985	Williams Honda FWIO
1986	Williams Honda FW11
1987	Williams Honda FW11B
1989	Williams Renault FWI2C
1990	Williams FWI3B
1992	Williams Renault FWI4B

Other racing cars
1921/2	Sunbeam 3 litre straight 8
1934	Frazer Nash 1.5 supercharged
1934	Maserati 8CM
1935	Derby Maserati
1935	Maserati V8RI
1936	Alfa Romeo Bimotore
1936	Auto Union
1946/7	ERA E type
1948	Alta
1948	Maserati 4CLT
1948	Cisitalia Porsche 360
1951	Osca V12
1955	250F Maserati
1955	A type
1955	Connaught B type
195?	2 litre Connaught
1958	Maserati 250F
1958	Studio Tecnica Meccanica
1959	Cooper Climax T51
1977	LEC
1959	Aston Martin DBR4
1960	Cooper Climax
1961	Porsche 718
1961	Ferguson Climax P99

1961/2	Scarab
1962	Porsche 804
1962	Cooper Climax T60
1963	ATS
1966	Cooper Maserati T81
1966	Eagle Climax
196?	Lola Climax
	Supercharged Alta
1970	March 701 chassis no 1
1970	Tyrrell 001
1971	Tyrrell 003
	Tyrrell 006
1975	Shadow Matra
1976	Hesketh 308D

The Wheatcroft Williamson cars
1971	Formula Three March Holbay Ford
	March BMW 732
	GRD Holbay Ford Formula Three Car
	Wheatcroft R26

The Indycar & Midget racing collection of non-GP cars
1885	Benz Motor Wagon
1894	Panhard et Levassor
1902	Panhard et Levassor
1907	Thornycroft no. 27
1908	Thornycroft no. 10
1911	Cottin et Desgouettes
1911	Rolls-Royce Silver Ghost
1924	Doble Steam Powered
1924	Delage
1931	Bugatti Royale
1931	Doble Model F
1935	Austin-twin Cam
1936	Bugatti type 57
1939	Austin side valve

Motorcycles
1921	Harwood bicycle with engine	KN 6544
1922	Douglas 2 cylinder	
1927	Norton Pacer	
1950	Sunbeam S8	
1980	Jock Taylor combo	

Bicycle
| 1896 | Penny Farthing |

Commercial
| 1939 | Merryweather fire engine | GXA 95 |

Entrance to Donington Park Motor Museum, home of the largest collection of Formula One racing cars in the world.

Some of the many McLaren racing cars on display at Donington Park, Leicestershire.

Displayed in this photograph (Mercedes West and McLaren Hall) are two of the five halls which, together, house the largest collection of Grand Prix cars in the world. (Courtesy Donington Grand Prix Collection)

A John Player Special racing car at Donington Park, Leicestershire.

Tom Wheatcroft, founder, at the entrance to the Donington Grand Prix Collection, with his first acquisition, a 1949 Ferrari 125. This is an ex-works car which was driven by Luigi Villoresi in the Italian GP in 1949. (Courtesy Donington Grand Prix Collection)

A general view of Hall Four. (Courtesy Donington Grand Prix Collection)

Snibston Discovery Park, Ashby Road, Coalville, Leicestershire, LE67 3LN.
Tel. 01530 510851. Keeper: Stuart Warburton.

Leicester is 32 miles northeast of Birmingham. To get to the Museum, follow the A50/A511 northwest from Leicester to Coalville. From junction 22 on the M1, follow the A511 to the Museum, or take junction 13 from the M42/A42.

The purpose-built exhibition hall of the Museum of Science and Industry occupies the site of the now closed Snibston Colliery, and comprises 100 acres of landscaped countryside with woodland, fishing and picnic areas. The Museum, which has many commercial vehicles, covers two sites and tells the industrial history of Leicestershire. Open: daily from 10.00am to 6.00pm, April to October, 10.00am to 5.00pm, November to March. Closed Christmas Day and Boxing Day. Many outdoor facilities are free. Facilities include golf centre, woodland, lakes and picnic areas, outdoor science childrens' play area, gift shop and cafe and baby changing facilities. Facilities for the disabled include toilets, Braille labels, touch-table exhibits and taped guides. The exhibition hall is all on one level and wheelchairs are available. Parking is free for cars and coaches.

MOTORCARS

1965	BL Mini Traveller Electric (Snibston)	DAE 137C

VEHICLES

1911	Leyland tower wagon	BC 1078
1935	Partridge Wilson electric van	AWK 230
1938	Morris Merryweather fire engine	BJU 790
1939	AEC Renown bus	CBC 921
1956	Harbuilt electric milk van	NUT 508

Admission: adults £4.75; children £2.95; OAPS £3.25; family ticket (2 + 3) £13.50. Group rates available.

Stanford Hall Motorcycle Museum, Lutterworth, Leicestershire, LE17 6DH.
Tel. 01788 860250. All enquiries to: Robert Thomas.

Location: east of the M1 exit at junction 18 or 20 to the B5414. Stanford Hall is about half a mile north of Stanford on Avon.

Set in many acres of parkland overlooking the River Avon, Stanford Hall, built in the 1690s for Sir Roger Cave, is still the home of his descendants. It is one of the architectural gems of the period and the splendour of the internal rooms may be seen on a guided tour. After a long search for suitable premises, two founder members of the Vintage Motorcycle Club opened the Motorcycle Museum in the stable block in 1962. The original collection has grown to about 60 motorcycles, mainly 'loaned' machines which, on occasion, may be returned to their owners. Attractions include a walled Rose Garden, a full-size replica of an 1899 flying machine - 'The Hawk' - the Old Forge, Craft Centre, nature trail and, lastly, a splendid 14th century church. Open: Easter Saturday to the end of September, Saturday, Sunday, Bank Holiday Mondays and the Tuesday following, 2.30pm to 5.30pm. On Bank Holidays and special event days the Grounds and Museum open at 12 noon and the House at 2.30pm.

The Stable Tea Room serves light meals and snacks. There are facilities for the disabled, including toilet. Access to the House is difficult; although, once on the ground floor, all of the five principal rooms may be seen. As entry to the tea room is via 25 steep steps, a downstairs room may be made available by arrangement. All other areas are easily accessed. Car and coach parking is free.

Logo and drawing of Stanford Hall.

Admission (including House and Grounds): adults £4.00; children £2.00. Rose Garden, Flying Machine, Old Forge and Craft Centre: £2.20 and £1.00. Additional charge for the Motorcycle Museum: £1.00 and £0.35.

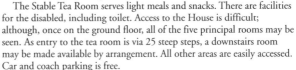

MOTORCYCLES

Year	Machine	Year	Machine
1914	Douglas 350cc	1938	Wickstead Supercharged Triumph
1915	Harley-Davidson 1000cc and sidecar	1939	Velocette Model 'O' 600cc
1915	Indian 1000cc	1939-62	Wilkinson 600cc
1920	James 225cc	1940	Gilera Ex-WD 600cc
1920	P & M + sidecar 500cc	1944	BSA M20 Ex-WD 500cc
1922	Norton 16H 500cc	1947	Norton Model 18 500cc
1923	Beardmore Precision 250cc	1950c	BSA Bantam 125cc
1924	Raleigh 350cc	1954	Triumph Tiger 100 500cc
1925	Scott 2 speed	1957	Lambretta 150cc
1926	James V twin 500cc	1957	Zundapp Bella Scooter 150cc
1926	Rex Acme 350cc	1958	Triumph Tiger Cub
1927	Royal Enfield Model 201 225cc	1959	Ariel Golden Arrow Sports 250cc
1927	T. Meeten Francis Barnett 172cc	1959	Ariel Red Hunter 350cc
1927	Sunbeam 500cc	1959	Excelsior Villiers 149cc
1928	AJS K7 OHC 350cc	1960	Heinkel Scooter
1929	Norton CSI 500cc	1960	Norton Model ES 490cc
1929	Speedway Scott 500cc	1962	BSA Gold Star (Export) 500cc
1929	Velocette KTT 350cc	1962	Triumph Tigress-twin scooter 250cc
1930	Rudge Whitworth Ulster 500cc	1963	Triton 500cc
1930	Rudge TT Replica 350cc	1963	Vincent Supercharged 1400cc
1932	Cotton JAP 500cc	1964	Honda Benley CB92 125cc
1934	Rudge 4 valve 250cc	1965	BSA Beagle 75cc
1935	Excelsior Manxman 250cc	1970	Triumph Bandit DOHC-twin 350cc
1935	Sunbeam Model 95 500cc	1972	Puch Moped 49cc
1936	Norton Model 16 500cc	1972	Triumph Craig Vetter X75 750cc
1938	BSA Gold Star 500cc	1975	Batavus Go-Go moped 48cc
1938	Manx Norton 350cc	1975	Peugeot 101T moped

1977	Jawa-twin 350cc
1980	Ducati Desmo 900cc
	Norton-Villiers-BSA, prototype 500cc
	Two-wheel-drive experimental
	Greeves Oulton 350cc
	Triumph EGLI 650cc
	Velocette KTT Mk IIX 350cc
	LE Velocette 150cc

	Norton Dominator 650cc
	Ducatti Desmo
	JAP Speedway 500cc

MOTORCARS

1931	Morgan 'Yellow' 1100cc
1958	Messerschmitt cabin scooter 200cc

One of the world-famous British motorcycle marques, a beautifully-prepared Inter Norton 500cc ohc racer. (Courtesy Stanford Hall Museum)

Stanford Hall with the Motorcycle Museum on the right. This museum was founded in 1962, after a long search for suitable premises, by the Founder of the Vintage Motorcycle Club. The Hall, with its beautiful grounds, is well worth a visit. (Courtesy Stanford Hall Museum)

Leicester City Fire Brigade Museum Society, Leicester.

Tel. 01530 242902. Secretary: Ivan Crockett.
Correspondence address: Pool Tail Bungalow, off
Wallace Drive, Groby, Leicester, LE6 0GD.
Registered charity: 502245

Leicester is 32 miles northeast of Birmingham, from junction 21 of the M1 motorway.

Formed after the closure of the Auxiliary Fire Service (AFS), the Society exhibits have grown to comprise some 14 appliances. There is a large collection of other fire service memorabilia, to which the Society is constantly adding. The Society is committed to supporting local charity events and fire service functions, and its aim is to establish a permanent museum for the collection. For viewing arrangements, please contact the Secretary.

The Collection includes:

1939	Austin K2 auxiliary towing vehicle	GXA520
1951	Dennis F12 pump escape	AJK200
1954	Austin K6 A type	MCV917
1956	Bedford RLHZ Green Goddess	PGW310
1957	Ford Thames, Wadham body	RGX91
1962	Bedford TK fire appliance	436CNV
1962	Commer Q4 transportable water unit	SXF509
1962	Dennis F27B Magirus 100ft ladder	700EJF
1963	Dennis F38 pump	769GJF
1963	Bedford Merryweather turntable ladder	RFA868
1966	Land Rover Series II	FUT237D
1972	AEC Mercury HCB body	CRY999K
1981	Dodge pump ladder HCB Angus body	RBC722W

Admission: free but donations welcome.

Allied Forces Museum, Main Road (Church Road), Stickford, Boston, Lincs, PE22 8ES.

Tel. 01205 480317.

Boston is 50 miles north of Cambridge.

The Collection includes motorcycles and heavy vehicles. No further information was available at the time of writing, so it may be that the Collection is private. Enquire at the local Tourist Office before arranging a visit.

Geeson Brothers Motorcycle Museum, 2, 4 and 6, Water Lane, South Witham, Grantham, Lincoln, NG33 5PH.
Tel. 01572 767280/767386.
Owner: George E. Geeson.

The Museum is located 51 miles northwest of Cambridge, on the A1, halfway between Grantham and Stamford, South Witham is half a mile to the west.

This museum houses 86 British motorcycles made by 24 different manufacturers and dating back to 1913. The collection and restoration to near-new condition of motorcycles has been a hobby of the owners for 27 years. Open: just six days a year; ring for actual dates. Parties by appointment. Car and coach parking at the roadside.

Refreshments are available in the workshop and tea towels and mugs are for sale. Toilets available although no special disabled facilities.

MOTORCYCLES (manufacturers)

AJS	Barnett
Matchless	Rudge
Ariel	Whitworth
Metisse	Hesketh
Brough Superior	Sunbeam
New Hudson	Humber
BSA	Triumph
Norton	Levis
Campion	Velocette
Panther	
Corgi	
Raleigh	**OTHERS**
Douglas	Lambretta scooter
Royal Enfield	Messerschmitt bubblecar.
Francis	

![GEESON BROS MOTOR CYCLE MUSEUM]

Admission: adults £1.50; children £0.50.

Len Geeson, at the entrance to his museum. His love of motorcycles and his enthusiasm for restoration led, with the help of his brother and many others, to the display you are able to see today. (Courtesy Geeson Brothers Motorcycle Museum)

Lincolnshire Road Transport Museum, Whisby Road, Lincoln, LN6 3QT.

Tel. 01522 500566. Curator: Paul Porter.

Located on the bypass just outside Lincoln, which is 34 miles southwest of Hull, the Museum is in North Hykeham, approximately 3 miles from the centre of Lincoln, on Whisby Road which links the A46 Lincoln bypass with the B1190 (Doddington Road).

The Lincolnshire Road Transport Museum was founded in 1993. However, the concept and gathering of vehicles has been going on for 40 years, via the auspices of the Lincolnshire Volunteer Vehicle Society. The present custom-designed museum building is also directly attributable to the Society's efforts, as it matched, pound for pound, the grant aid given: the Society's members are rightly proud of the end result. The present vehicular stock of around 45 cars, motorcycles, buses and lorries, ranges from the 1920s to the early 70s, Any necessary maintenance or restoration is carried out on site by Society members. The Society organises two Open Days each year and participates in local rallies and exhibitions.

Open: in winter on Sundays from 2.00pm to 5.00pm, and summer Monday to Friday, 12.00pm to 4.00pm; Sunday, 10.00am to 4.00pm.

The Collection:

MOTORCARS

Year	Model	Reg
1927	Humber 14/40	FE9852
1928	Austin 12 open tourer	TL48
1930	Singer Junior saloon	WL9794
1932	Austin 7 saloon	JV 1447
1934	Austin 16 saloon	AFY 376
1936	Austin 18 saloon	JV 4936
1936	Standard Flying 12 saloon	TL 5367
1937	Austin 10 saloon	VL 8960
1937	Ford V8 shooting brake	FW 9805
1937	Vauxhall 12 saloon	CWE 684
1939	Jaguar SS 2.5 saloon	BUT 7
1939	Morris 10 saloon	AVL607
1947	Austin 10 saloon	CVL212
1953c	Triumph 1500 saloon	FVO714J
1956c	Morris Oxford saloon	WE 1214
1966	Hillman Super Minx estate	HBE 554D
1967	Ford Cortina Mk 11 estate	PML 745E
1969	Daimler 2.5 V8 saloon	THA 313G
1969	Ford 1600XL Capri	MVE 397H
1971	Morris 1000 van	MFE 454J
1972	Reliant Scimitar sports hatch	HFN 854K

MOTORCYCLES

Year	Model	Reg
1950	AJS 500cc	DVL 992
1965	Honda moped 90cc	CFW 43C
1975	Honda moped 50cc	OTL 245P

BUSES

Year	Model	Reg
1927	Leyland Lion PLSCI	KW 474
1929	Chevrolet LQ	TE 8318
1929	Leyland Lion LTI	VL 1263
1929	Leyland Titan TDI	WH 1553
1930	Leyland Badger TA4	KW 7604
1930	Leyland Lion LTI	TF 818
1935	Leyland Tiger TS7	FW 5698
1940	Bristol L5G	FHN 833
1941	Leyland Titan TD7	BFE 419
1946	Bristol K6A	DBE 187
1946	Leyland Titan PDI	AHE 163
1948	Guy Arab 111	DFE 383
1949	Bristol K5G	ONO 59
1949	Bristol KSG	HPW 133
1949	Daimler CVD6	OHK432
1950	AEC Regal 111	FFU 860
1950	Bedford OB	LTB 907
1952	AEC Regent 111	FDO 573
1954	AEC Regent 111	OLD 714
1955	Bristol Lodekka	LFW326
1961	Leyland Titan PD2/41	RFE 416
1964	AEC Regent V	952 JUB
1967	Leyland Panther PSURIIIR	EVL 549E

COMMERCIAL

Year	Model	Reg
1927	Dennis 4-wheel lorry	YU 5455
1934	AEC Monarch 4-wheel tipper	TL 3513
1941	Leyland Retriever recovery	Not reg.
1942	Leyland TD7/Merryweather, 100ft turntable	GLW 419
1948	Austin 4-wheel lorry	KVS 559
1949	Bedford 4-wheel flatbed	DVL 577
1951	Albion 6-wheel box	FTL I38
1951	Albion 6-wheel box	FTL 277
	AEC Mammoth Major	Not reg.

Admission: free, although donations are accepted. Disabled access and free parking.

A Lincolnshire Road Museum 1930 Leyland Lion LT1 with Roe B30F bodywork. (Courtesy Peter Durham of *Classic Bus* magazine)

Museum of Liverpool Life, Pierhead, Liverpool, L3 1PZ.
Tel. 0151 207 0001.
Liverpool Museum Transport Curator: Sharon Brown.

Liverpool is at the end of the M62 motorway, from the M6 motorway.

Here will be found the first Ford 105E Anglia - registration number 1 KF - manufactured in 1963 at Halewood. It has had two owners from new and has covered 73,000 miles. Ford Motor Company bought it in 1969 from the last owner and presented it to the Museum. There is also an example of a car built by the William Lea Motor Co. of Liverpool, a 1900 Liver Phaeton with a Benz engine. A collection of memorabilia charts Liverpool life over the years. Open: all year round from 10.00am to 5.00pm, except 23rd to 26th December inclusive and New Year's Day.

Facilities include disabled access, shop, toilets and refreshments from the nearby Maritime Museum. No parking.

Admission to the transport section of the Liverpool Museum is via the '8 pass,' with the transport exhibits at present in the basement section. Halewood, on the Mersey, has been producing Ford cars for many years and the Museum has several interesting Ford cars in its collection. With redevelopment to another site, this Museum will be closing during 1999 and the vehicles stored until a new site is available, so it is necessary to check whether it is still open if you plan a special visit.

Exhibits include:

1929	Leyland motor pump escape, operated by Liverpool Fire Brigade until 1947, and known as the 'Leaping Lena' because of its roughness when starting from rest!	KD6614
1940	Atkinson 4FC flat wagon, brewery dray believed to be the oldest surviving Atkinson Ford D series, Liverpool Salvage Corps Tender	FVP479
1954	Rolls-Royce Silver Wraith Limousine	OKF1
	Ford Escort 1.6L 5 door saloon, millionth made	Never registered
	Ford Consul Corsair Deluxe (this model was the only one produced exclusively at Halewood)	96MOJ

Admission to the transport section of the Liverpool Museum is via the '8 pass, which allows entry to 8 city museums; it costs £3.00 with concessions and a family pass costs £7.50 for 2 adults and up to 3 children.

A great example of the 1954 Rolls Royce Silver Wraith Limousine in Liverpool Museum's transport section.

The first Ford Anglia 105E to be
built at Ford's Halewood works
on Merseyside in 1963, and now
in the Museum of Liverpool Life
at The Pierhead, Liverpool.

BT Museum, 135, Queen Victoria Street, London, EC4V 4AT. (Correspondence only.)
Tel. 0171 248 7444.

The historic collection of BT (formerly British Telecom) is a unique
vehicular history of transport associated with telecommunications.
Unfortunately, the Collection has now been dispersed for storage to
various BT motor transport depots throughout the UK. BT now only
rarely loans vehicles from the Collection for display purposes. Examples of
the old green Post Office Telephone van make up most of the Collection,
as well as some yellow British Telecom and a few grey BT vehicles.

BT is currently reviewing its plans to display the Collection; ring the
above number for details.

The Collection includes:

Year	Vehicle	Reg.	Year	Vehicle	Reg.
1936	Albion lorry	CXN247	1980	Bedford HA 6 cwt van	CHV 683V
1938	Morris 8 van	ELO688	1982	Roadphone	NYP115Y
1947	Morris Z van	JLD717	1984	Morris Ital 6 cwt van	A805UYYP
1947	Morris 30 cwt van	GYY107	1984	Leyland Sherpa demountable van	B257XUV
1950	Morris LCS van	JLE616	1992	Ford Transit van	J564VOM
1953	Morris 1000 van	NLW918	1992	Ford Escort car	J958TOP
1974	Bedford TK van	WRK384N	1933	BSA motorcycle combination	AGT23
1975	Bedford CF van	LGJ866P			
1977	Bedford PEU van	TUL264S			
1978	Dodge 15 cwt van	XYL71T	Plus other items such as mechanical aids, etc.		

Design Museum, Butlers Wharf, Shad Thames, London, SE1 2YD.
Tel. 01714 075261. Curator: Sue Andrew.

The Museum is located near to Tower Bridge underground station; cross Tower Bridge to get to it.

The Museum houses various collections, ranging from domestic appliances, graphics, ceramics and furniture, through to transport. As befits a design museum, the transport display includes some 'classics' and some *avant garde* designs. To complement the Design Museum's temporary exhibition programme and permanent collection, there is a continually changing display of cars on loan. During a visit, one of the authors saw a fascinating mix of ancient and modern cars on display. Always ring to determine availability and make of cars on show.

Open: Monday to Friday, 11.30am to 6.00pm. Weekends 12.00pm to 6.00pm. Open Bank Holidays, closed on Christmas Day.

Facilities for the disabled include toilets; there's also a shop and cafe, and car parking adjacent to the Museum.

Exhibits include:

MOTORCAR
1928   Auto Maxima

COMMERCIAL
Nissan S cargo van

Admission: adults £5.50; concessions £4.00; family ticket (2 + 2) £12.00. Group rates on application.

Imperial War Museum, Lambeth Road, London, SE1 6HZ.

Tel. 0171 416 5320; for information tel. 0171 416 5397. Marketing Officer: Lindsay Payne.

Location: via the underground the nearest tube stations are Lambeth North, Waterloo or The Elephant and Castle. Nearest rail stations are Waterloo or Waterloo East. Bus numbers: 1, 3, 12, 45, 53, 63, 159, 168, 171, 172, 176, 188, 344 and C10.

The Imperial War Museum contains much more than a small collection of military vehicles. However, as the Museum is intended to show the role of Britain and the Commonwealth in two World Wars, the vehicles are an important part. The display area - on the ground floor in a large exhibits gallery which rises through four floors of the building - contains the most important weapons and vehicles in the collection, including those on our list.

Open: 10.00am to 6.00pm. Facilities include a shop, toilets, disabled facilities and parking. Food also available.

Exhibits include:

Chevrolet 30 cwt truck, ex-long range desert group
M4 Sherman tank
Jagpanther tank destroyer
Daimler armoured car
British Mark V tank
British infantry Mark II 'Matilda'

Sherman V Tank M4 A4 at the Imperial War Museum, London. Outstations of this museum are at Duxford, Cambridgeshire and Wroughton, Wiltshire, where many other fine exhibits are to be found. (Courtesy Imperial War Museum)

Admission: adults £5.20; children under 16 free; OAPs/ concessions £4.20. Special rates for groups.

This German Jagpanther Destroyer from the 1939/45 war, and many other period military exhibits from the 1914/18 war, are displayed in the Museum. (Courtesy Imperial War Museum)

London Transport Museum, Covent Garden, London, WC2E 7BB.
Tel. 01713 796344.
Museum Director: Sam Mullins.
Web site: www.ltmuseum.co.uk

Location: By bus to the Strand or Aldwych, then tube to Covent Garden, Leicester Square or Holborn.

The London Transport Museum is comprehensive and imaginative. Set in Covent Garden's redeveloped Victorian Flower Market, the upper levels and glass walkway offer a panoramic perspective of historic buses, trams and trains. Complementing the vehicle displays are galleries housing original underground maps and posters. The Museum charts the story of London transport from the 1800s to the present day. Only a proportion of the Collection's 70 vehicles, 5000 posters and tens of thousands of other items are on display; the rest is held in reserve but, with the award of Heritage lottery money, will be made more accessible by way of special Open Days, computer or the Internet. There are many hands-on exhibits, working models, videos and touch-screen displays. For children there are fifteen 'Kids Zone' activities.

Admission: adults £4.95; concessions and children (5-15) £2.95; family ticket £12.00.

Open: daily 10.00am to 6.00pm, except Friday 11.00am to 6.00pm. Last admission 5.15pm. Closed 24th, 25th and 26th December. A lift and ramps allow access throughout the Museum for the disabled. There are toilets for the disabled, baby changing room, souvenir shop and transport cafe providing light snacks. There is also a new 'outstation' of Covent Garden at Acton; phone for details. Public car parking.

VEHICLES

1829	Shillibeer horse omnibus
1875	Tilling Knifeboard horse bus
1880	Stephenson horse tram
1888	'Garden Seat' horse bus
1910	West Ham electric tram
1910	'E1' type electric tram
1911	London General B type motor bus
1921	London General K type open top bus
1923	Tilling Stevens T53A petrol/electricity
1925	London General NS type 2 deck bus
1931	'Feltham' electric tram
1931	London General LT type 2 deck
1931	T type coach
1939	London United K2 trolley bus
1939	TF type single deck coach
1954	RT type 2 deck
1963	RM type 2 deck

1923	S type open top bus
1930	HR/2 electric tramcar truck
1931	ST type 2 deck bus
1931	A class trolley bus
1934	STL type 2 deck bus
1935	Q type single deck
1937	Fordson tractor
1948	Q1 trolleybus
1950	Aux. breakdown tender
1986	OV type single deck
1953	RF type single deck
1954	RT type 2 deck
1956	RM prototype 2 deck
1953	GS type single deck
1957	RM type 2 deck
1965	RCL type 2 deck
1966	FRM prototype 2 deck
1969	MBA type single deck
1970	DMS type 2 deck
1982	T type 2 deck

IMMEDIATE RESERVE VEHICLES

1906	De Dion L type open top bus

General view of the Main Hall showing just some of the exhibits at the London Transport Museum. This Victorian building was formerly the home of Covent Garden Flower Market. (Courtesy London Transport Museum)

Metropolitan Police Historical Museum (in formation), c/o Ray Seal, Metropolitan Police Historical Museum, Room 1317, New Scotland Yard, Broadway, London, SW1H 0BG. (postal address only).
Tel. 0181 305 1676.

Directions will be given by the Police once an appointment has been made for a viewing.

This is a museum in the making. It is hoped it will open at the old Bow Street Police Station in 2000 and is now located near Greenwich. At present, it is a private collection which can be viewed by prior appointment, although, even then, this is subject to police duties of the day. Drawings of police cars, uniforms, crash helmets, manuals, medals and other memorabilia are included in the Collection.

Exhibits intended for inclusion:

1937	Wolseley 14/56 patrol car
1939	Wolseley 12/48 patrol car
1948	Wolseley 18/85 patrol car
1953	Wolseley 6/80 patrol car
1957	Wolseley 6/90 patrol car
1964	Wolseley 6/110 patrol car
1969	Jaguar S-type patrol car
1971	Morris Minor Panda car
1973	Austin 1100 Panda car
1976	Rover P6 patrol car
1984	Rover SD1 patrol car
1984	Ford Transit incident van

Included in the motorcycles on display are:

1955	Triumph Speed-Twin
1959	Triumph 650 Thunderbird
1961	LE Velocette
1972	Triumph 650 Saint
1972	Triumph trials bike
1976	Triumph special escort bike
1980	BMW SEG bike.

National Postal Museum, Freeling House, Phoenix Place, Mount Pleasant, London, EC1A 1BB.

Tel. 0171 776 3636. Contact for information: Collections Manager.

The National Postal Museum is near the Barbican, Mansion House and St. Pauls, near to underground tube stations and served by frequent bus services. City Thameslink trains stop at the Old Bailey and Ludgate Hill.

Open: Monday to Friday from 9.30am to 4.30pm; closed at weekends and all Bank Holidays. Facilities for the disabled are limited and there is no parking on site. There is a shop and toilets. The National Postal Museum houses a vast collection of postage stamps, artwork, postal history, letterboxes and other artefacts. Due to limited space there may only be one or two vehicles on display. The Museum is seeking a permanent display area for its Historic Vehicle Collection, which is currently located in Gloucestershire.

Included in the Historic Vehicle Collection:

COMMERCIAL

Year	Vehicle	Reg		Year	Vehicle	Reg
1935	Morris Minor 6 cwt van	KXW507		1980	Bedford TK600 box van	DYY458V
1938	Morris 8 bullnose van	EXM446		1981	Austin Morris minivan	YYC873X
1945	Morris 8 Z van	LUL794		1981	Leyland Sherpa 150 van	AVX977X
1946	Morris commercial LES van	GYW270		1982	Leyland Terrier 600 box van	KHT899X
1948	Morris commercial LC3 van	JYY463		1982	Morris Marina van	PYO201X
1956	Morris commercial LC3 van	RLB517		1982	Renault Commando RG20	MYR482X
1961	Morris Minor 6 cwt van	194CXN		1983	Ford DA2114	GFB23N
1969	Land Rover series II	WLB882G		1983	Leyland Sherpa 150 van	A354TJD
1970	Replica 1901 Dennis 240 van	XLE304		1983	Commer HiLine post bus	WNJ479Y
1970	Reliant 21 E Robin supervan	DUU630J		1984	Leyland Sherpa 150 van	A69VUU
1971	Commer Karrier box van	GGO926J		1985	Bedford CF electric van	B368LCD
1972	Morris LDO 360 van	LYM228K		1985	Ford Escort 80 van	C371BYY
1973	Albion tanker	GOG584L		1985	Ford Fiesta van	B391TST
1973	Morris JO4 van	PGF256L		1986	Leyland Sherpa 240 hi top van	C281BYW
1976	Leyland EA 360 van	RLW561R		1986	Ford Escort 80 Mk 3 van	C891TLF
1977	Land Rover series III	OTX545R		1987	Bedford Rascal 30 van	D723NKK
1978	Bedford TK570	PWS798S		1987	Austin Maestro 80 van	D566TCW
1978	Commer PB minibus	SOP405S		1991	Ford Escort Mk 5 80 van	H341NPY
1979	Ford Transit van	AHJ1X				
1979	Dodge KC60 Mk I security van	DDU424T				
1979	Leyland EA 240 van	NGN699V		**MOTORCYCLES**		
1980	Leyland Sherpa 150 minibus			1965	BSA Bantam	
1980	Bedford TK600	DHV6V		1970	BSA Bantam	
1980	Commer PB van	GYE44W		1985	Kawasaki	
1980	Bedford HA van	KCW403W		1986	Steyr Daimler Puch moped	

A Morris commercial van, part of the Royal Mail vehicle collection. (Courtesy the Manager, National Postal Museum, London, copyright the Post Office)

Admission: free.

Royal Air Force Museum, Grahame Park Way, Hendon, London, NW9 5LL.

Tel. 0181 205 2266. Director: Dr Michael Fopp.

The Museum can be reached from the southbound exit of the M1 motorway. Follow the A41 Watford Way towards the North Circular Road. From the A5 and North Circular, there are brown tourist attraction signs to guide you to the Museum. There is a Thameslink rail station at Mill Hill and a London underground station at Colindale on the Northern Line. Buses depart from Victoria coach station, Buckingham Palace Road, London (797 Greenline service).

Britain's National Museum of Aviation contains many interesting transport exhibits, in addition to tracing the history of flight with its fine aircraft collection. Available facilities include a shop, 'Wings' licensed restaurant, mother and baby room, disabled facilities. Large free car park. Open: daily from 10.00am to 6.00pm (closed 24th-26th December and 1st January).

Exhibits include:

1963	AEC Mandator 4x2 - with Blue Steel Missile	78 AE 96
1958	Alvis Salamander Mk. 6 crash tender	23 AG 76
1940	Austin K2 ambulance	14775
1944	Austin K2 NFS fire tender	
1955	Austin K9WD 4 x 4 ambulance	55 AA 96
1961	Austin Princess Sheerline (undergoing restoration)	10 AB 92
1957	Bedford OX 10 ton tractor with Tasker Queen Mary trailer	06 AV 42
1940	Crossley Q 3 ton 4 x 4 crash tender	CJA309
1918	Crossley tender 11 seat personnel carrier	M14 629
	Daimler Ferret scout car composite	
1917	Ford Model T pick-up truck SD2563	M74 711
1966	Ford Zephyr saloon	25 Am 44
1942	Ford GPW 3 ton Jeep (USA)	GAP250
1943	Humber light reconnaissance car Mk.IIIA	135772
1935	Rolls-Royce armoured car HMAC Ajax	
1952	Scammell Scarab mechanical horse unit	19 AN 9
1955	Standard Vanguard Series I saloon	XMX633/55 AB 66

Some vehicles may be at the Museum's restoration centre at Cardington. In addition, various other vehicles are displayed at the Aerospace Museum in Cosford, Staffordshire.

Admission: special rates for families and groups, concessions for children, senior citizens, unemployed and students. Free admission for registered disabled and helper and serving RAF personnel.

A 1917 Model T Ford pick-up at the Royal Air Force Museum, Hendon, London.

An Austin K2 ambulance at the Royal Air Force Museum, Hendon, London.

*The nearest under-
ground station is South
Kensington (Circle,
District or Piccadilly
lines). Several bus
services also stop near the
Science Museum.*

The Science Museum, Exhibition Road, South Kensington, London, SW7 2DD.

Tel. 0171 938 8080 or 8008. (Recorded message on
0171 938 8111; disabled persons enquiry line: 0171
938 9788).
Assistant Curator of Transport Department: Ken
Shirt.
Web site: http://www.nmsi.ac.uk/visitors/index.html

The Museum tries to reflect current developments by constantly adapting
its displays and introducing new ones, so bear this in mind. At present
'The Gallery of the Modern World' is being prepared. Open: 10.00am
until 6.00pm every day except Christmas Eve, Christmas Day and Boxing
Day. There's a gift shop, toilets, disabled access, restaurant, picnic area and
book shop, but no parking facilities. Over one million people visit the
Museum annually so it's best to arrive as early as possible for your visit.

Land transport section exhibits will always vary relative to the
particular programme of exhibitions, but there are normally several
vehicles on display at the Science Museum.

We suggest that you also check page 149, the Science Museum,
Wroughton, near Swindon, Wiltshire. This houses the vast majority of the
land transport exhibits of the Science Museum and contains access details
for that site.

Exhibits may include:

JET 1, the world's first gas turbine car developed by Rover and based on the Rover 75. The engine
develops 200hp at 40,000rpm and uses a gallon of paraffin every 4 miles.

*Admission: adults
£6.50; OAPs/children
£3.50. Group rates for
15 or more.*

An unusual Amphicar, part of the Science Museum Collection.

A jumbo Rolls-Royce Silver Ghost Laundaulette, part of the Science Museum Collection.

Manchester Museum of Science and Industry, Liverpool Road, Castlefield, Manchester, M3 4FP.

Tel. 0161 832 2244. Curator: Alison Taubman.
Web site: http://www.u-net.com/set/msimanch

The Museum is in Castlefield, only minutes' walk from the city centre (follow the brown Tourist Board signs), and convenient for bus routes and Deansgate rail station.

The Museum of Science and Industry in Manchester is located in five large historic buildings. Each houses a major exhibition. These are entitled 'Air and Space Gallery,' 'Power Hall,' 'Station Building,' '1830 Warehouse' and 'Lower Byrom St. Warehouse.' Power Hall has the largest collection of steam mill engines in the world, and even smells the part! Many of the land transport vehicles displayed were made in Manchester. The Centre, in the basement of the main building, contains archive material on many topics, including transport. Shops, restaurant and cafe. Wheelchair access to 90% of the museum, sympathetic hearing scheme, accessible toilets. Car park £1.50. Open: every day from 10am to 5pm except 24th, 25th and 26th December.

The Museum Library and Record Centre is open Tuesday and Thursdays,1.00pm to 4.30pm and at other times by appointment

Exhibits include:

1896/98	LU-MIN-UM racing bicycle	
1900	Horse gig made by Cockshoot	
1904	Imperial motorcar	T1904
1905	Rolls-Royce 10hp 2 cylinder	AX148
1909	Crossley 40hp open drive limousine	J973
1912	Belsize motorcar	S3001
1913	Newton Bennett	N1
1916	Royal Ruby motorcycle sidecar combination	LX2037
1923	Harper Runabout 2.5hp	HR8999
1924	DOT motorcycle	FU2141
1926	Crossley Laundaulette 20.9hp	DS8082
1929	Crossley Six Shelsey	JK448
1935	Crossley Regis Six	BN685
1951	DOT motorcycle	FVY398
1994	Malc Cowle 'Town Hybrid' bicycle	

Admission: 1st to 21st January and 28th June to 14th October; adults £5.00, concessions £3.00. 22nd January to 27th June and 15th October to 4th June 2000; adults £6.50, concessions £3.50. (Group rates available throughout the season). Season tickets.

1904 Imperial 6hp, 2 cylinder with a front mounted engine and, usually, a four seater body. (Courtesy Museum of Science & Industry)

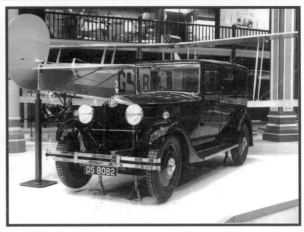

Entrance to the Museum of Science & Industry, Manchester. This is a very large museum which has many exhibits spread over several buildings. (Courtesy Museum of Science & Industry)

A superb example of a 1930 Crossley Laundaulette at the Museum of Science & Industry, Manchester. (Courtesy Museum of Science & Industry)

Manchester Museum of Transport, Boyle Street, Cheetham, Manchester, M8 8UL.
Tel. 01612 052122. Chairman: GMTS* Dennis Talbot.

Buses 59 and 135 run from the city centre, or it's a ten minute walk from the Woodlands Road Metrolink. Follow Castlefield signs from the M60/M66 junction and turn left onto the A6010, following the Museum signs.

The Museum houses a collection of over 70 buses, coaches and other vehicles from Greater Manchester, and evokes memories of the colourful buses from the towns of the area. Journeys to school, work, the cinema and longer trips to holidays by the seaside are recalled by the vehicles and displays drawn from the extensive archives and other collections. Many of the vehicles have been fully restored to original condition, whilst others may be viewed in the workshops undergoing restoration. The oldest vehicle on display is a Victorian horsedrawn bus. Local public transport history is brought up to date with the prototype Manchester Metrolink car.

Special events, rallies and working weekends are held throughout the year; phone for details. Open: Wednesday, Saturday, Sunday and Bank Holidays 10.00am to 5.00pm. Enquire about Christmas opening times.

Facilities include souvenir shop, tea room, toilets and baby changing facilities. Disabled access throughout. Free on-street parking available.

Greater Manchester Transport Society

BUSES/COACHES

1890	Horsedrawn bus	No reg.
1906	Brush D/D tram	No reg.
1921	Leyland G2	C 2367
1925	Tilling/Stevens TS4 bus	DB 5070
1927	Leyland Lion PLSC1	CK 3825
1928	Leyland Tiger TS1	VM 4439
1929	Leyland Lion PLSC1/1	VY 957
1930	Leyland Tiger TS2	VR 5742
1934	Leyland Titan TD3 chassis	AXJ 857
1935	Leyland Tiger TS7	JA 7585
1936	Leyland Cheetah LZ2	RN 7824
1938	Bedford WTB	EFJ 92
1939	Bristol K5G	AJA 152
1939	AEC Regent	BBA 560
1940	Leyland Titan TD7	JP 4712
1946	Bristol L5G	BJA 425
1946	Leyland Tiger PS1	HTB 656
1947	Bedford OB	HTF 586
1948	Crossley DD42/8S	JND 791
1948	Leyland Titan PD2/1	CDB 224
1949	Foden PVSC6	LMA 284
1949	Leyland Titan PD1/3	JNA 467
1950	Leyland Tiger PS1	PA 164
1950	Crossley Empire TDD42/2 t'bus	LTC 774
1950	Leyland Tiger PS2	MTB 848
1951	Leyland Titan PD2/3	JND 646
1951	Crossley Dominion TDD64/1 t'bus	JVU 755
1951	AEC Regent III	HDK 835
1951	Leyland Titan PD2/1	EDB 549
1951	Leyland Titan PD2/1	EDB 562
1951	Crossley DD42/7	EDB 575
1952	AEC Regent III	BEN 177
1953	Leyland Royal Tiger PSU1/13	NNB 125
1954	AEC Regent III	UTC 672
1955	Atkinson PD746	UMA 370
1956	Leyland Titan PD2/13	JBN 153
1956	Leyland Titan PD2/12	PND 460
1956	AEC Regent V	NDK 980
1957	Leyland Titan PD2/20	NBU 494
1957	Leyland Titan PD2/30	DJP 754
1958	Guy Arab IV	116 JTD
1958	Guy Arab IV	122 JTD
1958	Leyland Titan PD2/40	TNA 496
1958	Leyland Titan PD2/34	TNA 520
1960	AEC Reliance	YDK 590
1961	Leyland Titan PD3A/2	HEK 705
1962	Daimler CVG6	TRJ 112
1963	Leyland Atlantean PDR1/1	REN 116
1963	AEC Routemaster	414 CLT
1963	Daimler CVG6K	4632 VM
1964	AEC Regent V	8860 VR
1965	Leyland Titan PD2/37	PTE 944C
1965	AEC Renown	PTC 114C
1965	Leyland Panther Cub PSRC1/1	BND 874C
1965	Daimler Fleetline CRG6LX	DDB 174C
1965	Leyland Atlantean PDR1/1	DBA 214C
1966	Leyland Titan PD2/40	FRJ 254D
1967	Leyland Titan PD2/40	JRJ 281E
1968	Leyland Atlantean PDR1/1	HVM 901F
1968	Leyland Titan PD3/14	KJA 871F
1968	Leyland Leopard PSU4/1R	KDB 408F
1969	Leyland Titan PD3/14	TTD 386H
1969	Leyland Titan PD3/14	MJA 897G
1969	Leyland Titan PD3/14	MJA 891G
1972	Leyland National 1151/2R	TXJ 507K
1972	Leyland Atlantean AN68/1R	VNB 101L
1973	Seddon Pennine IV	XVU 352M
1975	Seddon Lucas	GNC 276N
1975	AEC Reliance	HVU 244N
1984	Leyland Atlantean AN68	A706LNC
1986	Freight Rover 365	D63 NOF
1990	Metrolink prototype (rail)	No reg.

COMMERCIAL

1913	Lacre 2 ton van	AR 246
1926	Karrier recovery	YM 9410

Admission: adults £2.50; OAPs and accompanied children (5-15) £1.50; family ticket £7.00.

Greater Manchester Fire Service Museum, Maclure Road, Rochdale, Lancs., OL11 1DN.
Tel. 01706 341221/30330, 0161 735866.
Secretary: Bob Bonner.

Location: Rochdale is 10 miles north of Manchester.

The Museum, situated adjacent to Rochdale Fire Station, opened in 1983 and is supported by a Museum Society consisting of volunteer Fire Brigade members. Sixteen appliances, together with a large collection of equipment, photographs, uniforms, medals, insignia, models and other memorabilia, portray the history of fire-fighting in general, and Greater Manchester in particular. Parts of the Museum have been laid out to form a tableaux of exhibits in a realistic setting that includes a Victorian street frontage with an insurance office, a fire equipment supplier's shop and a Fire Station. There is also a 1940 Blitz scene. A comprehensive archive section is available. Since the Museum is operated by volunteers, prior arrangement to visit should be made by ringing the above number or writing to the Secretary. There's a souvenir shop within the Museum.

Exhibits include:

1741	Newsham manual pump	
1845	Barton manual pump	
c1847	Shand Mason manual pump	
1880	Shand Mason manual pump	
1900	Merryweather hose cart	
1900	Shand Mason curricle escape	
1902	John Morris hose cart	
1910	Shand Mason steam fire engine	
1929	Dennis/John Morris pump/escape	VR 3001
c1930	Merryweather Hatfield trailer pump	
1938	Dennis trailer pump	
1939	Dennis trailer pump	
1940	Dennis pump/escape	GBN 217
1941	Scammell wheelbarrow pump	
1957	Dennis/Metz 125' turntable	PDK 717

During summer months the appliances are displayed at local rallies, so it would be wise to check first if you wish to see a particular vehicle.

1957 Dennis/Metz 125ft turntable, ex-Rochdale Fire Brigade. In summer months the appliances are displayed at shows and rallies all over the country. (Courtesy Greater Manchester Fire Service Museum)

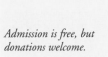

Admission is free, but donations welcome.

107

Caister Castle Car Collection, West Caister, Great Yarmouth, Norfolk. NR30 5SN.

Tel. 01572 787251. Curator: Brian Sewell.

Location: 18 miles east of Norwich and a mile north of Great Yarmouth on the A149.

Caister Castle houses a large private collection of motor vehicles, with exhibits from 1893 to the present day, including cars powered by steam, petrol and electricity, plus motorcycles, prams, childrens' transport, horsedrawn vehicles and other transport-related items. Includes some Americana.

Open: every day except Saturday, mid-May to 30th September, 10.30am to 5.00pm. Light refreshments available and free parking.

Admission (1998): adults £4.50; OAPs/ children £4.00; family ticket (2 + 4) £12.00; children under five free. Group rates on application.

The Collector's World of Eric St. John-Foti, Hermitage Hall, Downham Market, Norfolk, PE38 0AU.

Tel. 01366 383185. Owner: Eric St. John-Foti.

The Museum is located about 37 miles west of Norwich. Take the A1122 to Downham Market from Wisbech. At the second bridge outside Downham Market, turn left, pass through the automatic gates and along the drive to Hermitage Hall. Signposted.

Housed in the converted stable block of Hermitage Hall is a rather special collection of Armstrong-Siddeley cars, dating from the 1920s to when production stopped in 1960. Eric St. John-Foti has had a philosophy of never throwing anything away for many years; hence the cars and many other interesting collectables. Rooms are dedicated to individuals such as Dame Barbara Cartland and Nelson, whilst in another area there's a tableau of a Dickensian Christmas. Books, bottles, brass engravings, military items, tools, horsedrawn carts and many other items are displayed.

Open: from Easter to the last Sunday before Christmas, on Sunday, Friday and Bank Holidays, 1.00pm to 5.00pm. Full guided tour included, or a limited admission to car, cart farming collection, 'sensations' exhibition and brass rubbing collection, adults £1.00 and children £0.50.

Group visits at any time by appointment. Special events 12th-22nd December, 12.30pm to 4.30pm. There's a gift shop, tea room and free parking.

Admission (1998): adults £4.00; children £2.00; under-fives free.

MOTORCARS

Year	Description	Reg.
1937	Armstrong-Siddeley, black saloon.	AVH 125
1960	Armstrong-Siddeley, black saloon	244 EVE
1960	Armstrong-Siddeley, black limo	SMC 48
1958	Armstrong-Siddeley, grey saloon	PBO 106
1934	Armstrong-Siddeley, blue/black saloon.	AUB 887
1933	Armstrong-Siddeley, black/beige coupé	AGJ 603
1921	Armstrong-Siddeley, maroon limousine	NL 960

All cars are two axle rigid body.

Logo of The Collectors World of Eric St. John-Foti.
(Courtesy Eric St. John-Foti)

With an insatiable curiosity and a 'distaste for throwing things away,' The Collectors World of Eric St. John-Foti is a cornucopia of the accumulated possessions of a lifetime. This 1934 Armstrong-Siddeley saloon, with Eric St. John-Foti at the wheel, is one of several examples of the marque in his collection.
(Courtesy Eric St. John-Foti)

Muckleburgh Collection, Weybourne Military Camp, Weybourne, Holt, Norfolk, NR25 7EG.
Tel. 01263 588210.
Managing Partner: Jenny Billings.

Weybourne is 20 miles northwest of Norwich, and the Museum is about halfway between Wells and Cromer on the A149. Signposted.

The Muckleburgh Collection is based upon the old military camp NAAFI building, which has undergone several years of restoration. The Museum stands in 300 acres on the North Norfolk coast in one of the few original buildings on the site. There are fifteen working tanks, one of which, after expert tuition, you are able to apply to drive. There are also 150 armoured vehicles, guns, missiles and bombs, and 2500 other exhibits dating from 1782 to the present day. Several halls and rooms are dedicated to particular military themes from the Army, Navy and Air Force, with many rides and exhibits to be found outside the building. This Collection was winner of the 'Top Attraction in North Norfolk' in 1995 and Council Tourist award in 1994, 1995 and 1996.

Open: from the 14th of February until the 31st of October 1999. There are full facilities for the disabled, plus gift shop and licensed restaurant. Free parking 50 metres from the entrance. Coaches welcome.

Swiss-made 1960 PZ61 Main Battle Tank alongside a rare and complete WW1 machine-gun 'pill box' at Muckleburgh. (Courtesy The Muckleburgh Collection)

Exhibits include:

Canadian Sherman 'Grizzly' tank
Russian T34 with 88mm gun
Chaffee M24 tank
1960s Panzer 61 tank
1947 Patton M47 tank
Chieftain tank
1942 M13 half track
Stuart M3A1 'Honey' tank
Russian T55 tank
Churchill 'Crocodile' tank
Russian T55 bridgelayer
Saracen armoured car
Austin K2 Army ambulance
1941 Daimler MK1 armoured car with 2 pounder gun
1960 Ferrett scout car
4 x 4 amphibious jeep
American Diamond T 969A wrecker
Gama Goat personnel carrier
Bedford 3 ton QL truck
1940 Austin staff car
Alvis 'Stalwart' amphibious cargo carrier
Russian BTR40 1939

French White M3A1
1930s MOD BSA M20 motorcycle
Abbot self-propelled gun
WWII Naval 12 pounder gun
Sexton self-propelled gun
US 'Long Tom' 8 Howitzer
Morris Quad, 25 pounder gun and ammo transporter
Russian ZPU4 anti-aircraft gun
17 pounder British anti-tank gun
Chevrolet Portee with 2 pounder anti-tank gun
German 88mm ack ack gun
Argentinian 155mm Howitzer
French AMX13 tank with 105mm gun
Bofors gun
Argentine Rheinmetal ack ack gun
'Unimog' with Bazooka
3.7inch ack ack gun
Bloodhound missile
German V1 flying bomb
Anti-tank missile launcher AVF438
RAF Meteor NF11
1966 Thunderbird missile

Admission (1998): adults £4.00; OAPs £3.00; HM Forces £3.00; children £2.00; family ticket £10.50. Special party rates on application.

The Harry Dawson Hall at Muckleburgh. The tanks, which are all in working order, are a Chaffee M24, Stuart M3A1 (The Honey tank), Sherman 'Grizzly' and a Russian T34. (Courtesy The Muckleburgh Collection)

Norfolk Rural Life Museum, Gressenhall, Dereham, Norfolk, NR20 4DR.

Tel. 01362 860563. Conservation Keeper: Andrew McKay.
Tel. 01603 493637. Conservation Officer, Main Museum: David Harvey.

The Museum can be found 16 miles northwest of Norwich. From East Dereham travel north on the B1110, turn left after 2 miles onto the B1146 to Gressenhall, from where the Museum is signposted.

One of Norfolk's most prestigious museums is the Norfolk Rural Life at Gressenhall. Situated on a 50 acre site in the middle of the county, it offers much for both individual and family, including an early 1900s farm and woodland walk. The exhibits include an engine room, seed merchants, various rooms in a period cottage and a village shop, which are only part of a large display showing early rural life in Norfolk, and a working farm with old tractors. The Museum is home to an 1899 Panhard et Levassor once owned by Charles Stuart Rolls, joint founder of the world-famous luxury car firm. In June of 1899, Rolls 'raced' this car from Paris to Boulogne at an average speed of 23.2mph The car, donated to the Museum in 1936 by Herbert Egerton, is the only vehicle in the Norfolk Museum's Service collection. Its history is well documented, and photographs of the car in its original form, with C. S. Rolls at the wheel, are also in the archives of the National Motor Museum at Beaulieu. Restored to full working condition by a small team of volunteers, the car is on permanent display in the 'Craftsman's Row' area of the Museum.

Open: daily from Easter to the end of October. Usual facilities of souvenir shop, toilets (and for the disabled), tea room, free car parking; coaches by arrangement.

MOTORCAR	
1899	Panhard et Levessor
M22	

TRACTORS	
Oliver 90	No reg.
Fordson Major	No reg.
Alice Chalmers Model B	No reg.
Bristol Crawler	No reg.
Fordson	No reg.

Admission: adults £3.90; children £1.80; OAPs/concessions £2.90; family ticket £9.80 (2 + 2). Group rates by arrangement.

This 1899 Panhard et Levessor M22, once owned by C. S. Rolls, was, in June of 1899, raced from Paris to Boulogne at an average speed of 23.2mph. The only car in the Norfolk Museum Service collection, it was restored to full working condition by a small team of volunteers. (Courtesy Norfolk Museum)

Norfolk Motorcycle Museum, Railway Yard, North Walsham, Norfolk, NR28 0DS.

Tel. 01692 406266. Owner: George Harmer.

North Walsham is 14 miles northeast of Norwich, and the Museum is located in the railway station yard, on the right of the B1150 (Norwich Road) as you enter North Walsham.

The Museum is situated in a still active railway yard, and George Harmer, who has had a lifetime's interest in motorcycles, is still buying and restoring interesting machines for his collection. The Museum - a family business - has over 70 machines on display, with many more undergoing restoration. British motorcycles of the 1920s to the 1980s are the Museum's particular interest, and George Harmer is always keen to add new and interesting vehicles to the collection. Private motorcycle restoration work is accepted. Open: From Easter to the end of September, seven days a week, 10.00am to 4.30pm. October 1st to Easter, closed on Sundays; also closed Christmas, Boxing and New Year's Days. Toilets and wheelchair access, plus free car park.

MOTORCYCLES

1922	OK Bradshaw 350cc (oil boiler)
1922	Triumph SD 500cc
1930	AJS 500cc-twin port
1930	BSA Sloper 500cc side valve
1930	BSA Sloper 500cc ohv
1931	Rudge TT 500cc 4 valve
1932	BSA Blue Star 350cc-twin port
1934	Ivory Calthorpe 250cc
1934	Norton E.S.2, 500cc
1934	OK Supreme Flying Cloud 250cc
1934	Triumph 250cc-twin port
1935	Francis Barnett Cruiser 250cc
1935	Velocette MOV 250cc
1936	AJS 350cc coil ignition
1937	BSA Empire Star 250cc
1938	BSA Silver Star 350cc
1938	Francis Barnett 250cc, 4 stroke, ohv
1938	OEC Commander 500cc
1938	Rudge Special 500cc
1939	AJS 350cc
1940	Ariel 350cc ex-WD
1946	BSA C11, 250cc
1946	Velocette KTS 350cc ohc
1948	AJS 350cc
1948	Matchless 350cc
1949	Velosolex
1950	BSA Bantam D1, 125cc
1950	James Autocycle 98cc
1950	Sunbeam S.8, 500cc ohc
1950	Velocette LE 200cc
1950	Victoria Vicky
1951	Vincent Comet SC 500cc
1951	Vincent Rapide SC 1000cc
1952	BMW R67 600cc
1952	Panther 250cc
1954	Ariel Red Hunter 350cc
1955	BSA C10 250cc
1956	BSA C12 250cc ohv
1956	BSA Gold Star 500cc
1956	Douglas Dragonfly 350cc
1956	Excelsior Skotabyke 98cc
1956	Norman 150cc
1956	Panther Sloper 600cc
1956	Velocette 350cc MAC
1957	Matchless 500cc
1957	Norton Dominator 99 600cc
1957	Velocette Valiant 200cc flat-twin
1958	BSA Bantam D 14/4, 175cc
1958	Phillips Cyclemaster
1958	Phillips Gadabout
1959	Ambassador 250cc Villers 2T
1959	BMW R69 S Earles fork
1960	Berini
1960	Cotton 250cc
1960	Ducati Monza 160cc
1960	Matchless G9 500cc
1960	Norton Jubilee 250cc
1960	Royal Enfield Prince 150cc
1962	Capriolo 125cc ohc
1962	Raleigh Runabout
1963	NSU Supermax 250cc
1963	Royal Enfield Crusader 250cc
1964	NSU Quickly
1965	Mobylette
1968	Motobecane
1970	Gilera 50cc
1970	Triumph Tina scooter 100cc
1970	Triumph Trophy 250cc
1973	Ariel 3
1980	Benelli Quattro 250cc 4 cylinder
1985	Sinclair C5

MOTORCAR
1958	Powerdrive 3 wheel car, 322cc, two stroke

MISCELLANEOUS
Various cyclemotors, vintage bicycles and a collection of Dinky toys.

Admission: adults £2.50; OAPs £2.00; children (13-18) £1.50; under-13s free. Group rates on application.

Norfolk Motorcycle Museum logo and a Velocette ohc model.

NORFOLK
MOTORCYCLE
MUSEUM

...rt of the Norfolk Motorcycle collection ...classic motorcycles, which are restored ...on site. (Courtesy Norfolk Motorcycle Museum)

Sandringham House Museum and Gardens, Sandringham, Norfolk, PE35 6EN.

Estate Office, Sandringham, Norfolk, PE35 6EN.
Tel. 01553 772675.
Public Access Manager: Gill Pattinson.

Location: The Museum is signposted from the A148 and is 6 miles northeast of Kings Lynn.

Sandringham House and Museum are set in six hundred acres of woodland and heath, which provides beauty and colour throughout the seasons. The Museum, which was improved in 1995, contains Royal memorabilia ranging from family photographs to several cars which are still used by the Royal Family. Some rooms in Sandringham House are open to the public.

Open: 11.00am to 4.45pm daily from 1st April to 20th July and from 5th August to 3rd October. Wheelchair access throughout all areas and helpers admitted free. A small number of wheelchairs are available for loan. Guide dogs admitted. There's a gift shop, restaurant, tea shop and picnic areas. Free parking.

1900 Daimler 6hp (type A) Phaeton. Purchased by the future King Edward VII and later given a new bonnet and a professionally coachbuilt rear seat. Surrey top with fringe. (Courtesy Sandringham Estate Museum)

MOTORCARS

1900	Daimler 6hp type Phaeton	Used first by King Edward VII
1914	Daimler Brougham 45hp	Used by King George V
1924	Daimler Shooting Brake 57hp, 6 cylinder	Used by King George V
1929	Daimler Limousine 30hp, double 6 engine	Used by King George
1936	Daimler Shooting Brake 4.5 litre engine	Used by King George VI
1947	Daimler saloon 4 litre	Used by Queen Mary
1951	Ford V 8 Pilot Shooting Brake, 3.6 litre	Used by King George VI
1954	Rolls-Royce Phantom IV Landaulette 4675cc	Used by HM Queen and HRH Duke of Edinburgh
1961	Vauxhall Cresta 2262cc (MYT1)	Used for Royal staff and luggage
1961	Alvis TD21 coupé 2993cc	Used by HRH Duke of Edinburgh
1963	Rover 3 litre (VHW595H)	Used by HM Queen Elizabeth
1966	L/Rover station wagon LWB 109" Series IIA, 2625cc	Used by HRH at Sandringham and Balmoral
1969	Austin Princess Vanden Plas Limousine 3993cc. (NGN1)	Used by junior members of the Royal Family on official engagements
1984/5	Bedford electric van.	Used by HRH the Duke of Edinburgh for private trips around London

COMMERCIAL

1939	Merryweather fire engine	

Admission (House, Museum and Grounds): adults £5.00; OAPs/ students £4.00; children £2.00; family ticket (2 + 3) £13.00. Group rates for 20 or more paying in advance.

Sandringham Museum, housed in a converted stable block and improved in 1995, holds fascinating displays of Royal memorabilia from family photographs to vintage Daimlers, and an exhibition of the Sandringham Fire Brigade. (Courtesy Sandringham Estate Museum)

1939 Merryweather fire engine used by the Estate. (Courtesy Sandringham Estate Museum)

Fire Services National Museum, Weedon, Near Northampton. (in formation).
Tel. 01234 355453. Curator: Maurice Cole.

The Fire Services National Museum Trust is in the process of obtaining planning consent for the proposed new museum at Weedon, Northants, and hopes it will be open during the year 2000. It may have the name Fireworld and will tell the story of fire-fighting in Great Britain. Of the 45 appliances that the Trust owns, quite a number will be on display, from horsedrawn appliances to the vehicles of the seventies, plus water tenders, turntable ladders and crash tenders. Prior to the Museum opening officially, the Trust does have the occasional Open Day at Weedon, where the vehicles are stored. For details of these Open Days and for updated information about the Museum, please contact the Curator on the above number, or by post to 9, Morland Way, Manton Heights, Bedford, MK41 7NP.

Manor House Museum, Sheep Street, Kettering, Northampton. NN16 0AN.

Correspondence: c/o Tourist Information Centre, Sheep St., Kettering, Northampton, NN16 OAN. Tel. 01536 534381. Heritage Manager: Sue Davies.

The Museum is located centrally, and is next to the Parish Church.

Admission: free.

A small but interesting local history museum, covering Kettering Borough's past up to the present day. In particular the Museum explores the town's once thriving Victorian boot and shoe industry. Childrens' activities are run throughout the school holidays and there are themed family event days throughout the season. The Museum also proudly exhibits its one locally manufactured car.

Open: all year, Monday to Saturday, 9.30am to 5.00pm. Wednesday opening 10.00am. Closed Christmas Day, Boxing Day and Bank Holidays. Special interest group evenings by appointment only. The disabled can get to the first floor via a lift; unfortunately, toilets for the disabled are not provided. The Museum has a gift shop and there is adjacent pay and display parking.

Kettering Museum is small but well stocked with local interest items, including the only survivor of the original three Kettering Robinson cars manufactured in 1907.

MOTORCAR
1907   Kettering Robinson, one of only three manufactured.

Military Vehicle Museum, Exhibition Park Pavilion, Newcastle-On-Tyne, Northumberland, NE2 4PZ.

Tel. 01912 817222. Chairman of Trustees: John Stelling.

Location: via the Exhibition Park at the junction of the A6125 (A1) and the A6127(M).

The Museum is housed, uniquely, in the last remaining building from the 1929 Great Northeast Coast Exhibition. Upward of 50 military vehicles are on show, some of which are duplicated or not powered. Mostly they are pre-1945 and have been restored by members of the Northeast Military Vehicles Museum Trustees. Many other smaller items from the same period are displayed in the Museum.

Summer opening: daily, 10.00am to 4.00pm, winter: 10.00am to 3.30pm. Closed Christmas, Boxing and New Year's Days, and August Bank Holiday Sunday and Monday. There's a shop selling militaria, magazines, etc., cold drinks machine, disabled facilities (ramped access to the Museum only). Parking is adjacent to the Exhibition Park.

MILITARY VEHICLES

Argyle W/NG
Austin Champ
Austin K9, 1 ton 4 x 4
Austin 15cwt
Austin 10hp G/YH Utility
Bedford 3 ton, 4 X 4 QRL
Bedford 15cwt
Bedford 3 ton, Green Goddess
Can-Am Bombardier
Chevrolet C15 15cwt truck No 11 cab
Chevrolet C15 15cwt truck No. 13 cab
Daimler Dingo
Diamond T M20
Dodge 15cwt 4 x 2 D15
Ferret armoured car Mk I
Ferret armoured car Mk II
Ford Jeep
Ford Universal Carrier

GMC 2.5 ton 6 x 6 CCKW 352
GM armoured car 15 cwt 4 x 4
Hillman 10hp 4 x 2 car, 1935 Hanomag truck
Humber Snipe
Leyland Hippo Mk XI, 10 ton 6 x 6
Matador tractor 4 x 4
Mercedes truck
Minerva 4 x 4 GS
Morris C8/AT and 17lb anti-tank gun
Morris Commercial CDSW 30cwt 6 X 4
Morris Commercial C8 tractor, 4 x 4, limber and 25lb field gun
Morris Commercial 1 ton 4 x 4
Saracen armoured car
White scout car
White multiple gun carriage M 16
Willys Jeep

Admission: adults £2.00; OAPs, children (5-16), unemployed and students £1.00; under-fives free.

Ford Universal carrier as used in the Western desert. The Museum was originally erected as part of the 1929 North East Coast Exhibition, and used as the Pavilion of Fine Art. It remains the only surving structure.

Bedford MWD 15cwt general service truck. All of the vehicles have been restored by enthusiasts of the Museum and most are in working order.

117

Gateshead is one mile south of Newcastle city centre.

Admission: free, but donations welcome.

The Northeast Bus Museum, Lean Lane, Wardley, Gateshead, Tyne and Wear, NE10 8RD. •

Tel. 0191 4172539. Volunteer Group Chairman: Ian Finlay.

This small museum is housed in a listed building and is not open on a regular basis. It has about a dozen buses, some in the course of restoration, and its main interest is to preserve buses used by North Eastern bus companies like Sunderland and Newcastle Corporations. It's possible to arrange a viewing by phoning the Chairman on the above number. The Seaburn Vehicle Display is an annual event which occurs on August Bank Holiday Monay. Then, about 45 buses, some 20 commercial vehicles and up to 100 classic cars take part. John Purvis is the Group's rally organiser and can be reached on 0191 5489829.

Newburn Hall Motor Museum, 35, Townfield Gardens, Newburn, Tyne and Wear, NE15 8PY. •

Tel. 0191 2642977. Owner: Dominic Pirelli.

Newburn is three miles west of the City of Newcastle upon Tyne.

Admission: adults £2.00; children £1.00. Group rates on application.

A private collection of some 300 cars and motorcycles that are representative of family motoring. There are about 50 vehicles on display at any one time, and exhibits are regularly changed. Some famous cars, like the Standard, Rover and Bullnose Morris which appeared in the film *Chariots of Fire*, are on show. Housed in a fascinating period building which was built by the Duke of Northumberland, the Museum is easily accessible to the disabled as it's all on one level. There's a limited amount of free parking, a cafe and toilets (not disabled). Open: all year except Christmas and Boxing Days, Tuesday to Sunday. Bank Holiday Mondays: open between 10.00am and 6.00pm.

Industrial Museum, Courtyard Buildings, Wollaton Park, Nottingham, NG8 2AE. •

Tel. 0115 915 3910. Assistant Keeper of Technology: Robert Cox.

Location: 46 miles northeast of Birmingham. By car drive west on the A609 Ilkeston

Housed in the stable block and estate buildings of Wollaton Hall are many items representing Nottingham's industrial history, from curtains to computers. These include the best collection of lace machines in the country, working steam engines, the Basford Beam engine, mining and

Road. Turn left into Wollaton Road 4 miles from the city centre. Using the M1 going north, turn east at junction 25 onto the A52 dual carriageway; the Museum is signposted from there.

Admission (includes admission to Wollaton Natural History Museum) Saturday, Sunday and Bank Holidays: adults £2.00; children £1.00. Weekdays free.

agricultural machinery and various forms of transport.

Open: daily, 11.00am to 5.00pm, April to October. 10.00am to 4.00pm, Saturday to Thursdays, November to March. There's Pay and Display parking in Wollaton Park grounds, plus coffee shop at the main entrance to the Park. Toilets are in the courtyard opposite the Museum. Wheelchair users have access to all displays except the upper floors of the Beam engine. A battery car may be booked for use in the Park. Disabled toilets available.

MOTORCAR

1904	Celer	AU 250

MOTORCYCLES

1921	Brough Superior Mk 1	AU 5437
1921	Campion	AY 8863
1922	Brough Superior racer 'Old Bill'	No reg.
1924	Raleigh	AU 9794
1935	Rudge Ulster	AWJ 885

1935	Brough Superior	AFS 401
1939	Brough Superior SS80	FTV 784
1958	Raleigh moped	263 GAE
1964	Raleigh Mk II Moped	No reg.
1965	Raleigh Super 50	GNU 361C
1967	Raleigh Wisp	No reg.

Plus nineteen pushbikes and a pair of carriages.

Woolaton Park Industrial Museum was originally an 18th Century stable block. The Museum reflects the many industries of Nottingham, including some intersting vehicles, and what it describes as the 'best collection of lace in the country.'

The only surviving Nottingham-manufactured 1904 Celer. It has an 8hp, vertical twin engine with automatic inlet valves, 3-speed gearbox and shaft drive.

This 1939 Brough Superior SS80 has one of the most famous names in world speed record history. The model was owned by distinguished public figures such as Lawrence of Arabia.

Nottingham Heritage Transport Centre, Mere Way, Ruddington, Nottingham, NG11 6NX.

Tel. 0115 940 5705. Chairman: Steve Powell.

The Museum is located 43 miles northeast of Nottingham.

Admission (1998): adults £2.50; children £1.50.

The Museum, contained within a country park, contains classic public service vehicles and several locomotives which steam on a one mile standard gauge circuit.

Open: Easter to October, Sundays and Bank Holiday Mondays, 10.30am to 5.00pm. Facilities include souvenir shop, cafe and parking.

Aston Martin Trust, PO Box 207, Wallingford, Oxfordshire OX10 9TU. (in formation).

Tel. 01491 837736. Secretary: Christine Shamock.

The Trust will be near Wallingford on the A329, off junction 7 of the M40 (London-Oxford).

The Aston Martin Owners Club has acquired a building in Oxfordshire to house its collection of archive material about the Aston Martin franchise and the making of cars as far back as the thirties, as well as displaying a few cars. The Club hopes to have the Museum open in 2001 and, until then, all enquiries should be made to the Secretary of the Trust at the address given above. In its present premises the Club is pleased to welcome visitors by prior appointment; contact 01353 777353.

Oxford Bus Museum, Old Station Yard, Main Road, Long Hanborough, Witney, Oxon, OX8 8LA.

Tel. 01993 883617. Secretary: Colin Judge.
web site: http://www.geocities.com/MotorCity/Downs/6995

Location: The Museum is located next to Hanborough rail station, which is on the main Paddington to Worcester line; several services do stop at the station. By road, it is on the south side of the A4095, which links Bicester, Woodstock and Witney. If you are bringing a vintage bus to an event, use only the A4095 as other local roads have low bridges.

Admission: £3 adults.

The Museum is run by a Trust and has been building up a collection over the past 30 years. Predominantly former Oxford City buses, there are many other interesting buses, too, including one from Hong Kong and another from Portugal. The main collection is housed in a 10,000 square foot building, with other vehicles, both complete and awaiting restoration, in the yard outside. A collection of bus memorabilia is also housed in the main display area. Open weekends only, there are some special days throughout the year when rides on the old buses are possible. A simple cafeteria is open on special days and there is a shop and toilets. The Trust says it will do all possible to accommodate disabled visitors provided prior notice is given. School and other group visits may be arranged by contacting the Secretary. You can join the Friends of Oxford Bus Museum for £10 per annum.

Exhibits include:

1885	46 seater double deck horse tram			1949	AEC Willowbrook single-decker	NJO703
1897	46 seater double deck horse tram			1952	AEC Regal Mk IV single-decker	SFC610
1915	Daimler Y type	DU4838		1959	AEC Park Royal double-decker	PFN868
1917	Daimler Y type	FC2602		1962	AEC Reliance Duple single-decker	850 ABK
1932	AEC Regal double-decker	JO5403		1961	Dennis Loline double-decker	304 KFC
1947	Bedford PCV parcels van	MJO187		1963	AEC Renown Park Royal d-decker	332RJO
1948	AEC bus from Lisbon			1971	Daimler Fleetline CRL6 d-decker	UFC430K

Fleet line-up of the Oxford Bus Museum. Formed in 1967, the Museum has collected over forty vehicles from a variety of sources. (Courtesy Oxford Bus Museum)

n AEC Reliance double-decker bus on show at the Oxford Bus Museum, near Witney, Oxfordshire.

A Morris Minor van in the livery of Oxford City Transport on show at the Oxford Bus Museum, near Witney, Oxfordshire.

Midland Motor Museum, Stanmore Hall, Bridgnorth, Shropshire, WV15 6DT.
Tel. 01746 762992. Curator: Keith Partridge.

Access to the Museum is off the A458 Shrewsbury to Stourbridge Road, just east of its junction with the A442 Telford Road. The Museum is approximately 2 miles out of Bridgnorth town centre.

Open all year round except for Christmas Day and Boxing Day, from 10.30am until 5.00pm. Light refreshments are available, plus shop, toilets and free parking. Easy access for disabled with a special entrance and toilets available. Tickets for the Museum also include entry to the 17 acres of Stanmore Hall Grounds. There are price reductions for parties, which should be booked in advance with the Curator. There's a touring park adjacent to the Museum where caravans, motorhomes and tents may be used subject to usual charges. The Museum has over 90 motor vehicles, which include many of the world's fastest motorcars. There is also a good display of classic motorcycles. The Museum is now licensed for weddings and can cater for up to 400 people. Storage and renovation services available. When you have had your fill of cars, just a short distance away in Bridgnorth are the steam trains of the Severn Valley Railway.

1920 Lacre L type road sweeper at the Midland Motor Museum, Bridgnorth, Shropshire.

A Rothmans Mitsubishi Pajero, winner of the 1992/3 Paris Dakar Rally, at the Midland Motor Museum, Bridgnorth, Shropshire.

Exhibits include:

MOTORCARS

Year	Car	Reg	Year	Car	Reg
1907	Rolls-Royce Silver Ghost	AX201	1973	Lotus Elan Sprint convertible	TNP256L
1912	Calthorpe Tulip Phaeton		1975	Lancia Stratos sports saloon	GNF97Y
1915	Calthorpe Tourer	DS8238	1976	Ferrari 308GTB	MPH70P
1920	Lacre L type road sweeper	800WJH	1978	Aston Martin V8	BRD622T
1921	Vauxhall 30/98 4.5 litre	TB3119	1978	Alpine Renault A310 2.7 V6	BOF769T
1924	Morgan 3 wheeler	DL6736	1982	De Lorean sports 2850cc	SPY100
1925	Bentley Red Label 3 litre	XY1464	1986	Reliant Scimitar GTC 2792cc	HMO43
1929	Ford Model A delivery van	RP8538		Humber	KP2085
1934	Lagonda M45 tourer	BU8558		Rothmans Mitsubishi Pajero 4WD -	
1935	Austin Ruby saloon	CMG609		winner of the 1992/3 Dakar Rally	
1939	Lagonda V12	GPK564		Jaguar XJ220	MMM1
1954	Nash Healey - 327 Corvette engine				
1955	Austin Healey BN1 100-4 sports car	DCC61			
1963	Austin Healey 3000 Mk. 2	1174KO	**MOTORCYCLES**		
1966	AC Cobra 7.0 litre	NXC837M	1915	Sunbeam 350cc	E2834
1966	Mclaren M4 Formula 2 racing car		1921	Rover 500cc built for the Isle	
1968	Chevrolet Stingray 5360cc	ALM581H		of Man TT races	
1969	Nomad BRM V8		1928	AJS K7	UP2402
1973	AC V8 coupé	65DOP	1938	Triumph Tiger 100	

A rare 1915 Calthorpe Tourer at the Midland Motor Museum, Bridgnorth, Shropshire.

A beautiful Lagonda M45 tourer at the Midland Motor Museum, Bridgnorth, Shropshire.

Oswestry Transport Museum, Oswald Road, Oswestry, Shropshire, SY11 1RE.
Tel. 01691 671749. Secretary: Cyril Mottram.

The Museum is located 10 miles southeast of Llangollen.

The Museum is a registered charity and staffed by volunteers. It has a collection of about 30 motorcycles ranging in date from the 1930s to the 1990s, plus bicycles and other memorabilia. The Museum is open seven days a week from 10.00am to 4.00pm and closed on Christmas Day and Boxing Day. There are toilets and ample parking. There is a step to be negotiated at the entrance but, for the disabled, the interior is on one level. The Museum organises two transport festivals each year; one on Easter Monday, the other on the last Sunday in September. On these occasions, motorcycles, classic cars and steam engines are present.

Admission: £1 adult; £0.50 for OAPs and children over 6; under 6s are free.

Blazes, The Fire Museum, Sandhill Park, Bishops Lydeard, Taunton, Somerset, TA4 3DF.
Tel. 01823 433964. Curator: Brian Wright.

The entrance to Blazes is approximately 100 metres from the West Somerset Railway.

Blazes is a museum devoted to fire-fighting through the ages. In addition to the fire appliances displayed, there is much in the way of memorabilia and, to please the young ones, a display of 350 model fire engines that have been collected from all over the world. Open: Easter to the end of October, 10.00am to 5.00pm, closed Mondays except Bank Holidays. There are toilets, a tea room, souvenir shop and disabled access and toilets. Parking.

Admission: £3.90 adults; £2.90 children; £2.30 OAPs; a family ticket costs £11.

Exhibits include:

c1960 Austin Gypsy four-wheel-drive fire appliance - ex-Avon Rubber Co.
c1960 Bedford fire appliance - ex-Transwynnfdd Power Station
c1970 Magirus Deutz turntable ladder appliance
c1970 Ford Transit based industrial fire appliance - ex-Amersham International
c1973 Dennis S12 fire escape appliance

Haynes Motor Museum, Sparkford, Somerset. BA22 7LH.

Tel. 01963 440804. Chairman: John H Haynes OBE. Curator: Michael Penn.

Location: 29 miles southeast of Bristol. From any direction on the A303, at the Sparkford roundabout, follow the brown 'Motor Museum' signs.

A modern, purpose-built museum which has. under one roof, almost every car you've ever loved, loathed or desired. There are racing cars, motorcycles and motoring memorabilia, plus many American cars and military and commercial vehicle. The Red Collection of sports cars is breathtaking and there are many rare, cherished classics. A great day out for all the family. Work has begun on a 7000sq ft extension to the Museum - the Millennium Hall - which will house a further 25 cars and have the theme of 100 years of motoring.

The 'Pit Stop' serves a full range of meals, and there's a picnic area, extensive gift shop, full access for wheelchair users and baby changing facilities. Free parking.

Open: March to October daily, 9.30am to 5.30pm. November to February daily, 10am to 4.30pm. Closed Christmas, Boxing and New Year's Days.

Admission: adults £4.95, OAPs £3.95, children £2.95. Group rates on application.

The Collection

MOTORCARS

1900	Clement 2.75hp Voiturette	BS 8050	1947	Allard K1	JGP 467
1903	Darracq Type 8hp rear ent.	CD 287	1947	Chevrolet Sp. Fltlne Aerosdn	UCW 833
1903	Oldsmobile	BS 8043	1948	Riley RMA 1.5 L. Saloon	JYT 819
1905	Daimler det. top	DA 175	1949	Cadillac Fleetwood Sedan	49 CAD
1910	Renault AX	AY 1524	1949	Sunbeam Tiger	GWE354C
1913	Empire Model 31	DS 7912	1949	Jaguar 3.5 litre	KLO 784
1915	Ford Model T	626 147	1950	Healey Silverstone	LLE 947
1917	Morris Cowley	PA 7788	1951	Jaguar XK 120	LSN 572
1917	Haynes Light 12	DS 7518	1951	Turner Sports, 2262	JDA 555
1919	Daimler Lht 30 Rep Phaeton	E 6821	1952	Aston Martin DB2	328 LNX
1920	Moon Model 642 Touring Car	No reg.	1953	Morris Oxford, 1622cc	TPE 440
1925	Citroën 5CV, Cloverleaf	TBA	1954	Hillman Saloon	RVO 229
1928	Rolls Royce 20hp	YW 7616	1954	Austin A40 Somerset	PPO 445
1929	Rolls Royce Phantom 1	UT 4778	1954	Fiat Topolino	WJO 528
1929	Lanchester Straight 8 Spts trr	UW 7666	1954	Sunbeam Talbot 90, 2267cc	TYJ 341
1929	Alpha Romeo GT 17/75	GF 3522	1955	MG TF	SCV 730
1930	Morris Oxford	MY 6380	1955	Chevrolet Belair	AWE 220
1930	Bentley 4.5 litre Dphd Cpe	GJ 8309	1955	Citroën Light 15 IIB Nomale	CSV 421
1930	Morris Minor	RFP 374B	1955	Ford Anglia Saloon	VHU 254
1930	MG M Type Midget 2 str spt	SC 6400	1956	Reliant Regal	POY 497
1931	Duesenberg Model J	SFF 402	1956	Heinkel Bubble car	PSY 506
1931	Austin 7 Special	AJN 244A	1956	Austin Healey 100/6 2639cc	UXK 146
1933	Triumph Pillarless Saloon	MJ 2219	1956	Bristol AC Ace	JSU 238
1933	Austin 7	JH 6017	1957	Triumph TR3A Sports	TYS 896
1934	Austin 16/6	FW 4968	1957	Jaguar XKSS Kit	Not Reg
1934	Austin 10/4	EG 1302	1957	Austin A35 Saloon 945cc	YYC 243
1934	Riley Special	JB 3363	1958	Standard Pennant 948cc	NBW 301
1934	Alvis Speed 20	OC 7618	1958	Wolsley 1.5	TOT 596
1934	Ford Model ABF 2043cc	AYF 923	1958	Facel Vega hk 500	898 FKG
1935	Morris 10/4	JK 4494	1958	Chevrolet Corvette	2R1R 166
1936	Cord Beverley	HBL 533	1958	Ford Fairlane Retractable	Not Reg
1936	Auburn 852 Boat tail Spdster	CSU 744	1959	Renault 750	XXL 238
1937	Lagonda LG 45	DLF 697	1959	Turner 950 Sports	JPV 686
1937	Oldsmobile L37 Sedan	GMC 332	1959	Cadillac Sedan de Ville	2E0 A290
1937	Ford Corvair Special	FT 4904	1959	Ford Edsel Estate	Not Reg
1938	Lincoln Zephyr 4 dr sdn sln.	ALB 301A	1959	Frogeye Sprite	XAD 377
1938	MG TA	HPH 9	1959	A-Siddeley Star Sapphire	JIF 621B
1939	Packard 120 dhc	Not Reg	1959	Ford Popular	MTK 424
1940	Buick Series 40, 2 dr coupé	LSU 526	1959	Ford Thunderbird Convertible	MSU 542
1942	Willys Jeep	SSU 819	1959	Jaguar XK150 3.4	911 VHX
1947	MGTC, 1250cc	JKA 577	1960	Messerschmitt KR 200, trike	MFO 769

Rover SD1 Estate, Haynes Motor Museum, Yeovil.

The Haynes workshop, where you can see mechanics working on the restoration and maintainance of museum vehicles.
(Courtesy Haynes Motor Museum)

1964 Abbot self-propelled gun to be found in the open.
(Courtesy Haynes Motor Museum)

A 1942 Willys Jeep.
(Courtesy Haynes Motor Museum)

1961	Aston Martin DB4	8328 UG
1961	Vauxhall Victor	397 PKN
1961	Ford Consul	375 NAE
1961	Ford Zephyr Custom	800 DFJ
1962	MGA Roadster	899 CXX
1963	Daimler SP 250 Dart	988 FLL
1963	Chevrolet Corvette	ABK 747A
1964	Lotus/Westfield 11	Not reg.
1964	Chevrolet Impala	Not reg.
1964	Trojan 2 whlr cabin cruiser 198cc	YEE 880
1965	Jaguar E Type fhc	FBP 708C
1965	Cadillac De Ville Convertible	2CEX 907
1965	Bentley S3 4 dr sln 6230cc	FYW 202C
1965	Fiat 600 D, 767cc	FW 23C
1966	Ford Mustang	Not reg.
1966	Lancia Flavia	DBY 113D
1966	Ford Anglia 997cc	FJT 472D
1967	MGB Sports Roadster 1798cc	KDE 286F
1967	Hillman Imp California	KDG 119E
1967	Triumph TR4A	SYC 51F
1967	Lotus Elan S3	FVV 2E
1967	MS Midget	SDH 673F
1967	Citroen DS	928 NP29
1967	Wolseley Hornet	UYO 206F
1967	Jaguar 2.4 litre Mk 2	SYV 422F
1967	Chevrolet Camero Convertible	UPM 615
1967	Humber Hawk 2267cc	RGF 600E
1968	Rochdale Olympic	CUP 77G
1968	TVR Tuscan V8	YBP 889G
1968	Hillman Imp Sln	LVM 306G
1969	Fiat 500 Saloon	WYB 123G
1969	Chevrolet Corvette	RTA 278M
1969	Dodge Charger	Not reg.
1969	Riley Elf	TOR 976H
1969	Marcos 3L	HHW 74G
1970	Triumph Vitesse Convt	YLR 34G
1970	Mercedes 280 SL	SWL 951H
1970	Austin 1800 Mk 2	THR 527J
1970	Triumph Herald Convertible	FYR 862J
1970	Ginetta G15	WRL 982J
1970	AC Frua 428	WNV964H
1971	Daf, 844cc	VTA 557J
1971	Rolls Royce Corniche	ERO 54
1971	Ford Escort Mex	WLJ 454K
1971	MG 1300	FYC 673K
1971	Humber Sceptre 1725cc	JGC 969K
1971	AC 428 Frua Convt. 7014	SPD 268L
1972	De Tomasa Pantera	HUM133K
1972	VW Beetle	MPF 790L
1973	Austin Maxi 1748cc	BDH 659T
1973	Jaguar V12 E Type	NFL 16M
1973	Porsche 911 RS Carrera	PCO 15L
1973	Jensen Interceptor Mk III	XYB 251M
1973	Pontiac Trans Am Firebird	Not reg.
1974	Cadillac Eldorado, 8 lt	KYC 549N
1974	Reliant Scimitar	TH 449M
1974	Mercedes Benz Coupé 450SLE	1CGH 606
1975	Triumph TR6	THJ 184N
1975	Inla Cosworth Fl	Not reg.
1975	Jenson Healey	KNJ 877P
1975	Daimler 66 Auto 2 dr cpe	LDN 243N
1976	Trabant Saloon 600cc	LBP 665P
1977	Rover 3500D Estate	SHP 549R
1978	Rolls Royce Silver Shadow 6 L.	XUK 1T

1978	Triumph Dolomite Sprint	LLC 398V
1978	Chevrolet Camaro Z28	YKO 224S
1979	Belle Piaggio Goods	VVB 420T
1979	Mercedes Benz 6.9 450 SEL	NGK 444V
1979	Lincoln Continental Town Car	Q40 NYA
1979	Ford Country Squire	GYB 377T
1981	De Lorean	2 MAGU
1981	Triumph TR8	TVC 59W
1981	Lamborghini Countach	742 TR
1981	Lotus Esprit Turbo	OP 679W
1982	Ferrari 400i	6000 RU
1982	Maserati Merak SS	OCW 77X
1985	Chevrolet Corvette	Not reg.
1986	Citroen 2 CV	D830 YRK
1987	Ford Sierra Cosworth RS500	Not reg.
1987	Ford Sierra Cosworth RS500	717 JMB
1988	Coulthard Wright long circuit cart	No reg.
1988	D Type Jaguar Replica	8989 LJ
1989	Fiat X19	F111 FYC
1989	Mini Moke	G113 DPE
1989	Ford Probe	2KYY 729
1990	Caterham 7	G886 PYA
1993	Jaguar XJS V12 6L Coupé	L668 GYK
1994	Van Diemen RF 84 Formula Ford	No reg.
1994	Bentley Turbo R	L924 AGE

MOTORCYCLES

	AJS	RXO 613
1914	BSA	WL 1493
1914	Sunbeam ohc	Not reg.
1919	ABC Skooter	MD 794
1922	Francis Barnett 147cc	XLJ 556S
1922	Hawker Blackburn	BY 9774
1925	Sunbeam Exp Race	Not reg.
1929	Velocette Dirt Track	Not reg.
1930	Velocette KTT Race	Not reg.
1933	Morgan SS 3 whlr trike	WNS 420
1937	Rudge Ulster	EXC 205
1939	Scott 596cc	ELX 966
1949	BSA Gold Star 348cc	DSV 738
1955	AJS 500cc twin	REO 613
1958	Harley Davidson Duo Glide	VYJ 815
1959	DMW Scooter	956 YRE
1963	Norton Model 50	53 UYD
1967	Velocette LE3	RCH 875F
1975	Honda combo	LRE 904P
1977	Triumph Bonneville	XYD 570S
1978	Mobylette	WRU 782S
1985	Sinclair C5	Not reg.

COMMERCIALS

	Bajaj auto rickshaw	Not reg.
1941	Chevrolet ½ ton pick up	LSK 639
1951	Bristol double decker bus	LTA 995
1954	Bedford Fire tender	YW 3313
1966	Bedford Hose layer	Not reg.

STEAM

| 1922 | Stanley steam car | DV 26 |
| 1931 | Doble steam car | 12 811 |

MILITARY

| 1934 | T34 Russian tank | |

A superb 1931 Duesenberg Derham tourer.
(Courtesy Haynes Motor Museum)

A 1959 Elva Courier in pre-race tableau. (Courtesy Haynes Motor Museum)

The Haynes 'Red Collection.' What fabulous cars! (Courtesy Haynes Motor Museum)

The Bass Museum Visitor Centre and Shire Horse Stables, Horninglow Street, Burton on Trent, Staffordshire, DE14 1JZ.

Tel. 01283 511000. Curator: Diana Lay.
Web site: www.bass-museum.com

Location: The Museum is approached from the A38 Derby to Birmingham dual carriageway.

The Bass Museum contains brewing and local history exhibits, and includes a static Brewery Transport exhibition, the Bass Vintage Vehicle Collection and the Robey Steam Engine Shed. There is also a detailed scale model of Burton on Trent in 1921. The Shire Horses display team is also based at the Museum.

Open every day except Christmas Day, Boxing Day and New Year's Day, from 10.00am until last admission at 4.00pm. There are facilities for people with special needs. Free parking. Parties of all ages are welcome by prior arrangement with Museum staff. There is a good restaurant and a coffee bar, plus fully-equipped function suites and a well-stocked shop.

A 1954 Albion FT3 flat-bed lorry at the Bass Museum, Burton-on-Trent, Staffordshire.

Exhibits include:

Year	Description	Reg.
1916	Sentinel steam wagon in Bass Ratcliff and Gretton livery	AW3407
1923	Daimler bottle car, built for Worthington and Co. publicity purposes. Only five were built and there is another at the National Motor Museum	XU177
1927	Morris Commercial delivery lorry in draught Bass livery	WK3323
1934	Morris Commercial lorry in livery of Corona soft drinks	NG6424
1949	Leyland Beaver brewer's dray in livery of Mitchells and Butlers	KHA699
1954	Albion FT3 flat-bed lorry in livery of R. White Lemonade	PGC 409
1984	Leyland Sherpa Museum van, Sherpa chassis with an Austin Princess engine	ALE1
1986	Bedford artic in flame and brown livery of Bass Worthington	C245YPX

Please note that most of the vehicles are on display in the Museum's outdoor arena and during winter months are kept under cover in the interests of conservation.

One of just five 'Bottle Cars' on a 1923 Daimler chassis built for publicity purposes for Worthington's beers. Now at the Bass Museum, Burton-on-Trent, Staffordshire.

Admission: adults £4.50; OAPs £3.00; children (up to 18) £2.00; family ticket (2 + 3) £12.50. Group rates (for parties of 15 or more) £4.00.

East Anglia Transport Museum, Chapel Road, Carlton Colville, Lowestoft, Suffolk, NR33 8BL.

Tel. 01502 518459. Secretary: Ken Blacker.

Located 19 miles southeast of Norwich, 3 miles southwest of Lowestoft on the A146 road. Turn left onto the B1384 to Carlton Colville]; follow brown direction signs. Nearest rail station is Oulton Broad North and Oulton Broad, though better to travel into Lowestoft and catch a bus: Eastern Counties L11 and L12 services run every 20 minutes weekdays to Carlton Colville Church. The L18 and L19 run direct to the Museum on Sundays at half-hourly intervals.

The East Anglia Transport Museum started with four tramway enthusiasts rescuing the body of an old tramcar in 1961, from which came the idea of a transport museum. Visitors can now view and ride on three principal forms of public transport from the early part of this century. Run entirely by volunteers, the Museum occupies an attractive 4¹/₂ acre site, surrounded on most sides by mature trees. Exhibits are displayed throughout the site in different locations. Trolleybus trams and the East Suffolk Light Railway travel around giving rides - included in the price of the entrance ticket - subject to staff availability. Along the Museum street are many buildings which have been constructed and various artifacts that have been collected: there is much of interest for all the family and at least two hours should be allowed for a visit.

Open at Easter and from May to the end of September. As opening hours are dependent on season, ring or write for a timetable. Special dates during 1999 are: 27th June: Bygones and Fire Services Event; 11th July: Bus Event; 1st August: Classic Car and Vehicle Event and 11th/12th September: Trolleybus Weekend. July 15th and 16th the following year will be Event 2000 - a once in a lifetime show! Facilities include Terminus tearooms, souvenir and bookshop. Limited disabled facilities. Free parking.

Admission: adults £4.00; OAPs and children (5 to 15) £2.00. Group rates (10 or more) on application.

TRAMS

Chassis/body

1904	Brill/Milnes	No. 14
1927	Preston McGuire/Blackpool Corp.	No. 159
1929	Beijnes/Beijnes	No. 474
1930	EMB/English Electric	No. 1858
1939	Maley and Taunton/English Electric	No. 11

TROLLEYBUSES

Chassis/body

1926	Garrett/Strachan and Brown	No reg.
1936	AEC/Metro Cammell	CUL 260
1938	Leyland/Leyland	EXV 201
1940	Chassisless/Metro Cammell	FXH 521
1947	Sunbeam/Weymann	BDY 809
1948	Berna/Hess	No reg.
1950	BUT/Metro Cammell	NBB 628
1951	BUT/Burlingham	ERV938
1953	*BUT/Weymann	LCD 52
1953	Sunbeam/Willowbrook	DRC 224
1956	BUT/Bond	YTE 826
1958	Sunbeam/Harkness	2206 01
1959	Sunbeam/Weymann	YLJ 286

Date entered service; built 3 to 4 years earlier

BUSES

1927	Leyland/Leyland	KW 1961
1947	AEC/ECW	GBJ 192
1948	Bristol/ECW	KAH 408
1950	Leyland/Park Royal	LLU 829
1962	Bristol/ECW	557 BNG

1969	AEC/ECW	YRT 898H

COMMERCIAL

1916	Thornycroft lorry	HO 2534
1929	Thornycroft lorry	TR 7746
1932	AEC tower wagon	TV 6749
1935	Shelvoke and Drewry, dustcart	DPF 432
1938	Lacre, roadsweeper	CSP 802
1942	Fordson tractor	No reg.
1949	AEC brewer's dray	DVG 395
1952	Scammell mechanical horse	19 AN 80
1956	Mercedes tower wagon	SG 2109
1957	Harding invalid carriage	VNG 441
1972	Atkinson tractor	JRK 610K

MOTORCARS

1936	Austin saloon car	BOV 673
1937	Austin London taxi	ELC 837
1943	Austin ex-military car	MMX 979

STEAM

1924	Aveling and Porter road-roller	E 5333
1926	Aveling and Porter road-roller	RT 2474

ELECTRIC

1922	Ransomes tower wagon	DX 3578
1935	Electricar bread delivery van	BYM837
1943	Ransomes forklift truck	No reg.
1948	Brush/NCB milk float	KGH 441

tside the tram sheds is a 1904 Brill/Mills tram and a 1916 Thornycroft lorry. Founded in 1965, the Museum - open to the public since1972 - is now a popular tourist attraction. (Courtesy East Anglia Transport Museum)

Bathgate Garage featuring a 1936 Austin and a soft top Austin set in a period garage scene. (Courtesy East Anglia Transport Museum)

Ipswich Transport Museum, Trolleybus Depot, Cobham Road, Ipswich, Suffolk, IP3 9JD.

Tel. 01473 715666. Chairman: Brian Dyes.

The Museum is located 39 miles south of Norwich, on the outskirts of the city.

In 1995, after many years of frustration, the Ipswich Transport Museum opened in the former trolleybus depot in Cobham Road, on the eastern outskirts of Ipswich. The Collection has over 100 major exhibits, all gathered locally: several are from the town's largest manufacturer, Ransomes. Two exhibition rooms tell the story of air, rail and water-borne transport in the area using models and photographs.

Open: every Sunday and Bank Holiday Monday from Easter until the end of November, as well as Monday to Friday during school holidays in that period. Party visits are welcome at other times; ring for details. Hours are: Sunday and Bank Holiday Monday, 11.00am to 4.30pm (last entry 4.00pm). Half-term and August, Monday to Friday, 1.00pm to 4.00pm (last entry 3.30pm). The Museum is fully accessible by wheelchair, and has a purpose-built toilet. There's also a gift shop and tea room serving light refreshments. Car and coach parking is available on site.

Admission (1998): adults £2.25; children £1.25; concessions £1.75; families (2 + 3) £6.00.

VEHICLES

Year	Vehicle	Reg
1904	Brush open-top 2-deck 4-wheel electric tram	
1910	Aveling and Porter roadman's living van	
1915	Ransomes MO50 Orwell battery/electric lorry, front wheel drive	DX 1664
1915	Ransomes MO70 Orwell battery/electric tipper, rear wheel chain drive	PV 6736
1923	Railless trolleybus	DX 3988
1923	Ransomes and Rapier prototype 'Standard' mobile crane	EN 154
????	Lacre road sweeper	EL 6093
1925	Barford and Perkins petrol engine lightweight roller	
1926	Ransomes, Sims and Jefferies D trolleybus DX5610	
1926	Ransomes, Sims and Jefferies D trolleybus, chassis only	DX 5617
1926	Garrett 'O' type trolleybus	DX 5629
1927	Tilling Stevens B9B bus	X 6591
1928	Tilling Stevens B10A2 chassis only	DX 7812
1928	Associated Daimler Co. Mdl. 425 bus	VF 2788
1929	Manchester lorry	DX 7800
1929	Austin 7 van	VP 6505
1932	Bedford WLB bus	WV 1209
1933	Ransomes, Sims and Jefferies D4 trolleybus	PV 817
1938	Dennis Ace bus	CAH 923
1938	Leyland Cub Limousine fire engine	PV 4974
1939	Bristol L5G bus	CVF 874
1939	Dennis New World	F/E EBJ 732
1940	Ransomes & Rapier 'S' mobile crane	KLA 640
1940	Ransomes & Rapier 'Centurn' m/crane	MVX 156
1941	Ransomes & Rapier 1t shop mobile crane	PV 6854
1943	Chevrolet C60S wrecker truck	JSJ 173
1943	Leyland Retriever with Coles mobile crane	
1948	Karrier 'W' trolleybus	PV 8270
1948	Smiths/N B milk float	PV 8337
1948	AEC Monarch tower wagon	PV 8580
1948	Daimler hearse	PV 8784
1949	David Brown petrol/paraffin 'Cropmaster' tractor	JRT 508
1949	Bristol L4G bus	KAH 407
1949	Bedford OB coach	PV 9371
1949	Allis-Chalmers Row Crop Tractor 0	BNM 727
1950	AEC Regent III bus	ADX 1
1950	Sunbeam F4 trolleybus	ADX 196
1950	Atkinson 8-wheel flatbed lorry	JCE 725
1950	Commer Avenger fire engine	KRT 920
1950	Ransomes, Sims/Jefferies 1 ton battery/electric	
1950	Ransomes, Sims/Jefferies FL 20 battery/electric forklift	
1951	Raleigh Cycle Trojan motor convertible	APV 164
1951	Morrison battery coal lorry	APV 94
1951	Ransomes, Sims and Jefferies battery/electric 'Runabout' crane	
1951	Bristol LSX4G bus	MAH 744
1952	Lister petrol-engined Autotruck	
1952	Ferguson diesel-engined tractor	
1953	AEC Regal IV bus Pk Royal B42D b/work	BPV 9
1953	Ford E83W pickup truck	CDX 691
1953	Mercury timber tractor	CDX 894
1954	Ransomes, Sims and Jefferies NU4 battery/electric platform truck	
1954	Dennis F12 fire appliance	PBJ 338
1961	Ransomes, Sims/Jefferies NR 15 forklift	
1962	Bristol HA6G articiulated lorry	427 EYO
1964	AEC Regent V bus	ADX63B
1964	Bristol MW6G coach	APW 829B
1965	Scammell Scarab articiulated lorry	BPV 428C
1965	Bristol FS5G bus	GNG 125C
1965	Field Rider market garden tractor and trailer	
1966	AEC Regent V bus	DPV 68D
1966	Scammell Townsman mechanical horse	JLE 280D
1967	Brush Pony battery/electric van	UPV982
1967	Spedworth F2 Superstox racing car.	

1970	Batric invalid carriage	
1970	Commer Maxiload flatbed lorry	PDX 307H
1971	Ransomes, Sims and Jefferies 'Motor Triple' lawnmower	
1971	AEC Swift bus	JRT 82K
1972	Land Rover, 6x6 accident rescue unit	Q913 EGV
1974	Karrier Bantam lorry	GGV 71N
1974	ERF tractor unit	GPV 323M
1974	Scania 110 articulated lorry tractor unit	
1976	Enfield electric car	LYV 135P
1976	Enfield electric car	NTU 810P
1976	Leyland Atlantean AN68 bus	MRT 6P
1979	Bedford TK furniture van	BRT 642T
1981	Enfield electric van	LYF 162X

| 1985 | Freight Rover Sherpa electric van | B974PDX |

TWO-WHEELED VEHICLES

1940	Raynal autocycle	PV 6532
1948	Triumph ladies bicycle, with Cyclemaster wheel	
1959	NSU Quickly moped	HPV 584
1965	Mobylette moped	CDX 184C
1967	Raleigh moped	GDX 72E
1970	Mobylette moped	NPV 26H
1979	Triumph Bonneville motorcycle	UJO 897T
1985	Sinclair C5 electric motorcycle	

Brooklands Museum, Brooklands Road, Weybridge, Surrey, KT13 0QN.
Tel. 01932 857381. Curator: John C. Pulford.
Web site: http://www.ipix.co.uk

The Museum is 10 minutes from the M25 motorway and is approached off the B374, which lies between the A317 Weybridge Road and the A245 Cobham Road. Byfleet rail station is nearby. Access is via Sopwith Drive, off Parvis Road.

Brooklands Museum resides on the site of the famous Brooklands Race Track, constructed in 1907 and the world's first purpose-built motor circuit. Many of the original buildings still remain and are maintained and improved by the Trustees of Brooklands Museum. Besides motoring exhibits, there is a section devoted to Race Track facilities and a Ladies Reading Room, which has Barbara Cartland connections. There is a comprehensive aviation display, as World War II Wellington bombers were made at the Vickers factory, then on the site. A fully-restored Wellington Mk IA bomber recovered from Loch Ness in 1985, a Hawker Hunter, Hawker Harrier, Vickers Varsity, Vickers VC 10, Vickers Viscount and a Vickers Merchantman are also exhibited. There are many organised motoring event days throughout the season. Open throughout the year from Tuesday to Sunday and Bank Holidays, 10.00am to 4.00pm (winter) and 10.00am to 5.00pm (summer). Closed 24th December to the 1st of January inclusive. There's a Museum shop, refreshment facilities and toilets, plus wheelchair access. Some of the many cars in the Museum are on loan, with the understanding that they may be returned to the owner for his own use. Also, the Museum rotates these cars, so if you want to see a particular vehicle, it's best to ring in advance of your journey. A recent addition is John Cobb's 24 litre Napier Railton.

Admission: adults £6.00; students and OAPs £5.00; children (5 to 16) £4.00; under-fives free; family ticket (2 + 3) £16.00. Entrance includes free parking and a free trail guide.

MOTORCARS

1898	Alien Runabout	Not reg.		1933	Duesenberg race car	No reg.
1900	Peugeot Voiture	RU5865		1933	Frazer Nash (half-scale model)	
1904	Siddeley two-seater tourer	No reg.		1933	Napier-Railton, 24 litre record car	No reg.
1907	Napier 24 hour run racing car	Not reg.		1934	Alvis Speed 20	No reg.
1910	AC Sociable	KT8655		1934	Riley Ulster Imp	KV9475
1912	Lorraine Dietrich Vieux Charles III	No reg.		1935	MG PA Sports	ALJ666
1914	Rolls-Royce Silver Ghost	No reg.		1935	Morris 8 saloon	No reg.
1928	Vauxhall Grosvenor R type	XV479		1937	Austin 7 Sports	No reg.
1930	Austin 7 Ulster	No reg.		1937	Morgan 3 wheeler	No reg.
1932	MG Midget	No reg.		1991	Shell McLaren F1 showcar	Not reg.

An early AA motorcycle and sidecar at Brooklands Museum, Weybridge, Surrey.

MOTORCYCLES

1910	Scott 486cc	No reg.	1939	Brough Superior 998cc	No reg.
1911	Scott 486cc	No reg.	1939	BSA with AA sidecar	No reg.
1913	Scott 532cc with sidecar	No reg.	1939	Velocette GTP 250cc	No reg.
1914	Scott	No reg.	1960s	RAC Norton and sidecar	No reg.
1921	ABC Sopwith	No reg.			
1922	Zenith Bradshaw	No reg.			
1927	BSA Sloper	No reg.	**MISCELLANEOUS**		
1927	Sunbeam 493cc	No reg.	ABC motorcycle engine		
1928	Douglas S6, sidecar and				
	Douglas 500	No reg.	**COMMERCIAL**		
1929	Grindlay Peerless - JAP	No reg.	1952	AEC, Regal IV BEA coach	MLL 721
1929	Scott TT 596cc	No reg.			

A 1933 Duesenberg single seater car on the restored Clubhouse internal weighbridge. (Courtesy Brooklands Trust)

The Barbara Cartland 'Pink Room' at Brooklands Museum, Weybridge, Surrey.

The 1933 record-breaking 24 litre Napier Railton, in this photograph being driven by John Cobb on the Brooklands Banking in 1997. (Courtesy Brooklands Trust)

The famous 1907 Brooklands Clubhouse (now a Schedu Ancient Monument) restored to original 1930s appearan the venue for all present-day Club activities. (Courtesy Brooklands Trust)

Cobham Bus Museum, Redhill Road, Cobham, Surrey, KT11 1EF.

Tel. 01932 868665 (Saturday and Sunday).
Curator: The Secretary, London Bus Preservation Trust.

The Museum is located 19 miles southwest of London on the A245 Byfleet Road, close to the A3/M25 junction.

Originating in 1966, the Cobham Bus Collection united under one roof those large passenger vehicles that were owned by individuals. The building was originally Depot 45, an outstation of Vickers Armstrong during the 1939/45 war. The Collection consists of around 30 vehicles, though numbers vary with the season as owners visit rallies. This combination of Trust and privately-owned vehicles represents the widest selection of preserved ex-London Transport motor buses in the world. Many of the vehicles, once members of large classes, are sole survivors of their type and are therefore unique. The Collection is housed in a working garage, in which several of the earlier buses have been totally rebuilt. A guide book is available. Open: April, most weekends subject to external commitments. Telephone before setting off. Parking and toilets provided. No facilities for the disabled.

BUSES ON SHOW

Year	Vehicle	Reg	Year	Vehicle	Reg
1925	Dennis 4 ton	XX 9591	1948	AEC Regent III	HLX 462
1930	AEC Regent I	GI 2098	1948	Bedford O-type	JXC 2
1934	AEC Regent I	AXM 693	1949	Leyland Tiger PSI	JXC 288
1934	Albion Valiant	LJ 9501	1949	AEC Regal IV	UMP 227
1935	AEC Q	CGJ 188	1951	AEC Regal IV	LUC 210
1936	AEC Regent I	CXX 457	1952	AEC Regent III	LYR 826
1936	AEC Regal	CXX 171	1952	Leyland Titan	MLL 685
1936	Leyland Cub	CLX 548	1952	AEC Regent III	LYR 910
1937	AEC Regent I	DLU 92	1952	AEC Regal IV	MLL 969
1938	AEC Regent I	EGO 426	1952	AEC Regent III	MXX 223
1938	AEC Regal	ELP 228	1953	AEC Regal IV	MLL 740
1945	Guy Arab II	HGC 130	1953	AEC Regal IV	NLE 672
1945	AEC Regent II	HGC 225	1953	Guy Special NLLVP	MXX 334
1947	AEC Regent III	HLW 177	1954	AFC Regent III	CDX 516
1948	AEC Regent III	HLX 410	1958	Leyland No. 3	SLT 58

Admission is free but donations welcome.

Dunsfold Land Rover Trust, Alfold Road, Dunsfold, Godalming, Surrey, GU8 4NP.

Tel. 01483 200567. Owners: Phillip Bashall Senior, Brian Bashall and Guy Henderson.

The Museum is located 29 miles southwest of London. 8 miles south of Guildford on the A281, turn right onto the B2130 around the airfield for Dunsfold and Dunsfold Land Rover Trust.

The Bashalls have the largest Land Rover collection - around 60 unique Land Rovers, all special in some way - in the world. None are production vehicles; most were prototype or development models. Phillip Bashall Senior still has the first Land Rover he bought in 1968. There is a large library which is open to enthusiasts by arrangement. Opening hours also by arrangement. There's a shop but no food, toilets or disabled facilities. Parking.

ROVER PRODUCTS

1950	Land Rover 80 station wagon original	
1953	Land Rover 80 (mint)	SPK 107
1955	Land Rover 86 fire engine	AFF 218
1958	Land Rover 107 station ex-Duke	539 EWL
1958	L/Rover 109 station wagon, Series 2	TBT 444
1958	L/Rover 88 No. 3, oldest Series 2	UAA 392
1959	Land Rover 109 No. 6 K/T	WCG 849
1960	Land Rover 109 station No. 9	AC
1960	Land Rover Series 2 diesel m/t	YLX 827
1962	Land Rover 129 prototype turbo	FYF 928C1
1964	Land Rover 109 APGP Wader	APB 963A
1965	Land Rover Forrest Rover, ex-CEGB	BNB
1965	Land Rover 88M/T petrol	6459 UR
1966	Land Rover 110 F/control ch. 1	NXC 511D
1966	L/Rover 110 B19 lwt prototype	VXC 100F
1966	Land Rover 88 M/T	GPM 493D
1968	L/Rover 101 prototype 6 cylinder	OAB 266P
1968	Land Rover 88 V8 prototype	BXC 975G
1970	L/Rover US spec l/h drive original	PXC 561J
1970	Range Rover prototype No. 16	YUB 162H
1970	Range Rover Press No. 46	PXC 342J
1971	L/Rover fire control fire truck	YWK 177K
1971	Land Rover Portugese prototype	HLF 110T
1971	Land Rover ex-British Aerospace	BNJ 272K
1971	Land Rover 88 No. 1	RXC 548J
1971	Range Rover original gold	DTX 666J
1972	L/Rover 101 No. 1 l/h drive 24v	BXC 676K
1972	Land Rover 101 No. 5 prototype	
1972	L/Rover 101 No. 1 r/h drive	PGC 941K
1972	Land Rover Series III chassis 45	KYX 682K
1973	Land Rover 101 pre-production No. 15	

1973	Range Rover Darien Gap	VXC 756K
1974	L/Rover 88 4 x 2 ex-Belgian Army	LPB 59N
1974	Land Rover 101 prototype No. 4	SPE 146L
1974	Land Rover 88 winch track test vehicle	
1974	Range Rover 6 x 4 Swiss fire truck	SRW
1976	Land Rover 101 crane	NPK 105P
1976	Land Rover prototype V8	
1976	Land Rover 100 4 door prototype	
1976	Land Rover Judge Dredd	
1978	Land Rover Santana 109 Mil.	CHP 912T
1978	Land Rover 100 station wagon prototype	
1978	Land Rover 100 prototype 5 door ST	
1978	Land Rover 100 V8 prototype 24v	BAC 779T
1981	Land Rover 88 Santana	Q946 HEX
1982	Land Rover 90 No. 1 prototype	CWK 30Y
1983	L/Rover No. 2 90 prototype r/h/d	CWK 40Y
1984	Land Rover 90 No. 3 prototype	A543 JPB
1985	L/Rover 110 Swiss prototype V8 efi	B27 TKV
1986	L/Rover 110 Llama prototype 4	Q276 DPG
1986	Land Rover 110 Llama prototype 2	C413 SNP
1988	L/Rover Discovery prototype l/h/d	C60 JKG
1986	Land Rover Llama prototype No. 1	
1986	Land Rover Llama prototype No. 5	
1992	Disco cutaway	
1994	Range Rover prototype left hand drive	
1996	Freelander prototype diesel 5 door	
1996	Freelander prototype petrol 5 door	
1996	Freelander prototype Mule Mystro	

Admission is free but donations welcome.

Amberley Museum, Houghton Bridge, Amberley, Arundel, West Sussex, BN18 9LT.

Tel. 01798 831370 (ask for the Transport Garage).

The Museum is located 4 miles north of Arundel on the B2139, adjacent to the BR station at Amberley. Frequent trains run from London Victoria and the South.

The Museum is in what was previously Amberley chalk pit. From 1840 to the 1960s, chalk was mined from this 36 acre site; its closure left a fitting site for an industrial museum. Today, artisans demonstrate many skills associated with boat building, the manufacture of clay pipes, blacksmithing, and so on. Similar displays can be seen of a narrow gauge railway, stationary engines, wireless collection, steam traction engines, domestic display and, within a vintage bus garage, part of a collection of vintage motor buses, plus many other exhibits. The site also offers the 'Seeboard Electricity Hall' which is a major exhibit of interest to all, but children in particular.

Open: March to 31st October, usually Wednesday to Sunday, 10.00am to 5.00pm. Daily opening during school holidays. There's a shop, tea room and picnic areas, toilets and disabled facilities. Free parking for cars and coaches.

A fully serviceable 1938 Bedford lorry, which is used mainly in and around the site.
(Courtesy Amberley Museum)

COMMERCIAL

1914	Tilling Stevens	1B 552*	Aveling DX6 diesel roller	No reg.
1920	Leyland chassis and 1928 Short		Mechanical road testing machine	JPX 595J
	Brothers 51 seat, 2 deck body	CD 5125*	Readymix road machine	PPM 499X
1923	Tilling Stevens open charabanc	TS 3A	Lansing Bagnell tow cars	No reg.
1924	Tramocar	BP 9822	Fordson standard road roller	DTP 185
1927	Dennis 30cwt single deck	VF 1517	Auto tow truck, diesel	No reg.
1927	Tilling Stevens single deck	MO 9324*	'Stop me and buy one' trike	
1930	Southdown	VF 6473*		
1930	Tilling Stevens single deck	VF 6805*		
1931	Leyland Titan, 2 decks	VF 7428*	**STEAM**	
1936	MG open sports car - visitor	ZA 68	Steam roller (Joan)	PX 2690
1938	Bedford lorry	DKN 544		
1964	Electric float	APN 992B	* *On loan from Southdown Omnibus Trust*	
	Titan single deck	EUF 184*		

1920 open top Leyland N-Type outside Steele's Garage. This vintage vehicle is used by the public for travelling around the varied and extensive display site. (Courtesy Amberley Museum)

Admission: adults £6.00; children (5-16) £3.00; under-fives free; OAPs £5.30; family tickets (2 + 3) £16.00. Reduced rates for booked parties.

Batemans, (National Trust), Burwash, East Sussex, TNI9 7DS.

Tel. 01435 882302. Contact: The Administrator.

The Museum's location is 36 miles southeast of London, 13 miles south of Tunbridge Wells on the A265.

This was a Sussex Ironmaster's house in earlier times, and Rudyard Kipling's home from 1902 to 1936. Kipling was an inveterate motorist and the Rolls-Royce on show (which he christened Duchess) was one of many he owned during thirty six years of motoring. All the rooms in the house are as he left them, and the garden he designed is surrounded by *Puck of Pooks Hill* country. All the family will enjoy this visit. Open: 27th of March to the end of October, Saturday to Wednesday, 11.00am to 5.30pm. Open Bank Holiday Mondays and Good Friday. A licensed tea room is open the same hours as the house. There's a picnic area, gift shop, wheelchair access to gardens and ground floor of the house. Wheelchairs and route map available. There are toilets near the ticket office. Other facilities include sympathetic hearing scheme, Braille guide and baby changing. Parking is free.

Admission: adults £5.00; children £2.50; family ticket (2 + 3) £12.50 . Group rates available. National Trust members free.

MOTORCAR
1928   Rolls-Royce Phantom I

Bentley Wildfowl and Motor Museum, Halland, Near Lewes, East Sussex, BN8 5AF.

Tel. 01825 840573. Manager: Barry Sutherland.
email: barrysutherland@pavilion.co.uk

Location: 7 miles northeast of Lewes off the A26, A22 and B2192. Well signposted.

The Bentley Estate covers 100 acres of countryside in the heart of Sussex. Quiet walks through the woods and parkland, by the lakes where the renowned waterfowl collection may be seen, can be enjoyed. Adjacent to the Bentley House (which is open for viewing) is the Motor Museum, which depicts the development of motoring from the earliest times and contains about 50 gleaming veteran and vintage cars and motorcycles, plus various other transport-associated vehicles. Open: 15th of March to 31st of October, 10.30am to 4.30pm (5.00pm in July and August). The House opens at 12 noon from the 1st of April to the 31st of October. Winter weekend opening is 10.30am to 4.00pm. The House and estate are closed during December and January. There's a gift shop, licensed tea

Admission 1999/2000: adults £4.20 (£3.20 winter); children (4-15) £2.50; under-3s free; OAPs/students £3.20; family ticket £12.50. (2 + 4); 10 per cent discount for parties of 11 or more; special rates for the disabled.

rooms, picnic areas and disabled facilities, including separate toilet area. The grounds are flat and wheelchair-friendly. There is a childrens' play area. Parking is free. Dogs allowed in the parking field only.

MOTORCARS

Many of these vehicles are privately owned, in good order and used by the owner. The Collection is therefore subject to change. If you are hoping to see a particular vehicle it's advisable to check before travelling.

1850	Horsedrawn hearse	
1901	Stirling Panhard	
1903	De Dion Bouton	
1904	Humberette 4.5hp	
1909	Alldays and Onions 10/12hp	
1909	Buick 4 cylinder	
1911	Buick 4 cylinder	No reg.
1912	Panhard et Levassor	
1912	Austin 15	
1912	Austin 10	
1914	Sunbeam	
1918	Ford Model T ambulance	
1921	GWK (friction drive)	
1922	Standard 2 seat tourer	
1922	Rolls-Royce Silver Ghost	
1923	AC Empire	
1923	Halford Special	
1923	Wolseley 2 seater coupé	
1924	Aston Martin long chassis tourer	
1925	Swift 10hp	
1927	Riley 9 Monaco 1087cc ohv	
1927	Rolls-Royce 20hp	
1927	Austin Heavy 12/4 (Gumdrop type)	
1927	Vauxhall 30/98	
1928	Ford Model A special coupé	
1928	Minerva type AK 32/34hp	AXO 204
1930	Bentley 4.5 litre, original	
1930	Rolls-Royce 20/25 Boat Tail Skiff	
1933	Morgan Super Sports JAP engine	
1934	BMW 315, 6 cylinder	
1934	Talbot	
1935	Morris Eight Series 1	
1936	Armstrong Siddeley 12hp 2 door coupé	
1936	Austin 7 Nippy 748cc	
1936	British Salmson	

1937	Bentley 4.5 litre, (cantilever hinges)	
1937	Lagonda 4.5 litre, Rapide	FYW 998
	Austin Twelve, late thirties.	
1950	Frazer Nash Mille Miglia 2 l, 120hp	NMY
1950	Jaguar Mk5	
1950	VW Beetle	
1952	Jaguar XK120	
1957	Aston Martin DB 2/4	
1957	Standard Pennant 948cc	
1959	BRM F1 Grand Prix	No reg.
1963	Austin Healey 3000	212 GLD
1971	Enfield electric prototype	
1972	GT6 Triumph	
1972	Maserati Mexico 4.7 litre	
1972	Volvo 1800 ES Sports saloon	
1973	Aston Martin V8	
1975	Lotus Esprit	
1981	DeLorean	D301 POV
1982	Micro concept car	

MOTORCYCLES

1908	BAT 990cc JAP	
1912	Matchless	
1921	Beardmore Precision Sports 350cc	
1922	Douglas 4hp-twin	
1922	McKenzie (autocycle)	
1928	Scott Flying Squirrel	
1929	Levis (six port)	
1939	AJS	
1940	Norton 490cc	
1950's	Sunbeam S7	
1950's	Sunbeam S8	
1955	Excelsior 98cc	
1963	Child's motorcycle (Cyclemaster Unit)	
1967	'Just Like Dads'	
1967	Raleigh moped	
1968/9	Solex (autocycle)	

The Museum also contains many other bicycles, tricycles, pedal cars and childrens' tricycles.

1921 G W K Friction Drive. (Courtesy Bentley Wildfowl Trust)

1950 Frazer Nash Mille Miglia 120hp. (Courtesy Bentley Wildfowl Trust)

1937 Lagonda 4.5 litre Rapide of the Motor Museum in front of one of the Palladian windows. Bentley is famous for its many attractions, not least of which are the wildfowl and extensive gardens. (Courtesy Bentley Wildfowl Trust)

Filching Motor Museum, Jevington Road, Wannock, Polegate, Sussex, BN26 5QA.
Tel. 01323 487838/487933/487124.
Owner: Paul Foulkes-Halbard

The Museum is 49 miles southeast of London, one and a quarter miles on the Friston road from the A22 at Polegate crossroads.

Set in 28 acres of woodland, downland and formal gardens, Filching Manor (mentioned in the Doomsday Book and before) has about 100 veteran, vintage and classic cars and motorcycles that may be seen. The owner maintains a remarkable and unique collection of the rarest sports and racing cars in the world, from a 1904 Mercedes 70hp race car, to two of Sir Malcom Campbell's Bluebirds, with many other distinguished marques. Memorabilia from the first 100 years of the motorcar is also on show.

Open: Easter to October, Thursdays to Sunday and most Bank Holidays, 10.30am to 4.30pm. Light snacks and drinks available whenever the Manor is open. Facilities include shop, car sales and consultancy and toilets. Disabled facilities available. Parking is plentiful and free, close to the Museum and Manor.

MOTORCARS		
1904	Peugeot	
1904	Mercedes 70hp race car	No reg.
1907	Corbin Vanderbilt	No reg.
1926	Bugatti T35 Targa Florio	FYN 36
1926	Bentley 3 litre	
1931	Alfa-Romeo 8C Mille Liglia	BGO 246.
	1935 Ford race car	LMG 613
	Rolls-Royce	
	Alfa-Romeo	CA 8519
	Alfa-Romeo	AUL 776
	MG Brooklands	No reg.
	Toyota Carina-based rally car	No reg

Admission: adults £3.00; children and OAPs £1.50.

Museum of British Road Transport, St. Agnes Lane, Hales Street, Coventry, CV1 1PN.

Tel. 01203 832425.
Managing Director: Barry Littlewood.

To get to the Museum, follow the brown Tourist Board signs from the Coventry inner ring road. The Museum is near to Coventry Cathedral and there are regular bus services. Coventry railway station is nearby.

The Museum, on two floors, has over 210 cars and commercial vehicles of varying types, 93 motorcycles and 240 bicycles. The Tiatsa Model World Show will enchant children and adults alike. There is a variety of set piece tableaux charting development of the motorcar and motorcycle from the early years. Coventry's contribution to the industry may be seen in the many famous marques in the display. Special exhibitions are held periodically. Richard Noble's record-breaking Thrust 2 is on display with accompanying audio visual programme. Open from 10.00am to 5.00pm throughout the year except Christmas and Boxing Days. A twelve month trial period of free admission during 1998 has been extended until March 2000. There's a cafe serving light meals and snacks, and a gift shop offering an extensive range of books and gifts. All of the Museum is accessible to the disabled. There are toilets (including disabled) and baby changing facilities. No parking at the Museum but there are public car parks nearby. Exhibits constantly move in and out of store and attend external events. Anyone wishing to see a specific vehicle is therefore advised to telephone in advance to check if it will be on display during their visit.

CARS AND COMMERCIAL				
1896	Peugeot Vis-A-Vis	Unreg.	1925	Lea Francis J type 10125	PP 5206
1897	Daimler Wagonette	O 9521	1926	Daimler 25/85hp	DF 450
1897	Coventry Motette Tri-Car	KJ 8	1927	Rover 16/50	WK 2242
1898	Daimler Phaeton	FRW 767	1928	Alvis front wheel drive	UL 2046
1899	Crowden Dog Cart	O 9527	1929	Standard Fulham	UK 70541
1901	Payne and Bates 'Godiva'	BWK 1	1929	Standard Fulham Display Chassis	Unreg.
1904	Riley Tri-Car	DU 458	1930	Standard Swallow Saloon	LJ 2793
1905	Daimler 45hp	DU 541	1930	Humber Super Snipe	GC 412
1906	Rover 6hp	BW 332	1931	Singer 10 van	JU 827
1907	Standard Roi De Belge	SMC 1	1931	Daimler M 16-20	SR 7933
1908	Hillman Coatelen 12/15	A 338	1932	Alvis 12/60	KV 286
1908	Riley 12/18	NS 105	1933	Austin Seven	BB 9207
1909	Maudslay 17	AM 1842	1933	SS Cars SS1	JE 187
1910	Humber 12/20	M 2755	1934	Singer 9	2310 DU
1910	Humber 16/24	EH 225	1934	Hillman Minx	ANU 460
1910	Maudslay 32	EJ 79	1934	Rover 12	AWK 402
1910	Swift 7hp	G 5118	1934	Riley Lynx	JU 4269
1911	Daimler A12	FL 921	1934	Triumph Gloria	BLP 622
1912	Crouch Carette	Y 1060	1935	Talbot 105	FPG 137B
1912	Siddeley Deasy Althorp cabriolet	T 2980	1935	Standard 16	BDH 484
1913	Morris Oxford	FN 1662	1935	SS Cars 1.5 litre	FA 6342
1913	Swift Cyclecar	P 9217	1935	Daimler - Queen Mary's limo	NYE 582
1915	Rover 12	AC 5278	1935	Riley Kestrel	MJ 9035
1920	Coventry Premier TourerHP 416		1935	Humber Vogue	BYN 641
1920	Alvis 10/30	BO 2481	1935	Hillman Aero Minx	BKN 602
1921	Calcott cabriolet	AU 9653	1936	Armstrong Siddeley 14	BKV 552
1921	Rover 12	MD 7969	1936	Riley Kestrel	BRW 3
1922	Morris Cowley	HP 4386	1936	Morris Eight van	CTV 274
1922	Shelvoke and Drewry refuse truck	KP 7670	1936	Humber Super Snipe	BWA 360
1923	Albatross Tourer	HP 6370	1937	Dennis Ace fire engine	CRW 345
1923	Humber Chummy	XN 2972	1937	Austin pedal car	Unreg.
1923	Ford Model T	Unreg.	1937	Standard 1 0	EBH 720
			1937	Daimler V4.5	DYH 950

A Humber Hawk, part of the extensive Rootes Group collection at the Museum of British Road Transport, Coventry, Warwickshire. (Courtesy Museum of British Road Transport)

Thrust 2 Land Speed Record car at the Museum of British Road Transport, Coventry, Warwickshire.

A side view of Thrust 2 at the Museum of British Road Transport, Coventry, Warwickshire.

A 1937 Dennis Ace fire engine at the Museum of British Road Transport, Coventry, Warwickshire.

The short-lived electric Sinclair C5 at the Museum of British Road Transport, Coventry, Warwickshire.

Year	Vehicle	Reg.
1939	Austin K2 fire engine	GLE 837
1939	Lanchester Sports saloon	BNT 823
1939	Rover 16	EFD 23B
1939	Morris Series E	DHO 899
1942	Hillman Utility	WDU 620
1943	Daimler armoured car	ONK 897P
1943	Hmber S. Snipe (ex-Montgomery's)	MSV 103
1944	Daimler CWA6 2 deck bus	EKV 966
1946	Coventry Climax ET 199 F/L	Unreg.
1947	Daimler - King G. VI's Laudaulette	YXB 99
1947	Standard 14	SVC 764
1948	Jaguar 3.5 litre dhc.	TMH 964
1948	Oak Tree App. 3 wheel tractor	Unreg.
1948	Maudslay Marathon II coach	JNB 416
1948	Standard 8	LDH 996
1948	Morris Series M	HON 490
1949	Coventry Victor Venus prototype	YDU 502
1949	Triumph 2000 Saloon	HVC 854
1949	Standard Vanguard Phase 1	ONO 427
1949	Lea Francis Westland	FWN 429
1950	Daimler DB 18	538 BAA
1950	Daimler CVD6 single deck bus	KOM 150
1950	Paladin Caravan	Unreg.
1952	Alvis TA21	MUU 446
1952	Armstrong Siddeley Whitley	LWK 927
1952	Maudslay Monarch lorry	NGJ 489
1952	Karrier Gamecock fire engine	PWD 121
1952	Triumph Mayflower	MOL 327
1953	Austin 3 way van	MKV 326
1953	Aston Martin DB2	MRU 200
1953	Lea Francis 14	MXM 784
1953	Hillman Minx MK V	ODU 328
1953	Rover 75	ODU 45
1953	Daimler CD650 2 deck bus	SRB 424
1953	Daimler Conquest	ODU 994
1953	Riley RME	NNX 330
1953	Humber Hawk MK V	OHP 608
1953	Humber 4 x 4 winch truck	JRA 214D
1953	Jaguar XK 120	MWY 431
1953	Milk float, electric	SJW 266
1954	Austin A40 van	KKU 791
1954	Sunbeam Mk III rally car	PWK 603
1954	Standard Vanguard Phase 2	PDU 194
1954	Rover 75	VWD 125
1954	Karrier Mini-Coach	PBC 734
1954	Kieft Formula 111 racing car	Unreg.
1954	Sunbeam Mk III dhc	VBH 787
1954	Triumph TR2	RRW 327
1955	Harper 55 invalid carriage	142 APJ
1955	Standard Super 10	PKV 8
1955	Morris Minor	PWK 197
1955	Singer SM1500	MBP 730
1956	AEC Mercury Tanker	TYO 690
1956	Austin A50	MUT 699
1956	Ferguson R5/2 prototype car	PHP 866
1956	Hillman Radford estate	BTR 824B
1956	Scammell Highwayman Tanker	SXC 341
1956	Singer Gazelle	VWK 158
1957	Jaguar XK 150	VRU 131
1958	Ferguson R4 prototype car	RPE 4
1958	Jaguar Mk VIII	VRW 685
1959	Commer BF ambulance	WKV 2
1959	Austin Gipsy fire tender	XKV 33
1959	Ferguson R5 prototype car	OWK 21
1959	Triumph Herald (ex-section)	Unreg.
1960	Morris Mini	598 HTO
1960	Sunbeam Rapier Mk III	7523 IJ
1960	Standard Ensign	4886HP
1960	Lola Mk 1 racing car	Unreg.
1961	Austin FX4 taxi	WDW 623
1962	Sunbeam Alpine rally car	9201 RW
1963	Daimler CVG6 2 deck bus	333 CRW
1963	Humber Sceptre	991 FLO
1963	Techcraft - BRM	Unreg.
1963	Jaguar Mk X	308 DUG
1964	Commer mobile police control room	AHP 319A
1964	Hillman Swallow prototype	Unreg.
1964	Ferguson MF35X tractor	697 CWK
1964	Morris Minor Traveller	CDU 208B
1965	Daimler Majestic Major hearse	CRW 761C
1965	Alvis TE21	EOL 595C
1965	Austin A40 Farina	EVJ 505C
1966	Hillman Super Imp	CEC 340D
1966	Humber Hawk	LLW 773D
1967	Hillman Super Minx estate	FFF 185E
1967	Triumph 1300	MOE 350E
1968	Alvis Stalwart military carrier	17 ET 45
1968	Triumph Spitfire	MAN 414E
1968	Sunbeam Alpine	PAC 554F
1969	Daimler V8 250 saloon	YPC 434G
1970	Jensen Interceptor Mk 11	BAM 52H
1970	Leyld Marathon gas turbine truck	Unreg.
1970	Triumph Vitesse	DDT 456H
1971	Hillman Avenger	WDX 269K
1971	Morris 1300	HMC 174K
1972	Daimler Sovereign	JLP 432K
1972	Triumph Dolomite Sprint	FRW 797L
1972	Morris Minor Post Office van	DFL 158K
1973	Daimler Fleetline open bus	PDU 125M
1973	Range Rover	GRW 158L
1974	Motor Panels a/f crash tender concept cab	Unreg.
1974	Rover Land Rover	PHP 93M
1975	Chrysler Centura	JVC 263N
1975	Jaguar E type	XHP 12S
1975	Ford Escort	HKX 936N
1975	Hillman Imp	LHP 878P
1975	Ford Consul 2000 cutaway	Unreg.
1976	Triumph TR7	TRR 447R
1977	Austin Allegro	VDU 499S
1977	Triumph 2.5 TC police car	SUK 530S
1977	Jaguar XJC	Unreg.
1977	Lotus Eclat	SFD 400R
1978	Daimler DS420 Limousine	WOM 366T
1980	Austin M/Metro	MPB909W
1980	Electric child's car - Europa	Unreg.
1980	Peugeot-Talbot Paykaan (Iran)	TEH 4383
1980	Sunbeam Lotus rally car replica	KKV 444V
1981	Talbot Lotus Sunbeam Rally	RAC 134W
1981	Thrust 2, record car	Unreg.
1982	De Loran	Unreg.
1982	Jaguar XJ12 prototype fire engine	RDU 941W
1982	Sunbeam Lotus Horizon Turbo	Unreg.
1982	Skate Car 'Spirit of Coventry'	Unreg.
1983	Rover SDI 'Kat' Conversion	A28 HAD
1983	Triumph Acclaim	A601 ATV
1984	Abbey Cat saloon	Unreg.
1985	Jaguar XJ40 prototype	C541 VRW
1985	Peugeot 405 SRI	F497 BWW
1985	Peugeot 205 T16 rally car	B555 SRW
1985	UDAP electric car	Q33 GRW
1986	Daimler saloon (XJ6)	D150 DKV
1986	Jaguar XJ40 prototype	Unreg.
1987	City Wheels electric car	E901 JVC
1988	Rover Land Rover County	F120 RKV
1989	Vega concept car	Unreg.
1990	Ford Sierra Cosworth rally car	Unreg.
1991	Baltic concept car	Unreg.
1991	Hot Dog concept car	Unreg.
1993	Jaguar XJ220	100 JAG
1993	Peugeot-Talbot electric minibus	K232 DAC
1994	Aston Martin DB7 prototype	Unreg.
1994	Peugeot 306 XSI prototype	Unreg.
1994	Peugeot 306 XSI prototype	Unreg.
1994	Peugeot 306 XSI prototype	Unreg.
1996	Concept 2096 car	Unreg.
	Lister auto truck	Unreg.

MOTORCYCLES

Year	Vehicle	Reg.
1899	MMC Tricycle	Unreg.
1901/3	Riley Moto-Bi	Unreg.
1903	Centaur	Unreg.
1903	Singer Moto-Wheel	Unreg.
1911	Rudge	AC 2966
1913	Humber Lady's	BL 4063
1913	Premier	M 5112
1919	Triumph LW	DS 6730

Entrance to the Museum of British Road
Transport, Coventry, Warwickshire.

...n 1898 Daimler, one of the 150 cars and 75
...torcycles in the largest display of British road
...nsport under one roof. (Courtesy Museum of
British Road Transport)

...bably made at the Coventry factory, this 1910
...nber Landaulette cost around £350 when new.
...ourtesy Museum of British Road Transport)

...72 Morris Minor van and a 1977 Triumph 2.5
...n cam police car. (Courtesy Museum of British
Road Transport)

Year	Make/Model	Reg.
1920	Hobart	AJ 4555
1920	Invicta	AC 7956
1920	Rover 350cc	CM 3371
1920	Stafford Mobile Pup	0 9568
1921	Triumph C	DU 8490
1921	Coventry Victor combo	HP 2860
1921	Kenilworth scooter	HP 3115
1921	Triumph H	NL 1897
1921	Triumph H	AH 7079
1922	Triumph R (Ricardo)	CE 9797
1923	Triumph R	NR 2445
1923	Firman	AU 4620
1923	Francis Barnett	DS 6731
1923	R and H Super Lightweight	NX 3648
1923	Wee McGregor	XO 7705
1924	Coventry B and D	HP 9172
1924	New Hudson combo	AU 7426
1924	Rudge	FL 3692
1924	Lea Francis-twin	PC 4598
1924	McKenzie Popular	HP 3718
1924	Triumph LW	DS 6732
1925	Humber De Luxe, x-section	Unreg.
1925	Rover 345cc	HJ 5123
1926	AJS G8	RW 5898
1926	Triumph P	RW 6415
1927	Norton H18	WK 1644
1927	Triumph N	TW 1507
1927	Rudge combo	WK 2037
1927	Francis Barnett 4	YC 1524
1928	Francis Barnett 4	CM 8001
1928	Rudge dirt track racer	Unreg.
1929	Triumph N	VC 918
1934	Francis Barnett Cruiser	KV 8572
1934	New Imperial	WV 5334
1935	Norton 18 combo	BOH 759
1936	Coventry Eagle ME	BWX 202
1936	Coventry Eagle Pullman	BKV 330
1936	Francis Barnett Stag	BKV 224
1937	Rudge Sports Special	FPC 996
1937	Sunbeam 9	ABK 607
1938	Rudge Ulster	ELJ 956
1939	Francis Barnett H45 Cruiser	EHP 431

Year	Make/Model	Reg.
1939	Triumph Speed-twin	EOE 356
1940	BSA M20	C 5120508
1940	James ML 17	HNX 263
1940	Norton 16H	51 FAU
1940	Rudge Autocycle	EVC 526
1946	New Hudson Autocycle	LNX 283
1947	Francis Barnett Powerbike	ODU 901
1947	Velocette MSS	EJW 639
1948	Ridley Electric	GKV 400
1948	Tippen invalid carriage	HWK 78
1948	Royal Enfield	HTX 439
1949	OEC	LTV 292
1952	BSA C11	RDU 219
1952	BSA C11	HUK 646
1955	Sunbeam S7 combo	LOP 281
1958	Francis Barnett Falcon	WHP 742
1958	James Captain	830 BTO
1959	Norton 350	485 ARH
1960	Triumph Tigress	969 BNX
1960	Triumph Cub	BNX 756B
1961	Greeves	339 MWL
1962	BSA C15	462 EAY
1962	Francis Barnett Plover 86	838 AVC
1962	BSA 500 Star-twin	908 PHA
1963	Caldicott Special	811 BHP
1963	James Scooter	579 BRW
1964	Royal Enfield Clipper De Luxe	350 VRT
1964	Triumph Tina scooter	701 BHP
1965	Raleigh moped RM6	CVC 373H
1965	Triumph Tina	EUE 534C
1965	Raleigh moped RM8	EAC 48C
1965	Raleigh Runabout moped	BRW 204C
1968	Lambretta scooter	SNX 406G
1969	Triumph Trident	UWD 761G
1970	Ariel/BSA motor scooter	OKV 466J
1971	Ariel/BSA K2	OKV 552J
1973	Triumph Tina truck	XWK 66M
1974	Triumph Tiger T100	XRW 964M
1976	Motobecane Moby moped	JOA 326N
1977	Triumph T140 Bonneville	VWK 467S
1990	Atlas Concept	Unreg.
1992	Omega Concept	Unreg.

A 1932 Alvis 12/60, listed at the time of launch as 'the company's last out-and-out sports
car.' (Courtesy Museum of British Road Transport)

Heritage Motor Centre, Banbury Road, Gaydon, Warwickshire, CV35 0BJ.
Tel. 01926 641188. Curator: Stephen Laing.

The Museum is 26 miles southeast of Birmingham on the B4100, half a mile west of junction 12 on the M40. It's signposted on and from the motorway. Nearest BR stations are Leamington, Banbury and Stratford approximately 10 miles away. A bus service goes from Stratford and Leamington.

The British Motor Industry Heritage Trust, with over 300 historic British motorcars housed in an outstanding new building at Gaydon, has little to rival it. Nearly 200 vehicles are on display at any one time; family cars to rare prototypes and racing models, from 1896 to the present day. The Centre also houses an extensive archive collection of British motor industry documents, photographs, journals and film. Whilst intended primarily for the motoring enthusiast, the rest of the family is not forgotten, as the 65-acre landscaped wooded site also incorporates a nature reserve, lake, adventure playground, picnic area and camping site. Special events are held throughout the year and there are corporate facilities for business functions.

Open: daily 10.00am to 6.00pm, April to October; 10.00am to 4.30pm November to March. Closed 24th, 25th and 26th December. For 1999 only, the Centre is closed New Year's Eve and New Year's Day 2000. A cafeteria serves hot and cold meals, and there's a gift shop selling motoring souvenirs. Facilities (toilets and a limited number of wheelchairs, etc.,) available for those with special needs and wheelchair access to all areas. An access guide can be provided by arrangement. There is ample free car and coach parking.

The Museum has many vehicles in reserve and may consequently rotate those on display. The following list is not a guarantee that a vehicle is on display or, indeed, even on site at the Heritage Motor Centre (this is particularly true of vehicles on loan to BMIHT). If you are travelling to Gaydon to see a specific vehicle, please contact BMIHT beforehand to check that it is on display.

David Burke pictured with an old police Wolseley at the Heritage Motor Centre, Gaydon, Warwickshire.

Admission: adults £6.00; OAPs/students £5.00; children (5 to 15) £4.00; under-5s free; family ticket £17.00. Discounts for pre-booked groups of 20+ available.

MOTORCARS

1888 Benz motor (replica)	1910 Austin 18/24 Endcliffe
1896 Wolseley Autocar No.1	1910 Austin 7hp
1896 Wolseley tricar	1911 Austin Town Carriage
1899 Royal Riley tricycle	1912 Rover 12hp Landaulette
1899 Wolseley 3hp voiturette	1913 Morris Oxford
1901 Albion A1 dog cart	1913 Standard 20hp Cheltenham
1901 Wolseley 10hp tonneau	1914 Austin 20hp Vitesse
1903 Albion A2 12hp wagonette	1919 Wolseley E2A Stellite
1904 Rover 8hp	1921 Morris F-type 'Silent Six'
1904 Thornycroft 20hp	1922 Austin Twenty tourer
1904 Wolseley 6hp Phaeton	1922 Rover Eight flat-twin
1906 Rover 6hp	1922 Standard 13.9hp SLO
1907 Austin 30hp	1923 Austin Seven Chummy
1907 Austin 40hp York Landaulette	1923 Morris Oxford tourer
1907 Riley Popular forecar	1923 Wolseley E3
1907 Riley 9hp V-twin	1924 Leyland Trojan tourer
1907 Rover 20hp tourer	1925 MG 'Old Number One'
1908 Austin 100hp Grand Prix racer	1925 Morris Oxford 'Red Flash'
1909 Albion A6 tourer	1927 Austin Seven Top Hat
1909 Riley 10hp V-twin	1927 Leyland Straight Eight, Parry-Thomas

927 Rover 16/50 coupé at the Heritage Motor Centre, Gaydon, Warwickshire. (Courtesy Heritage Motor Centre)

A 1948 Mark 1 Land Rover 80inch at the Heritage Motor Centre, Gaydon, Warwickshire. (Courtesy Heritage Motor Centre)

1936 MG NB Magnette at the Heritage Motor Centre, Gaydon, Warwickshire. (Courtesy Heritage Motor Centre)

The Heritage Motor Centre, Gaydon, Warwickshire. (Courtesy Heritage Motor Centre)

1927	Rover 16/50 coupé
1928	Austin Seven chassis and engine
1928	BMW Dixi
1929	Morris Minor tourer
1929	Rover Light Six 'Blue Train'
1929	Standard Nine Teignmouth
1930	Rover Meteor Corsica
1931	Austin Seven Swallow saloon
1931	MG 18/80 Speed Model
1931	Morris Cowley taxi
1932	Austin 12/6 Harley
1932	Wolseley Hornet EW
1934	MG PA Midget, sectioned
1934	Standard 10/12 Speedline
1934	Wolseley Nine
1936	Austin Seven-twin cam
1936	Morris Eight saloon
1936	Rover 14 Streamline
1937	Austin Fourteen Ascot
1938	Austin Seven Ruby
1938	MG EX 135
1939	Rover 14hp drophead
1939	Wolseley Eight
1946	Austin Sixteen BS1
1948	Austin A40 Devon sectioned
1948	Land Rover 80" No. 1
1948	Morris Minor MM, No. 1
1948	Rover P3 75
1951	Austin A90 Atlantic
1951	Riley RMB 2 litre saloon
1951	Rover P4 75 'Cyclops'
1951	Triumph Renown
1951	Wolseley 6/80 police car
1952	Austin Champ
1952	MG YB saloon
1952	Morris Oxford MO
1953	MG EX 179
1953	Morris Minor fire engine
1954	MG TF
1979	MG Midget 1500
1955	Austin A55 Westminster
1955	Austin A30 Seven
1955	Standard Eight
1955	Standard Vanguard Sportsman
1956	Rover T3 gas turbine
1957	MG EX 181
1957	Standard Pennant
1958	Austin Nash Metropolitan
1958	Land Rover Cuthbertson's conversion.
1958	Land Rover 88"
1958	MG ZB Magnette
1958	MGA-twin cam, sectioned
1958	Standard Ten
1959	Austin Mini 'Downton'
1959	Morris Mini-Minor No. 1, 621 AOK
1959	Triumph TR3
1960	Austin A40 Farina
1960	Morris Minor convertible
1960	Rover P4 100
1961	Morris Mini-Minor Traveller
1961	Rover T4 gas turbine
1961	Wolseley 15/60
1961	Wolseley 1500
1962	Austin A60 Cambridge
1962	Mini 'twini' Moke
1962	Riley Elf
1963	Morris Mini-Cooper Monte Carlo 33 EJB
1963	Rover BRM gas turbine racing
1963	Standard Ensign
1964	Morris Mini-Cooper Monte Carlo ASB 44B
1964	Mini ADO 34
1965	Alvis TE21
1965	Austin Mini, left hand drive sectioned
1965	Rover 3 litre coupé
1965	Rover 2000 (P6)
1965	Triumph Vitesse
1965	Vanden Plas 4-litre R
1966	Land Rover 109", military ambulance
1966	Morris Mini-Cooper Monte Carlo, LBL 6D
1967	Austin 1100 automatic

1967	Land Rover Shorland armoured car
1967	Rover P6BS
1967	Triumph 2000
1968	Land Rover SAS 'Pink Panther'
1968	Morris Mini-Minor
1969	Austin Zanda
1969	Austin Ant
1969	MG Midget, sectioned
1969	MG MGB roadster
1969	MG MGC GT
1969	MG MGB, sectioned in 2 halves
1969	Mini 9X prototype
1969	Morris Minor Traveller
1969	Triumph GT6
1970	Austin Maxi rally car
1970	Range Rover No. 1.
1970	Mini, ADO 70
1970	Triumph 1300
1971	Range Rover, 'Darien Gap.'
1971	Morris 1800 S
1971	over P6B 'S', sectioned
1972	Leyland Crompton Electricar
1972	MGB GT,SSV 1
1972	Rover P5B
1972	Triumph Dolomite Michelotti
1982	Austin Allegro 1.5HL
1983	Austin Maestro
1983	Land Rover 1/2 ton
1974	Mini Clubman, SRV4
1974	Morris Marina, SRV2
1974	Triumph TR6
1974	Vanden Plas 1300
1974	Wolseley Six
1975	Land Rover 101, fwd continental
1975	Rover SDI estate
1975	Wolseley 2200
1976	Mini 9X
1977	Triumph Stag
1978	Triumph Lynx
1978	Triumph-March F3
1978	Triumph TR7 Unipart V8
1978	Triumph TR7 V8
1979	Mini Clubman estate
1980	Austin Metro 1.3HLS
1980	Triumph Spitfire 1500
1980	Triumph Dolomite Sprint
1980	Vanden Plas 1500
1981	Land Rover 110" station wagon, sectioned
1981	Rover ECV 3/1
1981	Triumph TR7
1985	MG Metro 6R4
1985	MG EX-E
1986	RoverCCV concept car
1987	Land Rover 90 'crocodile'
1987	Land Rover 90 rolling chassis
1987	Land Rover Llama, box van
1989	Land Rover 6x6, 'Perentie'
1989	MG DR2/PR5
1989	Rover 214GSi
1990	Mini ERA turbo
1991	Land Rover, 'Camel Trophy'
1992	Mini Cord
1993	MG RV8
1993	Rover 214GSi, sectioned
1994	Land Rover 'Judge Dredd' ex-films.
1995	Land Rover 'Judge Dredd' City Cab
1995	MG MGF
1995	Mini 1.3i 'Car of the Century'
1995	Rover 214Si

MOTORCYCLES

1911	Rover Imperial motorcycle
1915	Rover Imperial motorcycle
1985	Sinclair C5

VEHICLES ON LOAN TO BMIHT

1904	Lanchester 20hp tonneau
1924	Rolls-Royce 20hp tourer

1924	Rolls-Royce Springfield Silver Ghost		1960	Austin Healey 3000 Mk 1
1925	Bentley 3 litre		1961	Morris Minor 1000
1925	Rolls-Royce 20hp		1962	MG MGA 1600 Mk II
1928	Austin Seven Avon Sportsman		1966	Rover/Alvis, 'Gladys'
1929	Rolls-Royce Phantom II Piccadilly		1969	Vanden Plas Princess ex-Royal
1932	Austin Seven Swallow tourer		1970	Lucas electric taxi
1932	MG J2		1971	Rover P5B ex-Royal
1934	Triumph Gloria Monte Carlo		1972	Towns Minissima
1935	MG PB		1976	Jaguar XJ 5.3C 'Big Cat'
1936	MG SA		1976	Towns Microdot electric
1937	Wolseley 14/56 police car		1978	Austin Princess Ogle Triplex
1939	MG WA		1978	Towns Wooden Hustler
1948	MG TC		1980	Lucas Bedford electric dormobile
1950	Alvis Ferret scout		1984	Rover SDI police car
1950	Alvis Saladin armouredd		1986	Land Rover Himalayan rally
1950	Alvis Saracen personnel		1987	Towns Tracer
1951	Marauder tourer		1992	Williams FW 14B GP car
1952	Austin A30 convertible		1993	Jaguar 'C' type replica
1952	Standard Vanguard Mk 1			
1954	Austin A40 Somerset		**MOTORCYCLES**	
1954	Land Rover 86" fire engine		1970	Norton Commando RAC
1958	Jaguar 3.4, Mk 1		1987	Norton Interpol RAC
1959	Austin Healey 3000 rally car			

1967 Special 3.5 litre Rover P5 built for Prime Minister Harold Wilson. It had extra large ashtrays in the back seat area. (Courtesy BMIHT, Heritage Motor Centre)

c1966 Land Rover 4 x 4 110inch on the off-road demonstration circuit at Gaydon. (Courtesy BMIHT Heritage Motor Centre)

Each of these Minis won the Monte Carlo Rally: number 37 in 196 with Paddy Hopkirk at the wheel; Timo Makinen in 1965 in numbe 52 and Ranuno Aaltonen in 1967 in number 177. (Courtesy BMIHT Heritage Motor Centre)

John Carter 1930s period garage. Normally, period cars are shown undergoing maintenance. (Courtesy BMIHT Heritage Motor Centre)

Graham Hill and Jackie Stewart in this Rover/BRM achieved 10th place the 1965 Le Mans 24-hour race. (Courtesy BMIHT Heritage Motor Centre)

The Jaguar Daimler Heritage Trust Centre, Browns Lane, Allesley, Coventry, Warwickshire, CV5 9DR.
Tel. 01203 402121. Curator: Tony O'Keefe.

The Exhibition Centre is accessed from the A45 Birmingham to Coventry Road; just follow the signs for Brownshill and Browns Lane Plant. The new Jaguar plant entrance can be found off the second exit off the roundabout on Coundon Wedge Road.

A superb new exhibition hall opened in October 1998 to display some of the 120 cars in the Jaguar Daimler collection, and included in the older exhibits are Swallow and Lanchester models. Some 30 cars are on display but many of the vehicles in the Collection are on loan, so please check before travelling to see a specific model. Another exhibition hall is due to open at Jaguar's Castle Bromwich plant, which is in Chester Road, Castle Vale, Birmingham, where 15-20 cars will be on display. The exhibition hall is open to the public during normal working hours, Monday to Friday, with early closing at 1.00pm on Friday.

There are facilities for the disabled (including toilets) and a very good souvenir shop on site. Toilets available and, although there is parking, it is a long walk from the car park to the exhibition hall. No refreshment facilities. Group bookings and special functions with catering and weekend visits may be arranged with the Curator (Tel. 01203 202870). As many Jaguar customers arrange a factory tour in conjunction with a visit to the Heritage Collection, it is advisable to book with the Heritage Collection receptionist before travelling.

JAGUAR

Year	Model	Reg	Year	Model	Reg
1928	Austin Swallow	DS 6866	1982	XJ12 fire tender	RDU 941W
1933	SS 1 coupé	JE 187	1983	XJRS	Not reg.
1933	SSII Swallow	JN 2763	1984	XJS	A672ADB
1935	SS Airline	AWR 564	1984	XJS Group A ETC	Not reg.
1935	SSI saloon	BHX 234	1984	XJS police car	A329KJHP
1937	SS2/5 saloon	CDU 700	1984	XJS pace car	B503TAC
1938	SS100	ERB 290	1985	XJ40	C541VRW
1949	MKV saloon	NPC 557	1985	XJ40	Not reg.
1949	MYV dhe	SSU 113	1985	XJ40 fire tender	Not reg.
1950	XKI 20 ots	NUB 120	1986	XJ6 4.2	D402GAP
1952	XKI 20 lhe	LWK 707	1987	XJS Cabrio	E763KYX
1953	XKI 20 ots	OOF 748	1987	XJS Cabrio	E8SONAC
1953	C-type	NDU 289	1987	XJS convertible	E481JAC
1954	D-type	OVC 501	1988	XJS convertible	BARBIE
1955	MKVI 1	M464 HYV	1988	XJR9	Not reg.
1956	D-type	393 RW	1988	XJ220 concept car	Not reg.
1958	MKI left hand drive	Not reg.	1988	XJ40 lwb	F795ORW
1958	XKISO the	327 FPA	1988	XJ41	Not reg.
1965	S type	EXT 979C	1988	XJ41	Not reg.
1966	XJI3	Not reg.	1988	XJ42	Not reg.
1967	E type left hand drive	RUE 419	1988	XJ42	Not reg.
1967	MY 1 1	GHG 61 SF	1989	XJS 4x4 Turbo	G974BRW
1969	XJ6 SI 4.2	PBP 42G	1990	XJR12 (wooden)	
1970	420G	TWF 593H	1992	XJ40 Estate	J199TAC
1971	E type	WHP 205J	1992	XJ220	K994YUD
1974	E type Group 44 left hand drive	Not reg.	1993	XJRS	K619KDU
1974	E type	HDU 555N	1993	XJI2S111	K529DDU
1975	XJS	OOM 555R	1994	XJ40 coupé	M690CRW
1976	XJI2 Broadspeed coupé	Not reg.	1994	XJ40	M94FVC
1976	XJI 2 Broadspeed coupé	Not reg.	1996	XJS	P4OXJS
1977	XJI2 coupé	XRW 119S	1996	XJS	P6OXJS

Admission is free.

145

1950 Jaguar XK120 at the Jaguar Daimler Heritage Trust, Coventry, Warwickshire. (Courtesy Jaguar Daimler Trust)

1997	XJ12 (300)	P6OSOV
1997	XJ6 (300)	P30OWKV
1969	Jaguar 240	XRE1386
1996	XJ6 police car	N610SWK
1997	XJ6 supercharged	P76ONRW

DAIMLER

1897	Phaeton	AD1897
1899	Phaeton	TSN1900
1900	Mail Phaeton	A7
1903	Phaeton	AP221
1906	Open Tourer 35hp	DUS41
1911	TA12	FL921
1911	TA23	DUI
1913	30hp Yellow Peril	AE4
1913	Laudaulette	Not reg.
1921	Bass bottle car	XX2120
1922	Open Tourer	MB286
1924	Shooting Brake	CYF663
1929	DD6 Brougham	Not reg.
1935	LQ220	CHK479
1936	Shooting Brake	Not reg.
1937	E20 saloon	JGCIS4C
1939	El 5 saloon	HBB540
1949	DE27 Limousine	A3179
1949	Laundalette	Not reg.
1949	DBI S convertible	AAX 318A
1949	DE36 Limousine	Not reg.
1952	DBI S	3777 F

1952	Consort	XMX 667
1955	Sportsman	SOE 283
1956	DK400 Limousine	TOX 1
1961	SP250 Dart	4777 JW
1964	Majestic Major	AHC 8I5B
1973	DS420 Limousine	1 GLC
1973	Vanden Plas XJ12	VGY 215M
1975	Sovereign XJ6S 11	UEV 34N
1984	DD6	B432 VYO
1986	XJ40 Daimler	D15O DKV
1986	XJS Daimler	Not reg.
1992	DD6	K530 DDU
1993	DS 420	L420 YAC
1996	Century 300	P100 WKV
1996	Corsica	Not reg.
1966	Daimler V8 250	FTA 848D

LANCHESTER

1901	12hp Tonneau	FRW 766
1904	20hp Tourer	O 1230
1933	10hp Saloon	ABH 784
1950	LD1O	HTR 282

In addition to the above, there is a Triumph motorcycle on loan from the Coventry Museum which is attached to a Swallow Sidecar.

The new Jaguar Daimler Heritage Trust Centre, Coventry. (Courtesy Jaguar Daimler Trust)

Atwell-Wilson Motor Museum, Downside, Stockley Lane, Calne, Wiltshire, SN11 0NF.

Tel. 01249 813119. Curators: Richard and Hasell Atwell.

The Museum is arrived at from junctions 16 or 17 of the M4, from where head south until you meet the A4 road. Calne is between Chippenham and Avebury on the A4. Follow the brown motor museum signs; the turning to Stockley Lane is between the Talbot Inn and the Jolly Miller pub.

It's easy to miss this fascinating motor museum with more than its fair share of American cars, as it's housed in a modern building at the side of a private residence in Stockley Lane. There is a 17th century water meadow walk also on the site.

Open: 1st April to 31st October, Mondays to Thursdays, 11.00am to 5.00pm and Sundays from 11.00am; 1st November to 31st March, Mondays to Thursdays, 11.00am to 4.00pm and Sundays from 11.00am to 4.00pm, also open Good Friday. Phone for details of special rates for pre-booked parties. Parking and toilets available.

Part of the Atwell Wilson motor collection. (Courtesy Atwell-Wilson Museum)

Admission: adults £2.50; children £1.00; OAPs £2.00.

Exhibits include:

MOTORCARS

1924	Model T Ford 2.8 convertible left hand drive
1934	Alvis Speed 20, 2 seater
1931	Singer Junior 4 door saloon
1932	Morris Major
1933	Morris Major 6 saloon
1933	BSA 10hp saloon
1934	Vauxhall 14-6, 4 door saloon
1936	Ford Model Y saloon
1937	Buick Albemarle C.O. Series 40
1946	Austin 10hp saloon
1947	HRG 1.5 litre sports car
1948	Rover P3 75 saloon
1949	Triumph 2000 Roadster (Bergerac style)
1953	Ford Anglia
1953	Ford Consul saloon
1954	Rolls-Royce Silver Wraith Mk I saloon
1954	Ford Popular 1100cc, 3 speed
1956	Ford 100E Anglia
1958	Ford Prefect saloon
1958	Austin A55 Cambridge saloon
1959	Rover P4 105 saloon
1961	Plymouth Fury 5.2 auto
1961	Bedford CA Romany Martin Walter dormobile caravanette
1963	Riley Elf
1964	Chevrolet Nova
1966	Morris Minor 1000 convertible
1966	Volkswagen Beetle
1967	Daimler Majestic Major 4.5 litre limousine
1967	Daimler Sovereign 4.2 litre automatic limousine
1967	Ford Anglia 105E Super 1200cc
1967	Ferrari 330 P4 (replica)
1967	Cadillac Sedan de Ville 7.0 litre automatic
1968	Mercury Park Lane
1968	Renault 4
1972	Ford Escort Mark I
1973	Opel Manta S
1973	Jaguar E-type 2+2
1975	Jensen Interceptor III
1975	Lincoln Continental Mk. IV 7.5 litre automatic
1976	Cadillac Sedan de Ville
1977	Toyota Crown Custom
1980	Cadillac Fleetwood Brougham diesel V8
1981	Cadillac Fleetwood
1982	Ford Granada 2.1 diesel saloon
1983	Ferrari Mondial 308, 5 speed
1986	Ford Capri III 2.0, 5 speed
1989	FSO Polonez Prima saloon
1990	Ford GTD 40 (replica)

MOTORCYCLES

1949	HRD Rapide 1000
1949	BSA Bantam
1954	Norton 600
1957	Matchless 350
1959	Velocette, police style
1964	BSA 650

COMMERCIALS

1942	AEC Matador
1954	David Brown '30' diesel Master Tractor

One of a pair of Cadillac diesels at the Atwell-Wilson Motor Museum, Calne, Wiltshire.

An early Martin Walter Dormobile at the Atwell-Wilson Motor Museum, Calne, Wiltshire.

A selection of the motorcycles on display at the Atwell-Wilson Motor Museum, Calne, Wiltshire.

A few cars from the Atwell Wilson collection. For the sharp-sighted: a 193_ Vauxhall 14/6 and a 1937 Buick Albemarle CO Series 40. (Courtesy Atwell Wilson Museum)

Science Museum Wroughton, Wroughton Airfield, Swindon, Wiltshire, SN4 9NS.

Tel. 01793 814466. Site Curator: Francesca Riccini.
email: f.riccini@nmsi.ac.uk.
Web site: http://www.nmsi.ac.uk/collections/
treasures/lgeobjs.html

The Science Museum is located 33 miles east of Bristol, just south of Swindon off the A4361, or from junction 16 of the M4.

Described as an 'out station' to the London Science Museum, Wroughton houses the larger objects from its Road Transport, Civil Aviation and Agriculture collections. The Festival of Transport Open Day attracts over 400 vintage and classic cars, commercials, buses and bikes, and attractions include auto-jumble, trade displays, helicopter rides and childrens' fun fair. Special event days are arranged throughout the summer that involve all of the Museum's collections.

Unless otherwise stated, the Science Museum's collections are open to view on event days only, and a copy of the season's events leaflet may be obtained by writing to the Site Curator. On site there's ample space for cars and coaches and there is special parking and toilet facilities for the disabled at each hangar. Some exhibits may be touched by the visually handicapped. Mobile catering on site.

A minimum group of 30, at £3.00 per head, may visit at any time by arrangement; other group entry fees by arrangement, pre-booked school visits free. Always ring to confirm.

MOTORCARS

Year	Car	Reg.	Year	Item	Reg.
1895	Daimler-Maybach	No reg.	1922	BSA combo	R 9399
1897	Lanchester	A 259	1925	Harley-Davison and sidecar	K 2643?
1899	MMC Daimler	FC 53	1925	Ner-Á-Car	ON 312
1899	Stanley steamer	FC 153	1928	BSA	YU 6689
1903	Humberette	FHP 822	1928	Douglas B28 2.75hp	
1903	Peugeot Baby	CT 179	1935	Brough Superior 11-50 combo	BLW 981
1903	Vauxhall	A 719	1940	BMW R51, 500cc	AST 572
1906	Ford Model N	D 1434	1951	Sunbeam S7	
1909	Rolls-Royce Silver Ghost	LD 3092	1952	Velocette LE 200	
1913	Morgan cycle car	MC 7722	1953	BSA Golden Flash	BSA 650
1924	Bentley Red Label trr	XW 8863	1954	Douglas Dragonfly	730 AFC
1937	Lanchester	EKJ 614	1959	Raleigh moped	
1950	Rover JET 1 gas turbine	JET 1*	1959	Arial Square Four	PDR 495
1950	Bond Mini Mk A	BKS 448	1959	Velocette Valiant	384 FRO
1950	Morris Minor MM	EFE 53	1960	Royal Enfield Super Meteor	541 ALR
1955	Connaught racer	No reg.	1961	DKR Capella scooter	
1960	Citroën DS 19 auto guide	YXU 845	1961	BSA and combo, ex-AA	576 BLT
1960	Ford Model T	PP 7963	1963	Arial Leader	
1963	NSU Spider	EYU 446C	1964	Honda CB92 Benly Supersport 125	CBL 80B
1964	Ford Cortina auto	BRA 669B	1964	AJS-twin	RW 4648
1967	DAF 44 Shell fuel cell	ATE 79E	1965	Honda Cl00	
1967	Ford Comuta COMUTA	No reg.	1967	Raleigh Wisp moped	
1986	Trabant P601	D799 NCV	1969	Honda CB750	GVX 50H
????	Lotus Excel, unit no. 26OF	No reg.	1978	Yamaha XS 1100cc	
			1982	Honda CX 500cc turbo	?????

MOTORCYCLES

Year	Item	Reg.
1889	Hildebrand steamer	
1894	Wolfmuller	
1899	De Dion Bouton	
1904	Triumph	VC 1123
1905	FN 3hp 4 cylinder	AA 6911
1905	Indian	
1905/6	Quadrant 3hp	
1909	FN 2hp single/shaft-drive	LR 977
1911	Indian	
1915	Rudge Multi	
1920	Zenith Gradua	DC 1930

BUSES

Year	Item	Reg.
1928	Leyland Lion PLSC1	JCP 6OF
1929	Leyland Titan TD 1, 2 decker	DR 4902
1931	AEC Regal	VO 6806
1939	AEC 2 decker trolleybus	CPM 61
1940	Saurer Alpine CRD, Swiss reg	FR 1347
1943	Guy Arab II	DHR 192
1948	Leyland Titan PD2/1 bus	KPT 909
1953	Bristol LS	OTT 55
1963	Bedford VAL14 coach	504 EBL
1973	Leyland National	BCD 820L

* Sometimes displayed in London.

COMMERCIALS and UTILITY				
1910	Renault taxi, type AG	CD 2922	1950	Bedford MLD lorry	FAP 698
1919	Albion A10 lorry	XA 8315	1956	Bedford BBC outside broadcast van	SUU 483
1922	Unic taxi	XL 6671	1957	Rotinoff GR7 Atlantic tractor	RPY 767
1926	Vulcan VSD 2 ton lorry	TU 3024	1961	Morris Minivan	82 PAF
1929	Ford Model A horse box	MY 1704	1968	Foden S21 6 x 2 flat bed	GTU 906G
1929	Gamer WDL 6 lorry		1969	Winchester Mk 3 taxi	AMP 618H
1931	Foden 6 ton dies. lorry	LG 7186	1970	Foden 8 wheel tanker lorry	BUU 990H
1934	AEC Mammoth Major 8 tractor	AKB 320	1976/8	Foden/Rolls-Royce quiet heavy	
1939	Bedford 0, arcticiculated tractor trailer	JV 8266		vehicle	AUV 468T
1939	Harrods electric van	FYM 836	1982	Bajaj Autorickshaw type 22	DLR 6575
1948	Leyland Beaver X-ray van	OPL 840		Ford BB mobile library van	AKK 521
1949	Fordson 7V 2 ton lorry	ONO 514			

Bradford Industrial Museum, Moorside Mills, Moorside Road, Bradford, West Yorks, BD2 3HP.

Tel. 01274 631756. Senior Keeper, Technology: Eugene Nicholson.

The Museum is signposted from the Bradford ring road (A6177) and from the Harrogate Road (A658). Nearest motorway access is from junction 26 of the M62. Frequent bus services include bus numbers 614 and 634 from the Tyrls bus stop and 608 and 609 from Bank Street (both departure points in the Centre of Bradford), and Minibus number 896 from the Interchange. All services stop at Moorside Road.

Housed in an original spinning mill, the Transport Gallery contains cars made at the former Jowett factory in Bradford, which ceased production of Jowett cars in 1954. The Museum, in addition, houses six motorcycles, a working Shire Horse team and original weaving and spinning exhibits. The mill owner's house and mill workers' 'back to back' cottages are also part of the Museum. Many other items of engineering associated with this period are exhibited.

Open: Tuesday to Saturday 10.00am to 5.00pm, Sunday 12.00pm to 5.00pm. Closed Mondays except for Bank Holidays. Closed Good Friday, Christmas and Boxing Days.There's a cafeteria, baby changing facilities and gift shop, and the disabled have access to most of the Museum. Disabled toilets and wheelchair available. Good car parking.

MOTORCARS			MOTORCYCLES		
1913	Jowett 2 seater sports, 6.4hp	AK 3261	1912	Scott trials 3.3hp	AK 222
1927	Jowett Long 2 seater, 2 cylinder, 7hp	RT 3303	1922	Scott 'Sociable' 3 wheeler	SS1922
1929	Jowett 7/17hp fabric 4 dr sal, 748cc	UA 9158	1926	Bradley and Scott and sidecar	
1935	Jowett Kestrel saloon 745cc 4 stroke	AAK 162	1927	Scott 'Flying Squirrel' 498cc	JJ 8042
1951	Jowett Bradford utility	NTV 826	1954	Panther and sidecar	STE 782
1952	Jowett Javelin saloon, 1486cc	NKA 866	1969	Panther	XWX 17G
1953	Jowett Jupiter 2 seater sports, 1486cc	BHG 501			

STEAM		
1928	Wallis and Stevens, Basingstoke, Advance Steam Roller	OT 820

COMMERCIAL		
1929	Jowett Bradford van	LJ 1652
1948	Jowett Bradford van chassis 2 cyl	KTB 520
1950	Jowett Bradford ice cream van	LAT 141
1953	Jowett Bradford van, 1005cc engine	KCJ 778

TRAMCAR	
No. 104, circa 1930	

Admission: free, but groups are asked to book visits in advance.

The fascinating Jowett/Bradford collection at Bradford Industrial Museum, Yorkshire.

Bradford Industrial Museum logo.

A Jowett two seater, part of the Jowett/Bradford collection at the Bradford Industrial Museum, Bradford, Yorkshire.

Bradford Industrial Museum.

A 1922 Scott Sociable at the Bradford Industrial Museum, Bradford, Yorkshire.

The car transport gallery of the Bradford Industrial Museum showing, in the centre, a locally-made 1953 Jowett Jupiter two seater sports. (Courtesy Bradford Industrial Museum)

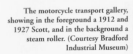

The motorcycle transport gallery, showing in the foreground a 1912 and 1927 Scott, and in the background a steam roller. (Courtesy Bradford Industrial Museum)

The Craven Collection of Classic Motorcycles, Brockfield Villa, Stockton-on-the-Forest, York, YO32 9UE.

Tel. 01904 488461. Owner: Richard Craven.

The Collection can be found 10 miles northeast of York.

The Collection comprises over 200 motorcycles, ranging in date from 1918 to 1983, plus memorabilia. Open only at Bank Holiday weekends between 10.00am and 4.00pm. Group visits at other times can be arranged by phoning the owner on the above number.

Admission: £2.50.

Eden Camp, Modern History Theme Museum, Malton, North Yorkshire, YO17 6RT.

Tel. 01653 697777. Museum Director: Steve Jaques.
Web site: http://www.edencamp.co.uk

Access to the Camp is off the A64 York to Scarborough road at the junction of the A169 to Pickering. Eden Camp is 18 miles from York.

As the address signifies, this is a World War II ex-prisoner of war camp which has steadily enlarged its visitor attractions to embrace all aspects of World War I. In 1998, Eden Camp won the English Tourist Board Visitor Attraction of the Year Award. The various aspects of WWII are covered in detail: the U-boat menace, Bomber Command, and so on. At the Camp is a military vehicle section which is constantly growing. Disabled access is good, and parking is free. Refreshments are served in the 'prisoners' canteen,' 'officers' mess' and the 'Garrison Cinema Bar.' There is a two-part assault course for younger visitors and one for Tiny Tot commandos. Open: between 15th January and 13th February, Mondays to Fridays from 10.00am to 5.00pm, last admission 4.00pm. From 14th February the camp is open 7 days a week until 23rd December.

Admission: adults £3.50; children and concessions £2.50, with a £1.00 reduction for groups over 10. Note that during term-time, school visits may be in progress.

MILITARY VEHICLES

Russian T-34/85 Medium Tank	Scammell British heavy recovery vehicle
GMC Truck	1941 Austin K4 pump escape fire appliance
White M16 Half Track	Churchill tank
Leyland Hippo Mk II	Bren gun carrier
Schutzenpanzerwagen SdKfz 251	Ferret scout car
Green Goddess fire appliance	
DUKW amphibious vehicle	
Sherman tank	Plus a number of artillery guns and V1 rocket

The Fire Police Museum, Peter House, 101-109, West Bar, Sheffield, S3 8PT.

Tel. 0114 249 1999. Secretary: David Purcell.

The Museum is located 33 miles east of Manchester, at the junction of the A57 and the A61 in the heart of Sheffield.

This museum, set on three floors in a Victorian Fire/Police Station, was opened in 1984 by South Yorkshire Firemen. In 1900, the Fire and Police services were a combined force. Since inception the Museum has enjoyed educational charity status, is run and managed by volunteers and is entirely independent of external funding. Over the years, thousands of children and young people have visited the Museum for fire prevention education. Fire appliances range from a 1794 manual pump to the latest, a 1974 HCB Angus, plus many other exhibits. Open to the public every Sunday and Bank Holiday from 11.00am to 5.00pm throughout the year. At other times by prior arrangement.

There's a souvenir shop and cafe selling hot/cold drinks and light snacks. Disabled access is limited, though there is a toilet. Special childrens' play area and free car parking at the rear of the Museum. Nearby on-street coach parking.

Part of the Museum's collection at a local Gala.
(Courtesy Streetlife)

FIRE APPLIANCES

Year	Appliance	Reg.	Year	Appliance	Reg.
1794	Sun Insurance Brigade manual 8 man	No reg.	1956	La France, American pump	US REG.
1854	Merryweather 16 man, horsedrawn	No reg.	1963	Opel Blitz breathing apparatus tender	BHE 955B
1882	Shand Mason, horsedrawn steamer	No reg.	1969	AEC Merryweather, wheeled pump	OET 333H
1918	Leyland, pump wheeled escape	CH 7699			
1936	Leyland, turntable ladder	AVB 1	1974	Bedford HCB Angus pump	GOT 877N
1942	Austin, war time towing vehicle	GLT 683	1984	Dennis RS 133 pump	B106 DET
1949	Commer Carmicheal, pump escape	EFK 63			

Built in 1900 as a Fire/Police Station, this fine Victorian building has, since 1985, housed the Sheffield Fire/Police Museum. (Courtesy Streetlife)

Admission: adults £2.50; children £1.50; family ticket (2 + 2) £6.50; under-3s free.

Keighley Bus Museum, Denholme House Farm, Halifax Road, Denholme, Bradford, West Yorkshire, BD13 4EN.

Tel. 01282 413179. Secretary: David Jones.

The Museum is 33 miles northeast of Manchester, situated behind the Parish Church off Halifax Road, Denholme, (midway between Keighley and Halifax on the A629). Buses run frequently from Keighley, Halifax and Bradford and all stop at the Church.

The Keighley Bus Museum Trust Limited is a registered charity devoted to increasing awareness of Britain's public road transport heritage, the preservation of historic vehicles and other artifacts. This collection of privately-owned vehicles comprises over 30 buses and ancillary vehicles, representing almost all of the principal British manufacturers and many of the best-loved models from the period 1927-1976. Some have been lovingly restored, many more are subject to constant improvement, whilst others are stored beyond the grasp of the scrap man. The KBMT welcomes visitors on Open Days, or informally on Tuesday or Thursday evenings and all day Sunday throughout the year. If you are travelling from a distance, please ring the above number in advance, to ensure that someone will be on site to show you around. KBMT buses sometimes operate free services, often in conjunction with the Keighley and Worth Valley Railway. On Christmas Day the Museum regularly provides a comprehensive free bus network throughout Keighley and the surrounding areas. Free parking. Vehicles within the Museum are close together, hence disabled access is limited. The KMBT organises and attends a wide range of events throughout the year. If you wish to see a particular vehicle - and since the vehicles are privately owned - it's best to ring to ensure you are not disappointed.

BUSES

Year	Vehicle	Reg.	Year	Vehicle	Reg.
1927	Leyland Lion PLSC	KW 2260	1962	Leyland Leopard	PJX 232
1931	Leyland Lion LT3	TF 6860	1962	Leyland Titan PD2/37	PJX 43
1938	Leyland Titan TD5	CFM 354	1963	Albion Nimbus NS3AN	RJX 250
1939/49	Leyland Titan TD5	RN 8622	1964	AEC Regent V	6220 KW
1938/50	Bristol K5G	CWX 671	1966	AEC Regent V	ENW 980D
1946	Bristol LL5G	LWU 886	1966	Bristol Lodekka FS6B	NWU 265D
1948	Bristol L6A	HOD 30	1966	Bristol Lodekka FS6B	KWT 642D
1949	AEC Regent III	NNW 492	1966	Daimler Fleetline	KVH 473E
1949	Crossley DD42/7	EVD 406	1967	Bristol RELH6GB	TWW 766F
1949	Crossley SD42/7	DBN 978	1967	Bristol RESL6G	YLG 717F
1950	AEC Regent III	NUB 609	1967	Daimler Fleetline	HNW 131D
1951	AEC Mandator (tower)	MBH 388	1969	Leyland Titan PD3A	LAK 309G
1951	AEC Regent III	LYR 533	1972	Daimler Fleetline CRL6	XAK 355L
1952	AEC Regent III	HKW 82	1973	Bristol RELL6G	OWT 776M
1953	Bristol KSW6G	LWR 424	1976	Leyland Atlantean AN68/1R	MUA 870P
1953	Leyland Royal Tiger PSU1/3	AEK 514			
1954	Bristol LS6G SVS 904 nee'	OTT 90			
1948/60	Sunbeam F4	FWX 914	**RECOVERY VEHICLES**		
1955	Bedford SGB	PGK 872	1952	AEC Militant Mark I	YFF 950
1955	Leyland Titan PD2/11	UUA 214	1968	Foden S36	UCH 10G
1956	Daimler CVG6	VTU 76			
1956	Daimler CVG6	GJX 331	**GUN TRACTOR**		
1956	Atkinson Alpha PL745H	XLG 477	1940c	AEC Matador	No reg.
1957	Leyland Titan PD2/20	KAG 856			

Admission is free but donations welcome.

155

KEIGHLEY BUS MUSEU**M**

Above - Logo of the Keighley
Bus Museum. Right - The 1956
Daimler CVG6, which has a
centre entrance, is owned by the
Trust Secretary, (Courtesy
Keighley Bus Museum Trust
Ltd)

Kelham Island Industrial Museum, Kelham Island, off Alma Street, Sheffield, S3 8RY.

Tel. 0114 272 2106. Collections and Access Officer:
Catherine Hamilton.

*Alma Street is off
Corporation Street,
Sheffield, and is
approached from the A6.*

Housed in a former generating station, the Museum tells the story of
Sheffield's industrial development, and displays a wide range of the city's
products: 'Made in Sheffield' is a mark of quality recognised throughout
the world. Visitors are able to watch expert self-employed craftsmen at
work in a Victorian street scene within the Museum. There is an 'Energy
Zone,' a hands-on area for children aged 7 to 13 that teaches them about
energy. For steam engine buffs, a 12,000hp River Don engine normally
gets up steam twice daily. Open: Monday to Thursday, 10.00am to
4.00pm and on Sundays 11.00am to 4.45pm. Closed Fridays and
Saturdays. Last admission one hour before closing.

Shop and cafe on site. Disabled access to main galleries - phone for
more details. The Shalesmoor Supertram stops nearby.

*Admission: 1999 rates
are currently under
review but are likely to
be adults £3.50; OAPs/
children £2.00; family
ticket £7.00; disabled
and special needs, free;
group rates available.*

TRANSPORT EXHIBITS

1921	Richardson 8/10hp tourer - made in Sheffield	U9296
1922	Wilkin motorcycle and sidecar, with Blackburne engine	
1926	Ner-A-Car - built by Sheffield Simplex	

Melham Mills Bus Museum, Mersey and Calder Bus Preservation Group, Meltham, Huddersfield, Yorkshire.

Tel. 01422 364494. Secretary: Mark Knott.
Address for correspondence: 79, The Arches, Claremount, Halifax HX3 6LD.

Directions will be given when viewing arrangements are made.

Members of the Group collect and restore classic coaches and buses which were used in the North of England. The vehicles are kept in an old David Brown factory near Huddersfield, and take part in the Heart of the Pennines Vintage Bus Rally, which is held on the first Sunday of May and last Sunday of October.

Enthusiasts who would like to see the vehicles should contact Mark Knott on the above number.

Museum of Army Transport, Flemingate, Beverly, Humberside, HUI7 0NG.

Tel. 01482 860445. Curator: W. A. Dugan.

The Museum can be found 8 miles north of Hull on the outskirts of Beverley; follow the A1079 Hull road.

Two acres of Army road, rail, sea and air exhibits are displayed in two exhibition halls. Over 70 vehicles, and the last remaining Blackburn Beverly aircraft, are the results of the The Royal Corp. of Transport's quest to "collect and restore British Army vehicles." There are a variety of wheeled exhibits, including Field Marshall Viscount Montgomery's Rolls-Royce and a pink, multi-purpose Army Land Rover, plus a saddle tank steam engine, an operating narrow gauge railway, special 'explore' vehicles and restoration workshop. An archive library and information centre are also on site. Special effort has gone into the provision of entertainment for the children - as you will see ...

Open: daily 10.00am to 5.00pm. Closed 24th-26th December only. The Museum has a gift and souvenir shop, cookhouse for snacks or full meals, and 90 per cent of it is accessible to the disabled; special toilets available. Childrens' parties by arrangement. Parking for cars and coaches; the charge is refunded to Museum visitors.

Admission: adults £4.00; senior citizens £2.50; family ticket (2 + 2) £10.00. Group discounts available.

There are many duplications of the listed vehicles, in addition to items which are not 'powered' transport, hence they are unlisted. Additionally, there's a Beverly aircraft and all types of railway rolling stock.

MUSEUM
of
ARMY TRANSPORT

A tank from the childrens' play area, an ex-RAF Blackburn Beverly, and one of two Rolls-Royce motor cars ascribed to Field Marshall Viscount Montgomery all feature on the front of a leaflet about the Museum of Army Transport.

MOTORCARS

1939	Rolls-Royce Wraith, ex-Field Marshall Viscount Montgomery
1941	Humber Snipe, also used by Field Marshall Viscount Montgomery
1960	Humber Super Snipe 4x2 saloon, Series 5
1962	Austin Mini Moke
1967	Rover 3.5 saloon staff car
1967	Morris Minor 1000 Traveller
1969	Daimler Limousine 4x2

OTHER SERVICE VEHICLES

AEC Matador 4 x 4 0853
Albion ST works vehicle (LEC)
Austin Champ FFR FV1800
Austin FV16013 4 X 4 k2 ambulance
Austin truck Loadstar (K4) 3 ton 4x2 (LEG)
Austin K9 4x4 wireless vehicle
Austin K6/A recovery 6x4
Bedford MWD 15cwt 4 x 2 CL
Bedford OY 4 X 2 3 ton
Bedford QL 4 X 4 office
Bedford 3 ton 4 x 4 QLT TCV
Bedford truck OX Civ truck (LEG)
Bedford 3 ton 4x4 RL truck (LEG)
Bedford QLR 4x4 radio vehicle
Bedford RL 6 ton GS 4x4 mine cab
Bedford OSBC 3 ton tipping truck
Bison Wolds wagon
Bushmaster LVT Mk3 (Buffalo)
Carrier Universal No. 1
Centurion Mk V tank
Comet tank
Daimler armoured car
Daimler Dingo scout car
Daimler armoured car
Diamond T980 50 ton 6x4 tractor
DUKW 353
Dynatrac oversnow racked vehicle
Enfield Auto 8000 eletric car
Ferret scout
FNAS 24 TRI car
Ford heavy utility Talbot ambulance 75
Fordson Thames 3 ton 4 x 4 GS
Hillman light utility 4 x 2
Humber 1 ton 4 x 4 armoured ambulance (Pig)

Humber 1 ton 4 x 4 armoured truck
Humber 1 ton 4 x 4 armoured truck (Pig) SQU
Humber 1 ton 4 x 4 wireless FV1604(A)
Humber, heavy utility 4x4
Hunting Harrier 4 x 2
JAB Ultra light weight
Jubilee tip wagon
'Kitchener' coach
Land Rover (medium stressed platform)
Land Rover 1/4 ton GS 4X4, Series 3
Land Rover (Royal ceremonial)
Land Rover 109 'Pink Panther', ex-SAS
Land Rover 4 x 4, 1 ton
Land Rover a/c ldr MOY
Leyland 10 ton 6x4 'Hippo' 2B (LEG)
Leyland water cannon
Leyland Charioteer Mk 7 Mod B FV4101 tank
Leyland 3 ton Mach. retriever
Michigan tractor wheeled FLRT (heavy) 175DS
Morris commercial 8cwt 4 x 2
Morris 5cwt Gutty
Morris commercial CFD 6 X 4 30cwt
Morris commercial CD 30 cwt
Morris commercial CD 6x4 30 cwt
Morris truck commercial 4 x 4 GS
Saracen APC wheeled FV610
Saracen APC 6 X 6 FV610
Scammell 3x2 mechanical horse (LEG
Shoreland armoured APC (LR)
Simplex 20hp tractor
Snowtrac Transartic expedition
Thornycroft Mighty Antar Mk l tractor
Triumph 3 wheeler
Volvo BV 202E Oversnow
White M5 half track truck

MOTORCYCLES

Corgi folding scooter
Matchless 350cc, sectioned
Matchless 350cc
BSA M20, sectioned
BSA Goldstar, sectioned
Triumph TRW Mk 3
BSA B40 Mk 1
BSA Gold Star B40
Triumph 750cc

A 1939 Rolls-Royce Wraith, previously used by Field Marshall Viscount Lord Montgomery when he landed in Europe on D-Day plus three. (Courtesy Museum of Army Transport)

A Mk 3 Ferrett recce vehicle descending a ramp in front of a Humber 1 ton wireless van. (Courtesy Museum of Army Transport)

n ex-1939/45 mix of desert vehicles: a mber Box heavy utility, the nose of an ustin K6 recovery vehicle with a 1943 Jeep alongside. (Courtesy Museum of Army Transport)

A 1927 Morris Commercial GP vehicle. (Courtesy Museum of Army Transport)

North Yorkshire Motor Museum, Roxby Garage, Pickering Road, Thornton Dale, North Yorkshire, YO18 4LH.

Tel. 01751 474455. Curator: Derek Mathewson.

The Museum is 2 miles west of Pickering on the A170 Scarborough road.

Set in a 1916 garage, the Museum also services and sells veteran and vintage cars.

Open: daily 10.00am to 5.00pm, except for Christmas, Boxing and New Year's Days. Winter opening hours may also vary; phone to check.

The Collection

	MGA
1944	Thames 10cwt van
1929	Renault NN tourer
1938	Rover 12
1960	Humber Hawk
1970	Aston Martin DB6

Admission: adults £1.50; children £0.50.

Sandland Transport Centre, Belton Road, Sandtoft, Doncaster, South Yorkshire, DN8 5SX.

Tel. 01724 711391.

The Centre is 14 miles southwest of Hull.

There's a working trolleybus system at the home of Britain's single largest collection of preserved trolley and motorbuses, and a miniature working 7.25 gauge steam railway.

Open: from April to September, Saturday and Sunday pm, plus various other days throughout the year. Ring before travelling.

Admission: adults £3.00; children £1.50; family ticket £7.00.

Sheffield Bus Museum, Tinsley Tram Sheds, Sheffield Road, Sheffield, Yorkshire, S9 2FY.

Tel. 0114 255 3010. Marketing Director: Mike Greenwood. (Tel. 0114 248 9166)

The Museum is 33 miles east of Manchester on the A6178 Sheffield to Rotherham road, close to junction 34 of the M1 motorway. The Carbrook Supertram is approximately 200 metres from the Museum entrance. There's a bus service from Sheffield and Rotherham.

The Sheffield Bus Museum houses 25 vehicles in part of the former Tinsley tram depot, which is listed as 'historically significant.' The majority of the Collection is local and extremely varied, each vehicle being an important contribution to Sheffield's transport history. The full-size buses are complemented by various artefacts, including destination blinds, tram stops, old road signs, models, timetables and tickets. Buses from other parts of the country add a further dimension with their different colours and shapes.

Open: Saturday and Sunday afternoons (except Christmas). There is a shop selling transport-related items. Snacks and hot and cold drinks are on sale on special Open Days. Ramps allow access to all ground floor displays and shop, but no disabled toilet facilities. On-street parking.

Interior shot of Tinsley Tram Sheds showing a 1950 Leyland PD2/1 in the foreground. (Courtesy Sheffield Bus Museum)

TRAMCAR					
1926	Sheffield Tram		1962	Leyland PD3A/1	GHD 765
			1962	Daimler CVG6-30DD	TJV 100
			1969	Leyland PDR2/1	BWB 148H
BUSES and COACHES			1970	AEC Swift	DWB 54H
1940	Leyland TD7	WG 9180	1971	Leyland PSU4B/4R	AHA 451J
1947	Leyland PSI	JWB 416	1973	Leyland AN68/IR	UWA 296L
			1976	Ailsa B55-10	LWB 388P
1948	Leyland PSI	HD 7905	1976	Ailsa B55-10	PSJ 825R
1950	Leyland PD2/1	ACW 645	1985	Dennis Domino	C53 HDT
1950	Leyland ECPO/1R	MHY 765			
1952	AEC Regent III	OWE 116			
1954	Leyland PD2/12	RWB 87	**MISCELLANEOUS VEHICLES**		
1954	Daimler CVG6DD	KET 220	1941	AEC Regent grit wagon	GWJ 724
1955	AEC Monocoach	WRA 12	1944	Austin K2 ambulance	KYW 939
1958	Bristol LD6G	VDV 760	1948	AEC Regent III gritwagon	KWE 255
1959	AEC Regent V	TDK 322	1948	Fordson Major tractor	KWJ 681
1959	AEC Regent V	PFN 858	1949	Bedford OLAZ tower wagon	FET 195
1960	AEC Regent V	6330 WJ	1953	Leyland Comet lorry	RWE 101
1960	AEC Regent V	7874 WJ	1959	Daimler CVG6-30DD	TET 135
1961	AEC Reliance	1322 WA			

Special Open Days bi-monthly, Easter to Christmas. On these days admission is: adults £1.00; concessions £0.50; family ticket (2 + 2) £2.00. At all other times a donation box is used.

A 1958 Bristol LD6G. The Museum houses a large collection of buses in part of the Tinsley Tram Depot and is keen to attract new members. (Courtesy Sheffield Bus Museum)

161

Skopos Motor Museum, Alexandra Mills, Alexandra Road, Batley, West Yorks, WF17 6JA.

Tel. 01924 444423. Curator: Suzy Merrick

The Skopos Museum is in the centre of Batley. To get there, from junction 40 of the M1, head northwest towards Batley, through Dewsbury on the A638. Alternatively, drive southwest on the A62 from junction 27 of the M62.

Skopos Motor Museum contains some extremely desirable motors, from the Benz Patent Motor Wagon, built in 1885, to the Ferrari F40 and the only surviving Bramham cycle car. Over 50 cars are displayed in pleasant surroundings. The Museum has three large workshops/restoration bays where Skopos mechanics restore and repair vehicles new to the Museum. The Museum is also interested in aircraft, one of which, a full-size airworthy Sopwith Camel, can be seen undergoing construction from original blueprints. The Camel, once built to original specification, will join the Northern Aeroplane Workshop's finished Bristol Mono Plane and Sopwith Tri-Plane in the Shuttleworth Collection at Old Warden, Bedfordshire. The Museum is open, from 10.00am until 5.00pm, every day with the exception of Christmas Day, Boxing Day and New Year's Day.

Refreshments can be provided for an additional fee. There's ample free parking, a souvenir shop, toilets and easy access for children and the disabled.

Admission: adults £2.50; OAPs and children £1.50; family ticket (2 + 2) £5.00. Reductions of £0.50 per person for pre-booked groups of 10 or more in normal working hours. The Museum can also be booked for evening visits for groups of 25 or more.

MOTORCARS

Year	Model	Reg		Year	Model	Reg
1884	De Dion Tricycle	B8079		1955	Mercedes Gull Wing 300 SL coupé	RLX 11
1895	Delahaye	BS 8205		1955	Triumph TR3	5892 VX
1901	Sunbeam Mabley Voiturette	EI 5		1957	Riley Pathfinder	CHD 205
1902	Panhard Lavassor 4 cylinder	AA 161		1960	Buick Le Sabre	NV 5110
1904	Societe Manufacture Darrnes	BS 8008		1961	BMW Isetta	PFR 930
1904	De Dion Bouton	XL 16		1961	Jaguar E type	ONW 220B
1907	Lanchester	LN 7815		1963	Jaguar E type	DSS 313
1908	Napier	LB 5500		1963	Jaguar E type	NWR 633A
1910	Knox Racing Car	Not reg.		1965	Alfa Romeo TZ	ABM 337B
1910	Rolls-Royce Colonial	XE 5844		1965-70	Shelby Mustang GT350	AFM 398
1910	Rolls-Royce Pullman	JS 191		1966	Jaguar Mk 2	EVN 843D
1912	Berliet	NA 237		1967	Aston Martin DB6	GCP 246E
1912	Locomobile	31931		1968-9	Austin Princess 1300	TBD 352G
1913	Jowett 2 seater tourer	BT I595		1969	Ferrari GTS	No reg.
1922	Bramham cycle car	NW 2010		1969	Triumph TR5	WMF 1999
1925	Farman Torpedo	1 DAR 1		1974	Fiat 500	KUA 619L
1926	Morris Cowley	NE 7022		1976	Aston Martin	V85 ATA
1926	Sunbeam Super Sport	EN 7831		1978	Porsche 911sc	YJX 484Y
1927	Jowett 2 seater tourer	KW 292		1983	Ferrari F40	F4O NNO
1928	Riley Brooklands Sport	VF 6134		1984	Benz Velo	BE 515
1930	Bentley 41/2 litre Blower	GP 42		1984	De Lorean S1	J 1082
1931	Alvis	GG 4051				
1934/5	Ford Model C	CLG693				
1935	Bentley Saloon Hooper	BXO 18		**MOTORCYCLES**		
1937	Delage D6-75 Olympic	No reg.		1909	Scott MIC	SV 4856
1937	Mercury MIC	PNJ 953		1929	Coventry Eagle MIC	SV 5948
1937	Morgan 4-4	EMA 357		1949	Indian Brave	No reg.
1941	Daimler Ferret scout 33	BA 07		1960	Panther and Swallow sidecar	597 ORA
1949	MG TC Sports	LL 9969		1964	Royal Enfield Crusader	BVH 45B
1949	TVR No. 2	FFV 62		1965	Royal Enfield Olympic	JWX 20D
1949	Austin Devon	LHN 609		1965	Royal Enfield Continental GT	No reg.
1953	Jowett Javelin	MU 1395		1969	AJS Stormer MIC	No reg.
1953	Jowett Jupiter	LUG 347		1976	Kawasaki motorcycle	OHE 906R
1953	MG TD	FSK 442		1978	Silk motorcycle	GDB 964V

	Scott Super Squirrel MIC	No reg.

MISCELLANEOUS

1885	Benz Replica	
	Jaguar C type Replica	824DOT
1920	Leyland fire engine	No reg.
	Child's racing car CGW	
	Child's Blower Bentley	
1897	Faggots Hanson Cab	
1925	Monotrace Tandem	

1937	Delage mascot Spirit of Wind
1945+	Luton Minor
	3 Hammond organs
	5 tailors' dummies plus 5 period costumes
	6 paintings by Kathryn Ensall
	22 various cycles

AIRCRAFT

Farman bronze statue and stand

splendid-looking 1904 De Dion Bouton
epared by Museum staff, who also rebuild
intage aircraft! (Courtesy Skopos Motor
Museum)

General view of the light and airy Skopos
Motor Museum vehicle display. The Museum
shares the building with Skopos Mills Village.
(Courtesy Skopos Motor Museum)

lls-Royce Pullman of 1910: regal is the word that
rings to mind! (Courtesy Skopos Motor Museum)

A 1966 Jaguar Mk II, a model which has featured in
many TV series and films. (Courtesy Skopos Motor
Museum)

Streetlife, Hull Museum of Transport, High Street, Hull, HU1 1NQ.
Tel. 01482 613902. Keeper: Steve Goodhand.

The Museum is situated in Hull City, on the High Street close to Drypool Bridge.

When originally opened in 1925 and called the Museum of Commerce and Transport, this was claimed to be the first transport museum in the country. The Collection was built up by Thomas Shephard before the 1939/45 war and covered over 200 years of land transport. In the early 1980s, it was decided to develop, through five phases, a purpose-built museum - Streetlife! The first four phases are now open and phase five is scheduled for 2001. It is advertised as 'Hull's Noisiest Museum' and has motor vehicles from 1890 onwards, plus Hansom Cabs, fire engines, a road coach, trams, bicycles, early motorcycles and a variety of other items. Open: Monday to Saturday, 10.00am to 5.00pm; Sunday, 1.30pm to 4.30pm. Closed Good Friday, Christmas Eve, Christmas Day and New Year's Day.

The Museum is available for corporate hire, and facilities include gift shop, cafe, picnic area and gardens, plus disabled access. Parking unavailable at the Museum; the nearest multi-storey is 5 minutes' walk.

Streetlife, Hull's Transport Museum.

MOTORCARS			MOTORCYCLES	
1897/8	Panhard et Levassor 6hp Wagonette		1914	Rudge multi
1899	'English' Daimler	DS 6751	1914	Wall auto-wheel
1898	Coventry Motette 3hp		1919	Walls
1901	Marshall Benz 5hp	DS 6753	1923	Grigg scooter
1899	De Dion Quadricycle 2hp	DS 6752		
1900	Sturmey Voiturette			
1901	Gardner-Serpollet steamer	DS 6756	**COMMERCIAL**	
1901	White Stanhope steamer	DS 6755	1957	Jowett Bradford ice cream van
1901	Cleveland electric	DS 6754		
1907/8	Lanchester 20hp open tourer		**TRAM**	
1956	Morris Isis	OBE 378	1885	Kitson tram, ex-Portstewart Tramways,
1954	BMW Isetta	2417 RH	Northern Ireland	
1939	Morris 8	FKH 200/GFO 467		

Internal shot of Streetlife's spacious Transport Gallery showing the 1954 BMW Issetta, 1956 Morris Isis and a 1939 Morris 8 to the rear. (Courtesy Streetlife)

Admission: free from 1999.

Tolson Memorial Museum, Ravensknowle Park, Wakefield Road, Huddersfield, West Yorkshire, HD5 8DJ.

Tel. 01484 223830. Senior Officer, Museums: John Rumsby.

The Museum can be found 22 miles northeast of Manchester in Ravensknowle Park, one and half miles east of Huddersfield town centre, on the A629 Wakefield/Sheffield road.

The Tolson Museum's purpose is to paint a picture of Huddersfield's natural history, archaeology and history. 'Going Places,' the local history of transport and travel, contains 10 vehicles and 6 cycles. The cars, although few in number, are worth a visit, particularly as the David Brown was manufactured locally. Open: daily, Monday to Friday, 11.00am to 5.00pm. Saturday and Sunday, 12.00pm to 5.00pm. Closed Christmas Eve, Christmas Day, Boxing and New Year's Days and Good Friday. The Museum has a gift shop and, for the disabled, there's an adapted unisex toilet. The transport section (on the ground floor) is fully accessible to wheelchairs and there is a chair lift to the first floor (staff are happy to help). Stair/rail access or ramped access. Parking is free with reserved parking for the disabled.

1920s reconstruction of a Garage with the David Brown car and the 'valveless' engine beyond. (Courtesy Kirklees Museum Service (Tolson Museum))

MOTORCARS			TRACTORS		
1910	David Brown valveless	No reg.	1949	David Brown Cropmaster	HWY 955
1902	De Dion Bouton engine		1956	David Brown 30D Industrial	No reg.
1910	David Brown valveless engine				
1922	LSD three wheeler	CX 1059			
			CYCLES		
			1868	Velocipede	
MOTORCYCLES			1870	Ordinary	
1918	BSA 4.5hp	CX 2774	1880	Childs ordinary	
			1880	Singer Sociable	
1919	Phelon and Moore ex-RAF.*	DS 8912	1910	Dursley-Pedersen	
1920	Excelsior (parts only)		1930	Raleigh Superb	
1950	Phelon and Moore (Panther)				
	Redwing 100 engine		*(*On loan to Red Howe Museum, Tel. 01274 335100.)*		

1908 David Brown car and spare engine. The David Brown who manufactured this and many other cars between 1908 and 1915, also owned a Huddersfield factory producing 'gears,' This was his first venture into cars, which were also made in Huddersfield and sold overseas, pricipally in South Africa and Australia. His son, also David, later invested in Aston Martin (his initials being the 'DB' in the names of a succession of fine cars. (Courtesy Kirklees Museum Service (Tolson Museum))

Admission: free.

Yorkshire Air Museum, Halifax Way, Elvington, York, YO41 5AU.
Tel. 01904 608595. Vice-Chairman: Ian Reed.

To get to the Museum, from the York bypass take the Hull exit (A1079) and then an immediate right to Elvington (B1228); the Museum is signposted on the right.

The Yorkshire Air Museum was created in 1985, on the former RAF Elvington World War II bomber base, as a living memorial to the Allied Air Forces that served in Yorkshire. Although primarily an aircraft museum, there's also a collection of military vehicles on display. The Museum has a NAAFI-style, self-service restaurant, shop, free parking and disabled facilities. Open: throughout the year, 10.30am until 4.00pm, weekends and Bank Holidays until 5.00pm. Closed for one week at Christmas. The Northern Branch of the Victory in Europe Re-enactment Association is based at the Museum. Annual rallies attract over 400 vehicles: contact the Museum for details.

EXHIBITS INCLUDE:

1941 Karrier K6 4 x 4 cargo 3 tonner	1958 Commer Q4 'Bikini' unit
1941 Chevrolet CMP C15 4 x 4 cargo	1958 Lansing aircraft carrier tug
1941 Bedford QL aircraft refueller	1959 Daimler Ferret armoured car Mk2/3
1942 Bedford OY 4 x 2 cargo	1965 Daimler Ferret armoured car Mk2/6
1942 Austin K2 NAAFI wagon	1971 Pathfinder 35 ton fire engine
1948 David Brown aircraft tractor VIG2	(ex-Manchester Airport)
1949 David Brown aircraft tractor VIG3	
1951 David Brown airfield GP tractor	**MOTORCYCLES**
1953 Alvis Saracen APC	1962 Triumph 250cc Dispatch Rider
1953 Austin Champ cargo	1963 Triumph 250cc Dispatch Rider
1954 Morris Commercial 4 x 4 3 ton cargo	
1954 Austin K9 recovery vehicle	

Admission: adults £4.00; OAPs and children under 16 £3.00; infants free; family ticket £12.00. Winter opening hours may vary, so you should check before a visit.

CHANNEL ISLANDS
Jersey Motor Museum, St. Peter, Jersey, Channel Islands, JE3 7AG.
Tel. 01534 482966. Director: F. Michael Wilcock.

Located in the heart of St. Peter at the junction of the A12 and B41.

Opened in 1973, the Museum is dedicated to preserving historic motor vehicles of all types and, particularly, transport and other photographic records relating to the island of Jersey. The Museum has a policy of adding to its vehicle stock every year, and the Collection includes veteran and vintage cars, plus Allied and German World War II military vehicles.

Open: daily from the end of March to late October, 10.00am to 5.00pm (last admission 4.40pm). There's a souvenir and motoring memorabilia shop and refreshments at an adjoining hotel. Car parking is free.

Built at Cobham in Surrey in 1938, this Railton Straight 8 cost its original owner £575. (Courtesy Jersey Motor Museum)

MOTORCARS			CHILDRENS'		
1912	Talbot type 4CT	J 1912	1938	Bentley child's car	
1919	Carden Cyclecar	J 322	1963	Cheetah Cub child's car	
1925/6	Morris Cowley Bullnose	J 1333			
1926	Austin Seven Chummy	J 1056			
1926	Ford Model T	J 6386	MOTORCYCLES		
1927	Austin Twelve	J 1917	1927	AJS 350cc	J 3812
1929	Peugeot type 201	J 1497	1931	Sunbeam Lion 350cc	No reg.
1930	Bentley 8 litre	J 2803	1936	Sunbeam Model 8, 350cc	DPX 954
1935	Bentley 3 litre	J 10017	1948	Sunbeam S7 prototype	KOU 477
1936	MG PB Midget 9hp	J 3536	1955	Douglas Dragonfly 350cc	J 17766
1936	Morris 8	J 6139	1985	Sinclair C5 electric	J 2336
1936	Rolls-Royce Phantom III	J 6663			
1937	Standard Flying Ten	J 3076			
1937	Talbot 3 litre '110'	J 5110	COMMERCIALS		
1938	Lanchester Eleven	J 3680	1931	Chevrolet truck	J 5609
1938	Railton St. 8	J 16310	1935	Albion fire engine	J 4392
1942	VW Kubelwagen	WH 121703	1940	Fordson standard tractor	J 3187
1949	Triumph 2000 Roadster	J 4889	1942	Ford Jeep 4 x 4	J 41181
1961	Cooper 59 (racing)	Not reg.	1942	Mack prime mover,	
1964	Hillman Husky	BLC 989B		articulated tractor	No reg.
1972	Jaguar E type V12	J 8372			

1930 Bentley 8 litre. Only a hundred of these very fast cars were built. This one set an average speed of 108.2mph at the Ghent Speed Trial in 1968. (Courtesy Jersey Motor Museum)

1912 Talbot 16hp Tourer; one of the many fine vehicles on display in the Jersey Motor Museum. (Courtesy Jersey Motor Museum)

Admission: adults £2.50; children (5-15) £1.20; wheelchair handicapped free.

IRELAND (EIRE)
Museum of Irish Transport, Scott's Gardens, Killarney, Ireland.
Tel. 0035364 34677. Curator: Eileen Daly.

The Museum is located in the centre of Killarney.

The Museum is centred in the middle of Killarney town, opposite the railway station, and is unique in housing a private collection where the majority of exhibits are from the veteran period. One car alone will make your visit noteworthy; the 1907 Silver Stream. The only one built, (it was assembled in Ireland) it's still in original condition. The Museum includes a 1920s garage with tools, spare parts, oil cans and even a mechanic working on a car. There's also a huge range of exhibits, including automobilia and a range of old cycles.

Open: from April to October, 10.00am to 6.00pm (later by appointment). Private viewing with guided tour if required. Wheelchair access and free car and coach parking. Access to the Museum is through the coffee and souvenir shops.

MOTORCARS

Year	Car	Reg.
1901	Argyle, Phaeton body	No reg.
1902	Austin Wolseley	IT 1
1902	Oldsmobile, tiller steering	IO 65
1904	Germain 50hp, 6 litre	IK 2239
1904	Humber, single cylinder, 2 seater	DX 61
1907	Silver Stream	IO 1
1908	Siddeley 14hp	IK 528
1910	Adler12hp	IA 5413
1910	Wolseley Siddeley	O 4578
1910	Wolseley Siddeley (consec. chassis nos.)	CI 1
1910	Wolseley Siddeley	KI 825
1911	Minerva 26hp limousine	No reg.
1911	Buick, very early, wooden wheels	No reg.
1914	Wolseley limousine	EI 398
1922	Ford Model T	AI 2185
1922	Ford Model T, Tudor sedan, 24hp	IU 733
1923	Calcott, 4 seater	No reg.
1923	Peugot 7hp, 2 seater	IK 5747
1923	Wolseley 10, 2 seater	IY 1393
1925	Morris Cowley12hp	PI 3190
1925	Vulcan 20hp	UM 1534
1927	Rolls-Royce 20	Z 287
1928	Wolseley 12/32hp limousine	IU 1848
1930	Ford Model A 24hp	IN 1930
1934	Austin 7	ID 2393
1935	Morgan 3 wheeler, 8hp Ford engine	ZK 3981
1935	Ford Model Y (garaged)	Z 6033
1936	Austin 18hp	Z 6786
1969	VW 1600cc fastback	7477 YI
1981	De Lorean	XOI 7569

COMMERCIAL

Year	Vehicle	Reg.
1912	Merryweather fire engine	Y 1157
1930	Merryweather fire engine	No reg.

Admission : adults £3.00; children £1.00; OAPs/students £2.00; family ticket (2 + 2) £7.00; (2 + 3) £7.00. Group rates available.

This beautiful 1904 Germain has a 5 litre, 4 cylinder engine with low tension magneto ignition, double chain drive, four forward gears and reverse. The car is in completely original condition. The price, when new, was £970. (Courtesy Museum of Irish Transport)

Interior view of part of the Museum of Irish Transport showing part of its collection of vehicles and automobilia. (Courtesy Museum of Irish Transport)

This unique car has a 6 cylinder Gnome of Rhone engine with magneto ignition and shaft drive. Costing £2000 in 1907, the Silver Stream - the only one ever built - is said to be the rarest car in the world. It was assembled in Ireland by Cork-born engineer Philip Somerville-Large. (Courtesy Museum of Irish Transport)

169

National Transport Museum, Heritage Depot, Howth Castle, Demesne, Howth, Co. Dublin, Ireland.

Tel. 003531 847 5623. Curator: Michael Corcoran.

Located 5 miles east of Dublin, the Museum is 730 metres from Howth DART railway station and 360 metres from the bus stop opposite the Castle gates. Bus 31 from Lower Abbey Street will get you there.

Created by the Transport Museum Society, a voluntary organisation and registered charity, this Collection (of 150 vehicles at present) is Ireland's only comprehensive assembly of public and commercial road transport vehicles. The National Transport Museum at Howth Castle opened in 1986, and its exhibits record the Golden Age of commercial vehicles and the motor industry in Ireland. Many were made by now defunct manufacturers; several are rare or unique and some are the sole survivor of once familiar types.

Open: from May to October, Saturday, Sunday and Bank Holidays, 2.00pm to 5.30pm. 26th December to 1st January, 2.00pm to 5.30pm daily. June to September, Monday to Saturday, 10.00am to 5.30pm. Sunday 2.00am to 5.30pm. Last admission 5.00pm. Other times by prior arrangement. No food/drinks on site but refreshments nearby. Disabled access is limited and the site is level but has restricted space between exhibits. Although there's not a shop, cards and a few books are available from the admission desk. Plenty of parking for cars and buses.

Admission: adults £1.50; children/OAPs £0.50; families (2 + 5 or one car with 4 people) £3.00. Party rates available on request.

COMMERCIAL, PUBLIC TRANSPORT, FIRE & EMERGENCY, MILITARY VEHICLES

Year	Vehicle	Reg	Year	Vehicle	Reg
1883	Merryweather manual appliance	Not reg.	1945	Bristol K6A/Brush 59s O/T	FRU 305
1883	Single-deck tramcar	Not reg.	1945	Leyland Interim Beaver lorry	LI 3724
1900	Unvestibuled 46s tramcar	Not reg.	1947	Foden F6/70 drawbar tractor	ZH 1278
1901	Directors tramcar	Not reg.	1947	Leyland Tiger PS1/NIRTB 34s	GZ 7638
1902	Howth Mines/Peckham 73s O/T	Not reg.	1948	AEC Regal III/Park Royal 35s	ZH 3926
1921	Leyland FE fire appliance	IK 4246	1948	AEC Regent III/Park Royal 56s	ZH 3937
1927	Albion LC24 Lon, 2.5 ton	ZI 504	1948	Leyland Titan PD2/Leyland 60s	ZH 4538
1928	Bogie standard tramcar	Not reg.	1948	Leyland OPS3 Tiger chassis	ZD 7163
1928	International 10/20 tractor	ZI 1920	1949	Commer Avenger/Plaxton 33s	LTU 869
1928	Leyland PLSC Lion Chassis	TE 5110	1949	Guy BTX/Harkness 68s trolleybus	GZ 8547
1930	Barford and Perkins 'A' path roller	FL 9226	1949	Morris Commercial FV12/5P lorry	ZJ 723
1930	Leyland LT2 Lion lorry	AZ 5078	1950	Bedford PCV 12cwt van	MZ 6596
1931	Merryweather AA 85' ladder	ZI 7528	1950	Dodge 25cwt recovery	ZJ 8298
1933	Dennis Lancet Mk. I/DUTC 32s	ZI 9708	1950	Guy Arab III/Harkness 31s	MZ 7396
1933	AEC Regal Mk.I Chassis	Not reg.	1951	Bedford OB/Duple 31s	GUX 188
1936	Merryweather FE6 100' ladder	ZA 7706	1951	Commer Q/HCB fire tender	PBH 222
1936	Morris Magirus Turntable ladder	BYV 322	1951	GNR Gardner/PRV-GNR 33s	IY 7384
1937	Leyland Titan TD4/Leyland 58s	ZC 714	1951	GNR Gardner ambulance	ZL 2718
c1937	Thompson living van	Not reg.	1951	Leyland Tiger OPS3 tender	ZJ 5933
1938	Dennis 45cwt (Ace) gulley emptier	ZC 3934	1951	Morris-Commercial LC3 van	ZL 3383
1938	Landswerk L180 armoured car	Not reg.	1951	S and 'W' refuse freighter	ZL 7761
1938	Leyland Terrier armoured car	ZC 776	1952	Austin K9 lorry, 4 x 4	Not reg.
1939	AEC Mammoth Major 8 w, O386	BEW 102	1953	AEC Mammoth Major 8 wheeler	Not reg.
1939	Leyland K2 trolleybus, 70s	EXV 348	1953	AEC Matador 0853 recovery	ZL 1257
1939	Leyland RET retriever workshop	ZC 9394	1953	Daimler CVG6/Harkness 56s	OZ 6686
1939	Morris-Comml CDSW gun tractor	ZD 296	1953	Dennis F12 pump escape	ZO 8056
1940	Morris Quad gun tractor	ZD 3177	1953	Leyland Tiger PS2/CIE 39s	ZO 6857
1941	Ford V8 lorry	ZD 3202	1953	Leyland Titan OPD2/CIE 68s	ZL 6816
1941	Leyland FK8 chassis	ZD 2902	1954	AEC Regal IV/PRV-GNR 45s	ZY 79
1942	Chevrolet CMP 15cwt lorry	Not reg.	1954	Albion HD57 8 wheeler lorry	RLV 154
1943	Commer Q2 articiulated tractor	ZD 3423	1954	Leyland Royal Tiger/CIE 34s	ZO 6881
1943	Fordson 7V Tangye heavy pump	FI 3368	1954	Leyland Royal Tiger/CIE 39s	ZO 6949
1945	Austin K6 6-wheel lorry	ZD 4998	1955	Land Rover Series 1	2793 RZ

1930 Merryweather AA 85ft ladder, ex-Dublin Fire Brigade, as are many of the emergency vehicles forming the core of this Collection. (Courtesy National Transport Museum)

'60 Morris LD ambulance and a Bedford light ruck. (Courtesy National Transport Museum)

1955	Leyland Titan OPD2/CIE 68s	ZU 9241
1956	AEC Mandator 3473	KI 7150
1956	Dennis F8 pump/water tender	NIK 888
1956	Reo Gold Comet tipper	FIK 634
1957	Ford E83W pickup	ANI 243
1958	Leyland Titan PD2 tender	CYI 621
1959	Ford Thames 530E tipper	YYI 219
1960	Leyland Tiger Cub/Dundalk 45s	UI 8511
1960	Leyland Titan PD3/CIE 74s	HZA 230
1960	Morris LD ambulance/fire tender	PZA 406
1961	AEC Regent Mk. V/CIE 69s	HZA 279
1961	Leyland Hippo 20H. 11 tanker	Not reg.
1962	Austin Gypsy fire tender	FZD 783
1962	Sunbeam MF2B/Weymann 65s	299 LJ
1963	Albion Lowlander/Alexander 72s	404 RIU
1964	AEC Merryweather 100 foot ladder	RZE 117
1964	Ford Thames 800 van	HNI 295
1964	Leyland Comet CS3,1 R lorry	LHD 204
1964	Leyland Leopard L2/CIE 45s	NZE 598
1964	Leyland Titan PD3A/Dundalk 76s	NZE 620
1965	Bedford R chassis/cab	HZH 155
1965	Leyland 2 ton	IZI 3
1965	Leyland Leopard mobile hospital	EZH 64
1965	Leyland Leopard PSU/CIE 45s	EZH 17
1965	Leyland Titan PD3A/Dundalk 76s	NZE 629
1965	Scammell constructor tractor.	HZH 933
1966	Leyland Hippo drawbar tractor	MZI 227
1966	Leyland Leopard PSU/CIE 53s	EZH 231
1967	Bedford VAM/Duffy 45s	WZJ 724
1967	Bedford VAS/CIE 33s	EZL 1
1967c	Bedford Val 14/Plaxton 53s	VZL 179
1967c	Bedford S Green Goddess	855 LYI
1967c	Fordson Thames ET tower wagon	Not reg.
1967	Leyland Atlantean PDR1/CIE 78s	VZI 44
1968	Scammell Townsman tractor	MZL 723
1969	Reliant Ant 3-wheeler	CZU 301
1971	Unimog APC	2269 ZC
1972	Bedford VAL14/Duffy 38s	Not reg.
1973	Commer C Pantechnicon	7958 ZJ
1974	Bedford horsebox	UTI 866
1975	AEG Mandator tractor, 2TG4R	593 PRI
1975	Atkinson Borderer tractor	YAI 533
1975	ERF Pump water tender	43 NIK
1975	Guy Big J4T tractor	872 CIK

1975	L/land Atlantean AN68/van	
	Hool 74s	694 ZO
1976	Bedford CF/Hanion ambulance	708 GYI
1976	Dodge K/Carmichael WL	977 GYI
1977	Wrigley works truck	892 IZC
1978	Dennison truck	IZW 56
1979	Bedford TK750 van	575 TZH
1979	Bedford TM tractor	795 WZE
1979	Foden 6 wheel 100 ton tractor	497 WZE
1979	Ford Transit van	261 AZI
1979	Timoney arm'd personnel carrier	365 KZE
1980	Dodge Commando gulley emptier	80D 124
1981	Dennison articulated tractor	498 EZO
1981	Ford D 1311 lorry, Atlas crane	159 TZL
1983	Timoney Firefly water ladder	518 YZU
1984	Ford Cargo 1111, Simon hoist	TZG 194

STEAM

1889	Merryweather steam fire pump	Not reg.
1924	Aveling and Porter steam roller	IK 7224

ELECTRIC

1946	Morrison BM battery-electric van	ZD 5957
1948	Brush battery-electric van	ZH 9296
1953	Wilson battery-electric van	ZU 4894
1960	Austin Electricar DI van	HZA 23
1960	Austin Electricar D1B ambulance	XZA 471
1962	Smith's Commuter electric van	KZD 995
1964	Smith's Commuter electric van	HZH 660
1967	Smith's NCB battery-electric float	CZL 216
1970	Wales and Edwards 3 wheel electric	2401 YI
1971	Wales and Edwards 4 wheel electric	3335 ZC
1979	Cabac battery-electric van	GZY 997

HORSEDRAWN

1920c	2 wheeled horsedrawn van	Not reg.
1925c	Merryweather horsedrawn tank	Not reg.
1926c	4 wheel horsedrawn van	Not reg.
1930c	4 wheel horsedrawn van	Not reg.
1952	Horse drawn milk float	Not reg.

1948 Leyland Titan PD2 and a 1948 AEC Regent III. (Courtesy National Transport Museum)

Vintage and Classic Car Museum, Buncranna, County Donegal, Ireland.
Tel. 0035377 61130. Owner: Jim Bradley.

Located in Buncranna Town, overlooking the Lough.

A personal collection of vintage and classic cars, vintage motorcycles and many other items of historical transport. Some exhibits are 'on loan,' consequently stock changes.

Open: daily, 1st June to 30th September, 10.00am to 8.00pm. Toilets on site and there are some disabled facilities. Parking available.

VEHICLES
1929   Rolls-Royce 20hp Laundalette   Not reg.

1929 Rolls Royce Landaulette dressed for its secondary duties of wedding car. It forms part of a small collection which, like many others, changes from time to time. It's best to ring before visiting. (Courtesy Automobilia)

THE VINTAGE CAR & CARRIAGE MUSEUM
BUNCRANA
CO. DONEGAL, IRELAND
Telephone 077-61130 any time.
(Dialling code from N.I. 0003.)

Admission: adults £2.00; children £0.50. Group rates available.

ISLE OF MAN
Manx Motor Museum, Glen Vine, Crosby, TT Course, Isle of Man.
Tel. 01624 851236. Contact: Richard Evans.

Located at Crosby, on the TT course (A1),

Here can be found the history of the motorcar, illustrated mainly by unusual cars. Motorcars on display include such oddities as a Diamond

about four miles west of Douglas.

Wheel, Patton-Sunbeam, 1916 Detroit Electric, and advanced designs such as the Citroën-Maserati and the 1965 Peel Trident, the only Manx car. No access for the disabled. Parking available.

Open: 10.30am to 5.00pm, May to September, but the number of days it is open will vary, so check first by phone.

Admission: £1.00.

Murray Motorcycle Museum, The Bungalow, TT Course, Snaefell Mountain, Isle of Man.

Tel. 01624 861719. Owner: Peter Murray.
Address for post: Peter Murray, Santon Villa, Santon, Isle of Man. Tel. 01624 823223.

Located on the TT course (A18) about six miles from Douglas, going towards Ramsey.

Mr Murray Senior collected motorcycles for some years and stored them in a shed in his garden. Being pushed for space, he often worked on them with the shed doors open, allowing access to interested visitors. This was the beginning, in 1957, of the family museum. Obtaining a lease on a goverment-built, early-warning station (which was unused and on the famous TT circuit), the Murrays opened the present museum in this new location in 1969. About 130 motorcycles are now on display, ranging from record-breakers to the everyday machine. Additionally, a mass of memorabilia and historical photographs are displayed. Altogether a fine collection in a world-renowned location.

The Museum is open from mid-May to the end of September, seven days a week, 10.00am to 5.00pm. Refreshments are available, as are toilets. There's disabled access but no toilets. Parking available.

Admission: adults £3.00; children/OAPs £2.00.

MOTORCYCLES (specific machines)

1902	Kerry	
1903	Coventry Eagle	
1904	Humber	
1907	Rex	
1910	Rex Blue Devil	
1911	Zenith	
1913	Rex	
1914	Indian V-twin	
1924	AJS side valve	
1925	AJS side valve	
1925	Rex Acme 350cc, ex-Brooklands record-holder	
1937	Brough Superior SS100	
1951	Wooler flat four	
1957	Mondial racer	
1961	Honda racer, ex-TT	

1915	Harley-Davidson

MANUFACTURERS MODELS (general)
AJS
Royal Enfield
Harley-Davidson
Rudge
James
Scott
Ner-A-Car 2 and 4 stroke
Sunbeam
Norton
Triumph
OEC
Velocette

NORTHERN IRELAND
Route 66 Automobile Collection, 94 Dundrum Road, Newcastle, Co. Down, Northern Ireland, BT33 OLN.
Tel. 01396 725223. Owner: Mrs Sheila Parks.

Location: from the centre of Newcastle take the Dundrum Road towards Belfast. Route 66 is in a short cul-de-sac on the left, opposite the Barbican Esso filling station. Tourist Board signposted.

The Route 66 Museum has its home in a previously unused factory building and specialises in American cars and memorabilia. It reflects the personal interest of its founders, Mrs Sheila Parks and her husband, John, in American motoring and culture. The Museum is named after the longest (2400 miles), and most famous of all US roads. With only enough space to show 15 cars, the rest of the collection is housed off-site and, in turn, rotated through the Museum. A video cinema shows early American car advertisements and footage of the Mustang and Corvette. There's also a half-scale 'Batmobile' as used in the film *Batman*. Also various police badges, astronaut badges and native American memorabilia.

Summer opening hours: daily, 10.30am to 6.00pm. Off-season, Saturday and Sunday 2.00pm to 6.00pm. Refreshments available from an adjoining 'Diner.' The Museum has a souvenir shop, and parking is on-street and in a small bay opposite the Museum.

Sheila and John Parks with their 1990 Ford Crown Victoria ex-Sheriff's Cruiser.
(Courtesy Route 66)

AMERICAN CARS

1938	Ford Tudor De Luxe
1939	Hupmobile Skylark saloon
1949	Willys Jeepster
1953	Cadillac Series 62 convertible
1955	Ford Thunderbird convertible
1957	Chevrolet Bel Aire coupé
1958	Ford Edsel Ranger
1959	Cadillac Series 62 coupé
1965	Ford Mustang 2 door coupé
1966	Mercury Park Lane convertible
1978	Pontiac Trans Am
1981	Excalibur Series IV Phaeton

1984	Pontiac Firebird (Knight Rider style)
1990	Ford Crown Victoria (Sheriff's Cruiser)

VEHICLES IN STORE

1958	Studebaker Golden Hawk
1959	Ford Skyliner Retractable
1963	Corvette Stingray
1978	Lincoln Continental Mk V
1978	New York Checker cab
1985	Lincoln Town car (Cartier edition)
1988	Mercury Cougar 'Tiffany' customised

Admission: adults £2.50; children (5 to 16 years) £1.00; concessions £1.50. Special rates for groups.

Interior shot of the Route 66 Museum. Display vehicles are rotated with reserve stock, so if you want to see a particular vehicle, ring before departing. (Courtesy Route 66)

1981 Excalibur Series IV Phaeton. (Courtesy Route 66)   A 1949 Willys Jeepster 2.2 litre tourer. (Courtesy Route 66)

Ulster Folk and Transport Museum, 153, Bangor Road, Cultra, Holywood, County Down, BT18 OEU.

Tel. 01232 428428. Head of Transport: Michael McCaughan.

Located at two sites: Cultra Folk and Transport Museum, Cultra, Holywood, 4 miles east of Belfast, and Belfast Gallery, Witham Street.

The transport section of the Museum is only one of many on a 130 acre site. The exhibits represent Irish agricultural and domestic life in the last two centuries, including transport in its varied forms: road, rail, sea and water. The two separate transport collections present a unique cross-section of Irish transport history, and include vintage and classic cars, commercial vehicles, trams, trains, motorcycles and bicycles. Some are special, some are commonplace, but all have individual appeal. The Museum, standing in beautiful grounds on the south shore of Belfast Lough, appeals to all the family.

Open: April to June and September, Monday to Friday, 9.30am to 5.00pm, Saturday 10.30am to 6.00pm. October to March, Monday to Friday, 9.30am to 4.00pm, Saturday and Sunday, 12.30pm to 4.30pm. July and August, Monday to Saturday, 10.30am to 6.00pm, Sunday, 12.00pm to 6.00pm. There's a restaurant at Cultra Manor, plus picnic areas, Museum shop and toilets; also parking. Most of the indoor facilities are accessible to the disabled and there is a toilet for the disabled, too. Exhibitions and special events are held throughout the year. A few of the Museum's transport exhibits are listed below.

Admission: adults £4.00; children £2.50; family ticket (2 + 3) £10.50; concessions £2.80. Special price for groups by arrangement.

MOTORCARS	TRAMS
Chambers	Fintona horsedrawn
De Lorean	Bessbrook and Newry 'Toast Rack'
Amphicar	
DAWB	
	CARRIAGES
	Stage coach
MOTORCYCLES	Laundaus
1921 Levis	Pony and trap
1971 Yamsel	Jaunting car

SCOTLAND
Biggar Museum Trust, Albion Archive, 9, Edinburgh Road, Biggar, Lanarkshire, ML12 6AX.

Tel. 01899 221497. Curator: Brian Lambie.

Location: from the centre of Biggar on the A702 to the northeast, the Museum is signposted to the left.

The Biggar Museum Trust's interest in transport centres on the fact that one of the two founders of the Albion Motor Company, established in Glasgow in 1899 and absorbed into British Leyland in 1951, was born in Biggar. The name was dropped in 1972 but, following a management buyout, commenced trading again as Albion Automotive. The vehicles in the Museum reflect Albion products from the earliest times, including a bus used in the television series *Dr Finlay's Casebook*. The Albion Archive contains a vast collection of company records from 1899 to 1972. Open: daily by appointment. Light refreshments are available and there are restaurants nearby. Disabled access and parking facilities are good. Public car parks nearby. Souvenir shop.

This 1902 A2 Albion Dog Cart Car 8hp, third off the production line, was purchased from a collection which had been based in Hawaii. This fine example (CR 36) took part in the earliest runs of the Veteran Car Club of Great Britain. Courtesy Albion Archive)

VEHICLES		
1902	Albion dog cart	CR 36
1923	Albion Hotel bus	ES 5150
1931	Tipper	VD 389
1936	Travelling Home Bus	567
1938	Tipper	SV 1228
1943	Army truck	Not reg.
1965	Three axle truck	AXS 586C
1970	Fire engine	KTS 557H

A 1951 Albion FT37L Chieftain lorry, registration KRW 496, was originally built at Scotstoun in 1951 and spent most of its working life on farm haulage in the Penrith area. (Courtesy Albion Archive)

Admission is free.

David Coulthard Museum, Twynholm, Kircudbright, DG6 4NU.

Tel. 01557 860313. Management: David Coulthard Fan Club.

The Museum is located in the village of Twynholm on the A75 road between Newton Stewart and Kircudbright. It is approximately 80 miles south of Glasgow.

This is a new museum which was opened in February 1999 by the father of Grand Prix driver David Coulthard. Coulthard's father has collected memorabilia connected with his famous son's driving career, which started with go-karts when he was 12 years old. All of David's racing helmets, his driving suits and his many trophies are on display. The Museum is open from 10.00am to 2.00pm daily, Monday to Saturday, or by appointment. Closed Christmas and New Year holidays. There is a souvenir shop, toilets and parking. Some access for the disabled, but it's best to 'phone first.

Admission is free.

VEHICLE COLLECTION (single seater racing cars
Formula Ford
Vauxhall Lotus
Formula 3 Honda
Formula 3000
2 go-karts

Museum of Scotland, incorporating the Royal Museum, Chambers Street, Edinburgh, EH1 1JF

Tel. 0131 225 7534. Curator of Road Transport: Alastair Dodd.
Website: http://www.nms.ac.uk

Chambers Street is off South Bridge in Edinburgh and a short distance from Waverley Rail Station.

Admission: adult £3.00, concessions £1.50, children and visitors under 18 free. Admission is free on Tuesdays from 4.30pm until 8.00pm.

A striking new landmark in Edinburgh's historic Old Town, the Museum charts the History of Scotland, its land, people and achievments through the ages. In the Museum of Scotland, the Industry and Empire section includes numerous road transport exhibits, such as a Hillman Imp made in Scotland, a Saab with Scottish connections plus combine harvester, engines and steam trains. The Royal Museum also has many transport exhibits. All parts of the building are accessible to the disabled and there are lifts to all floors, also toilets (including disabled). Other facilities include sound guides, a rooftop garden with spectacular views, tower restaurant at rooftop level and a self-service restaurant in the Royal Museum. Shop.

Open all year, except Christmas Day, Monday to Saturday, 10.00am to 5.00pm, Sunday 12 noon to 5.00pm. Late night opening on Tuesdays until 8.00pm.

*Newton Stewart is 70
miles southeast of
Glasgow.*

*Admission: adults
£1.00; OAPs/children
£0.50.*

Glenluce Motor Museum, Newton Stewart, Wigtownshire, DG8 0NY.
Tel. 01581 300534. Contact: Bill Adams.

Contained in a range of farm buildings this is a collection of vintage and classic cars and 14 motorcycles, plus stationary engines. Restoration work is also on display. Open: from the 1st of March to the 31st of October, 10.00am to 7.00pm, and from the 1st of November to the 28th of February, 11.00am to 4.00pm. Closed Monday and Tuesday during winter. There is a shop, tea room and toilets, plus disabled facilities.

*The Museum is located
in the village of Alford,
on the A944, 22 miles
west of Aberdeen.*

*Admission: adults
£3.50; OAPs £2.50;
children £1.50; family
ticket (2 + 3) £8.50.
The entry ticket also
allows admission to the
Transport Gallery and
Railway Exhibition.*

Grampian Transport Museum, Alford, Aberdeen, Grampian, AB33 8AE.
Tel. 01975 562292. Curator: Mike Ward.

A collection of historic road vehicles, the earliest of which is steam powered. The Trust was able to provide a custom-built museum set adjacent to a large play area and car park. There are many exhibits specifically for children, including a Giant Mac snowplough, a vintage roller and, adjacent to the Museum, an adventure playground. There's also a driving simulator and videos showing motorsport and road transport history. Recitals are given by the Mortier Dance Organ. There is an extensive programme of summer motoring events.

Open: daily from 10.00am to 5.00pm, 28th March to 31st October. The Museum cafe conforms to these opening hours. The Museum shop sells motoring memorabilia and souvenirs and there is a large, free car park. The Museum and cafe are principally at ground level; wide aisles allow wheelchair access. Toilets available.

MOTORCARS					
1902	Argyll 8hp	RI 44	1921	Ford Model T coupé	RS 3870
1906	Arrol-Johnston 18hp	G 1481	1926	Swift 8hp, soft top	TS 5481
1907	Albion A3 Wagonette	KS 103	1928	Austin 7 Chummy	AEG 97
1912	Hispano Suiza Alfonso	K 1085	1929	Rolls-Royce 20/20	VX 4167

The Grampian Transport Museum entrance showing the car park in the foreground and the Museum to the right rear.

1931	Sunbeam van 2 seater	JU 2094
1934	Austin 10 hearse	AV 8358
1936	MG TA Sports Special	No reg.
1951	Land Rover Series1	PNW 72
1953	Bristol 403	OXM 576
1935	Riley saloon	MJ 9035
1958	Messerschmitt bubblecar	492 ALM
1956	MGA	FSV 972
1959	MG sectioned, chain and drive gear	
1963	Aston Martin DB4V Vantage	128 HYP
1963	Trojan bubblecar	LSO 154
1970	Morris Minor saloon	PSA 110J
1974	Jaguar E type V12 Roadster	AJW 30M
1976	Austin Allegro	LSO 198P
1976	Chevrolet Corvette Stingray	6666-16
1995	Ford Ecostar electric van	M979 XPU

MOTORCYCLES

1902	Beeston Humber	ST 25
1920	Clyno Model C	TS 2448
1921	Ariel combination	SA 3804
1921	New Hudson 2.25hp	SA 3361
1921	Triumph 2.5hp	DS 7503
1922	Harley-Davidson	Not reg.
1922	McKenzie 169cc, 2 stroke	Not reg.
1923	Raleigh 2.75hp	SR 3426
1924	Matchless 347cc	SR 4450
1928	Lea Francis 3.5hp	Not reg.
1929	Praga 500	Not reg.
1931	Ariel square four, 497cc	FD 6717
1934	Red Panther 250cc	GSV 286
1936	Maserati 6CM	Not reg.
1921	OK Junior flat-twin	PS 421
	BSA, in line V-twin	Not reg..
1943	BSA WD M20	JS 52
1956	Corgi folding scooter	Not reg.
1943	Excelsior Welbyke	Not reg.
1946	Moto Guzzi 250	Not reg.
1947	Ariel Hartley 350	Not reg.
1949	Douglas Dragonfly V	JCE 624
1950	Norton F'bed 250cc	Not reg.

1953	Maserati A6 GCM/250F	Not reg.
1957	Sunbeam S8	FYJ 699
1958	BSA Bantam racer	Not reg.
1958	Lohmann diesel bicycle	
1959	BSA Goldstar	734 LRA
1960	Ariel Arrow 250cc	Not reg.
1960	Triton 650cc	XSP 594
1961	NSU Supermax 250cc	Not reg.
1962	Honda CR110, 50cc	Not reg.
1964	Triumph T10 scooter	Not reg.
1964	Lambretta Li125, Series 2	DRS 459
1965	Rickman Mat. trials	Not reg.
1966	Bombardier WD	Not reg.
1966	LE Velocette	PUR 41D
1972	Honda CB750 K2	PVO 101M
1973	Kawasaki 21	DRS 94L
1977	Suzuki GT750A	RUL 509R
1978	Yamaha TZ750 racer	Not reg.
1979	Triumph Bonneville, 750cc	VAS 649cc
1983	Yamaha TZ 125H, 50cc	Not reg.
1986	Sinclair C5	Not reg.
1988	Honda RC30, VFR 750cc	Not reg.
1992	Honda RC40, NR 750cc	Not reg.

COMMERCIALS

1899	Cruden Bay Hotel tram	
1940	Ford Thames fire tender	FYY 160
1940	Mack snow plough 6 x 6	
	Saunderson agricultural tractor	SA 38
1950	Pashley ice cream trike	GAV 311
1957	Ferguson Antarctic replica	Not reg.
1960	Saracen armoured car	
	Leyland Atlantean 2 deck bus	NRG 154M

STEAM

1892	Aveling Porter Invicta steam roller, 7hp	SA 4464
1895	Craigie Vor Express steam trike	SA 16
1918	Foster steam tractor, 'Olive'	Not reg.

...rt of the display at the Grampian Transport Museum.

Museum of Transport, Kelvin Hall, 1, Bunhouse Road, Glasgow, G3 8DP.
Tel. 01412 872000. Curator: Alistair Smith.

Argyle Street is about one mile west of the city centre and leads to Kelvin Hall Sports Centre (signposted) and the Transport Museum. The nearest underground railway station is Kelvin Hall.

The Museum, containing almost 100 vehicles, is situated in the City of Glasgow and is devoted to the history of transport on land and sea. The land element contains a cross-section of the many types of wheeled vehicle used in Scottish transportation. Displays include a Glasgow street scene of 1938 and a period garage. The Museum makes a splendid day out for families. Open: Monday to Saturday from 10.00am to 5.00pm, Sunday from 11.00am to 5.00pm. Closed Christmas and New Year's Days. The Museum has a gift shop and restaurant, plus disabled access and toilets.

One of the sections of Glasgow Museum of Transport devoted to safer driving. Here a motorist can have his or her braking reaction tested against recommended stopping distances.

Admission and parking are free and there are free guided tours.

MOTORCARS

Year	Model	Reg
1896	Daimler Phoenix Wagonette	
1898	Benz Voiturette Comfortable	MS 36
1900	Argyll Voiturette	AR ?06
1900	Argyll Voiturette	XS 558
1902	Argyll light tourer	Y 246
1904	Albion Tonneau, type D	
1906	Argyll-Johnson 18 open	G 1481
1906	Lagonda Tricar	T 1115
1907	Argyll 10/12 tourer	G 1974
1910	Argyll Flying Fifteen	SD 4086
1912	Arrol-Johnson 15.9 tourer	LE 8582
1913	Argyll 15/30(G) tourer	SB 547
1915	Schneider tourer, replica	G 252
1915	Ford Model T	
1920	Arrol-Johnson 15.9 Model	SD 2146
1924	Austin 7 tourer type C	GD 310
1924	Galloway 10.5 coupé	MB 4268
1924	Beardmore tourer	
1926	Morris Cowley Bull Nose	UD 250
1927	Argyll 12.5 tourer	GD 9250
1928	Austin Big 12	JTF 1802
1931	Rolls-Royce Phantom II	GO 6444
1938	Morris 12/4 saloon	BGG 132
1938	Vauxhall 10 saloon	CUS 665
1938	Sunbeam Talbot 6	CGD 155
1939	Standard Eight saloon	CGE 908
1949	Morris 6 saloon	MMM 777
1949	Standard Vanguard Mk 1	GFH 977
1950	Morris Minor saloon	KDF 285
1951	Bentley Mk 6	GM 5425
1952	Triumph Mayflower saloon	MYW 642
1955	Ford Popular 103E	VS 6866
1955	Austin A30 saloon	SX 9574
c1957	BMW 300 Isetta	UCS 269
1959	Morris Mini Minor	221 OSM
1961	Jaguar 3.4 340	SCS 777
1963	Volvo P1800S Sports	AUN 508B
1963	Hillman Imp saloon	
1971	AC Model 70, 3 whl invalid car	GPG 721K
1977	Chrysler Sunbeam	XSU 367S

MOTORCYCLES

Year	Model	Reg
1913	AJS V-twin 800cc	G 6168
1914	Scott 532cc (water cooled)	
1918	BSA 55Occ	S 7895
1920	Triumph Model 20	
1920	Zenith V-twin	
1921	Triumph 550cc	SA 2743
1921	Ner-A-Car	SW 698
1921	Zenith V-twin 677cc	AE 8467
1923	New Gerrard 175cc (ex-TT winner)	
1925	BSA 329cc	
1927	Harley-Davidson	J D OD 6651
1929	Douglas (track racer)	
1931	Coventry Eagle 198cc	?? 3823
1934	Raleigh 487cc	
1936	Douglas E29	XS 2572
1938	Royal Enfield S L Deluxe	SC 9372
1939	BSA 500cc (ex WD)	
1939	Brough Superior SS80	CYS 962
1948	BSA B31	GFG 162
1946	AJS 500cc	KS 9504
1949	Vincent HRD	GGE 812
1949	Scott 596cc (water cooled)	KNA 405
1952	Sunbeam S8	KFG 903
1952	BSA Bantam D2	TUV 42
1953	Sunbeam S7 and Watsonian sidecar	UGG 236
1953	LE Velocette 192cc	GHS 397
1954	BSA M21 600cc and AA sidecar	PYE 206
1959	Norton Dominator Series 99	MWG 631
1962	Matchless 350cc	AVS 143
1968	Triumph Tiger 90 & Jet 80 s/cr	OGG 209F
	Royal Enfield 125cc	CRS 45
	BSA 250cc	SYS 673
	Ariel 500cc	AG 1335

Plus eleven scooters of differing types.

TRAMS

1898	'Room and Kitchen' No. 672	
1908	Standard 21E No. 779	
1924	Standard 21E No. 1088	
1926	'Bailie Burt' No. 1089	
1938	Coronation Mk 1 No. 1173	
1947	Maley and Taunton 45hp	
	Maley and Taunton 35hp, type 596	
1952	Cunarder, M and T type 596, No. 1392	
1958	Trolleybus TBS 18, No. TBS13 FYS 988	

Young Stephanie Howitt pictured in costume dress against the background of a Romany caravan, Part of the Glasgow Museum of Transport's permanent display of Victorian transport.

Founded in 1964, the Glasgow Museum of Transport moved to the present day premises in Kelvin Hall, Glasgow in 1983 where Scotland's premiere transport museum now has space to display its comprehensive exhibits of motorcycles, cars, trucks, buses and much more!

Glasgow Museum of Transport has a permanent display featuring the after-effects of car crime. Here, a graphic illustration of what happens when a person loses control of a vehicle is a stark deterrent to would-be criminals.

Moray Motor Museum, Lossie Bank Mills, Bridge Street, Elgin, Morayshire IV30 2DE.
Tel. 01343 544933. Owner: Tom McWhirter.

The Museum is 35 miles east of Inverness. In the centre of Elgin, turn north and follow the signs to the Museum, which is on the right just after the bridge over the River Lossie.

Housed in a converted mill building near the banks of the River Lossie, many of the cars in this collection are special to the owner and demonstrate an enthusiast's concern for the preservation of our motoring history. All are in full working order and are used frequently on the road or in competition. The motorcycles are, in the main, machines 'loaned' to the Museum. Again, all are operational and used in local events.

Open: daily from Easter to the October half-term, 11.00am to 5.00pm. Souvenirs may be purchased at the Museum ticket office. Light refreshments are available at an adjacent local cafe. Disabled access throughout the Museum. Disabled toilet. Parking free.

MOTORCARS		MOTORCYCLES	
1903	Albion	1904	Minerva 2hp
1903	Humberettie	1905	Rex
1904	Speedwell	1913	Clyno lightweight
1914	Ford Model T	1913	Douglas 2hp Model P
1914	Renault	1914	Ixion
1912	Daimler 2 seater dickie	1914	Triumph Model A
1921c	Alvis 10/25 sports tourer	1920	AJS Model D combo
1926	Ford Model T	1921	Royal Enfield sports
1926	Rover aircooled 8	1925	Excelsior tourer
1927	Rolls-Royce PI	1925	Raleigh
1929	Bentley 4 litre	1926	Rover sports
1932	Austin 7 Stadium boat tail	1928	AJS 'Big Port'
1937	Jaguar SS 100	1928	Rudge Special
1946c	HRG	1929	Scott
1949	Maserati Milano	1930	BSA E14 with sidecar BSA 11
1950c	Frazer Nash, Bristol engine	1947c	Sunbeam S8
1950c	Tojeiro Jaguar	1949	Manx Norton
1953	Jaguar XK 150 coupé	1949	Vincent HRD
1954	Lagonda, open racer V12	1952	Francis Barnett
1955c	Bristol 403	1953	BSA B31
1956c	Bristol 404	1955c	Douglas Dragonfly
1957c	Jaguar Mk 7	1963	Velocette Vogue
1963	AC Ace	1973	Norton Commando
1968	Jaguar E type, Series 11/2		
1970c	Tojeiro Bristol		Most of the motorcycles are loaned to the Museum,
1974c	Triumph Stag		so it might be wise to ring first if looking for a
			particular machine.

Admission: adults £2.50; OAPs £2.25; children £0.60; family ticket (2 + 2) £5.00.

Moray Motor Museum logo and a1937 Jaguar SS100, one of the Museum's 'faster' cars which is used in competition by the Museum's owner. (Courtesy Moray Motor Museum)

Moray Motor
Museum

nternal view of the
useum showing a few
f the many cars and
otorcycles on display.
ourtesy Moray Motor
Museum)

1939 SS100

Myreton Motor Museum, Aberlady, East Lothian, EH32 0PZ.
Tel. 01875 870288. Curator: M. Mutch.

Aberlady is 12 miles east of Edinburgh. Turn right at the junction with the A1 and the A6137 for Haddington. Three miles from the A1 at Haddington, turn right onto the B1377 for Myreton.

The Museum contains a varied collection of over 50 vehicles, the first dating from 1896. Motorcars, motorcycles, commercials, World War II military vehicles and automobilia are all on display, all in original condition and running order. Open: every day, except Christmas, from 10.00am onwards. There are toilets, parking, facilities for the disabled and a shop selling accessories. A catalogue and childrens' quiz books are available.

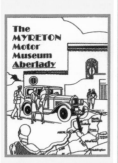

Logo of the Myreton Motor Museum.

MOTORCARS				
1897	Arnold Benz	Not reg.		
1899	General Electric Wagonette	Not reg.		
1900	Locomobile	Not reg.		
1909	Albion 16hp Wagonette	KS 103		
1909	Albion 24/30	SY 333		
1914	Morris Oxford de luxe	AR 4376		
1919	Ford Charabanc 14 seater	GA 3560		
1923	Arrol-Johnson 15.9hp	No reg.		
1923	Hillman Sports 10.4hp sports car	EM 1491		
1923	Renault 8.3hp cabriolet	SG 7867		
1924	Alvis 12/50 'Duck's Back' 2 stroke	XR 1856		
1924	Model T Ford van/pick-up	XG 9348		
1925	Morris Oxford	SE 36		
1925	Morris Commercial, type SW	PP 8805		
1925	Morris Oxford, 2 seater	SF 3681		
1926	Morris Oxford	YB 5628		
1927	Darracq DTS 15/40	YM 3968		
1927	Galloway	RP 4674		
1927	Rolls-Royce 4 seater tourer	P? ??42		
1928	Austin Twenty, ex-limo/truck	YU ??39		
1930	MG M type 2 door sports car	EO 4917		
1930	Morris Minor	No reg.		
1934	Austin light utility	OSH 512		
1934	Singer TT racing car	AK 483		
1935	Citroën Kegresse tracked			
	personnel carrier	No reg.		
1937	Wolseley 10hp 4 door saloon	FMP 610		

1939	Morris ambulance		JHY 965
1940	Morris Commercial 8cwt PU		
	wireless truck		No reg.
1940	Renault 17hp cabriolet		GGK 922
1941	Standard light utility 12hp		Not reg.
1942	Daimler scout car Mk. 11		F 48090
1942	Humber heavy utility		RAF 747
1942	Standard Beaverette		M 4815836
1943	Austin K2 ambulance		FSC 700
1943	Hillman light utility		M 797798
1952	Cooper Sprint racer		Not reg.
1954	Cooper Formula 3		Not reg.
1956	Hillman Minx		JST 906
1960	Wolseley 15/60 Farina		STY 380

MOTORCYCLES		
1912	Triumph TT	BB 817
1913	Henderson 1086cc	LF 2320
1926	Dunelt Model K 250cc	YP 9308
1928	AJS 498cc	SR 5196
1932	BSA Blue Star	SS 3504
1932	Sunbeam Model 90 493cc	FM 8806
1935	Triumph L2/1, 250cc	SY 5599
1938	Excelsior Manxman 250cc	Not reg.
1938	Sunbeam 250cc Sports, Model 17	BWS 618
1942	James 125cc	Not reg.
1943	Welbike, 98cc airborne scooter	Not reg.

A 1930 MG M crossing a local ford. The Myreton Motor Museum has provided vehicles to the film and television industry. The 1925 Morris Oxford, for example, was driven by Andrew Cruikshank in TV's *Dr Finlay's Casebook*. (Courtesy Myreton Motor Museum)

Admission: adults £3; OAPs £2; children £1.

1934 'TT' Singer. This car has a long racing history, having been raced at Ards, Le Mans, Donington, Montlhéry and Brooklands. (Courtesy Myreton Motor Museum)

A 1954 Cooper Formula III, the same type of car in which Stirling Moss started his racing career. (Courtesy Myreton Motor Museum)

The Motoring Heritage Centre, Loch Lomond Factory Outlets, Main Street, Alexandria, West Dumbartonshire, G83 0UG.
Tel. 01389 607862. Curator: Terry Kain.

The Museum is 16 miles northwest of Glasgow. Follow the A82 dual carriageway north from Dumbarton to the Stoneymollan roundabout, turn right onto the A811. Follow the signs towards Balloch and Alexandria. At the Balloch roundabout, turn right. The Motoring Heritage Centre is 500 metres along on the left.

The Museum building was constructed in 1905 for the expansion of the Argyll Motorcar Company which, at that time, was producing more vehicles than any other manufacturer in Europe. In 1908 after the death of Managing Director Alexander Govan, the company went into liquidation. It was reconstituted and prospered until it developed its own sleeve valve engine which ended in crippling patent litigation. In 1914 the company was finally wound up on this site; however, Argyll cars were made in Glasgow until 1928.

After thirty years as a Royal Navy torpedo factory (the torpedo which sank the *Belgrano* is said to have been made here) the factory became derelict. A six million pound reconstruction programme has now brought this magnificent 'A' listed building, with its seven hundred foot marble and red sandstone frontage, back to life, and cars once again feature as a commercial activity. The Museum shares the building with factory outlet shops and celebrates Scottish motoring with a fine gallery of cars from 1902 to the present day. Archive film on video, memorabilia and pictorial displays provide a further insight.

Open: 363 days a year, closed on Christmas Day and New Year's Day. There are souvenir shops, a restaurant and coffee shop. Disabled lift and wheelchair access. Free car and coach parking.

MOTORCARS		
1902	Bartholomew*	
1902	De Dion Bouton 6hp	
1910	Argyll 10hp*	
1911	Ford Model T*	
1912	Overland T59	
1925	Argyll 12.4*	
1926	Albion truck*	
1928	Humber 14/40	
1933	MG J2	
1935	Rover 10	
1950	J Potts racing car	
1954	Vauxhall Velox*	
1964	Electric Scamp*	
1964	Singer Chamois*	
1978	Parabug*	
1978	Argyll*	
1981	Lotus Sunbeam*	

1984	A C 3000*
1995	Subaru World Championship rally car, ex-Colin McCrae*

MISCELLANEOUS

1931	Thompson caravan*
1941	BMW motorcycle replica

*Vehicles built in Scotland or with strong Scottish connections.

Admission: adults £1.50; concessions £1.00; children £0.75; under-5s free

The renovated facade of what was the Argyll motor factory, now the Home of Motoring Heritage Centre and Loch Lomond factory outlet. (Courtesy Home of Motoring Heritage Centre)

Museum of Fire, Lothian and Borders Fire Brigade, Brigade Headquarters, Lauriston Place, Edinburgh, EH3 9DE.
Tel. 01312 282401. Curator: I. McMurtrie.

Located at Brigade Headquarters, Lauriston Place, Edinburgh.

The Museum of Fire was first formally established in 1963, inheriting, amongst many other valuable historic items, Firemaster Braidwood's Badge of Office, batons, Bosun's pipe and log books from 1824 to 1832. The Museum now occupies a fire station built in the 1900s - its third home; the moves have been necessary because of having to find room for additional vehicles, equipment and archive material. Whilst it was intended that the Museum be a record of the Borders Fire Brigade and its links with Edinburgh, it has a much wider-based interest and is now one of the largest collections of fire service appliances, equipment and memorabilia in Great Britain, if not the world. It has connections with Europe, the USA and the Far East. The Museum also has a large collection of fire service equipment and memorabilia from the fourteenth century to the present day. A large library and archive material is also available within Brigade HQ.

Open: by arrangement with the Curator. Toilets and disabled facilities. Parking at nearby public car parks.

FIRE APPLIANCES

1806	Manual engine	Not reg.	1936	Leyland Cub fire appliance	EW 9795
1824	Tilley manual pump	Not reg.	1939	Dennis Limousine pump	SY 6848
1830	Ridgeway manual pump	Not reg.	1941	Austin Standard towing unit	GLE 32
1860	Rose manual pump	Not reg.	1941	Austin escape carrying unit	GXA 797
1879	Dunbar manual pump	Not reg.	1941	Austin/Merryweather TL	GXN 247
1880	M/W H/D curricle fire escape	Not reg.	1950	Dennis F8 pump	KSF 404
1898	Shand Mason steam fire engine	Not reg.	1951/3	Dennis pump escape	Not reg.
1900	Morris wheeled escape	Not reg.	1959	Commer MK III	NES 448
1901	Merryweather Gem steam fire engine	Not reg.			
1910	Halley fire engine	WS 113	**MOTORCAR**		
1930	Dennis motor pump	AV 4203	1935	Austin Heavy 12 Hertford saloon	SL 1942
1936	Dennis New World Ace fire engine	SY 5885			

A 1930s Dennis fire engine.

Admission: free.

Northfield Farm Museum, New Pitsligo, Fraserburgh, Grampian, AB43 6PX.
Tel. 01771 653504. Curator: Thomas Hamilton.

The Museum is on the A950, just off the A98 Fraserburgh to Macduff road, about 32 miles north of Aberdeen and 8 miles southeast of Fraserburgh.

As the name implies, Northfield Farm Museum has many old farmhouse artefacts, plus about ten classic tractors, including a 1922 International, a Marshall and 'Little Alice,' which the owner still uses. Agricultural machinery from the early part of the century is on display and there's a carpenter's workshop, complete with old tools and equipment. A number of classic motorcycles are also on display. There are toilets and limited siabled access.

Open: May to September, 11.00am to 5.30pm.

A 1921 International Junior.

Admission: adults £1.50; OAPs/children £0.75.

WALES
Madog Motor Museum, Snowdon Street, Porthmadog, LL49 9DF.
Tel. 01758 712308. Curator: Bill Evans.

Porthmadog is 41 miles west of Llangollen.

This private museum is devoted to British vehicles; cars and motorcycles from vintage, post-vintage and classic periods. Additionally, the Museum has a large collection of posters, motor memorabilia, stationary engines, old pumps and tools, plus lots of associated collectables.

Open: weekdays from May to September, 10.00am to 5.00pm. Free car park. Please note that the building is not suitable for the disabled.

MOTORCYCLES

1920	New Hudson de luxe
	Levis Model 1K
	Montgomery Terrier
	Norton Model 18
	Norton 16H
	Norton Domiracer
	Norton Navigator
	Panther 100
	Raleigh Cyclemaster
1921	Royal Enfield 225cc
	Royal Enfield Crusader Sport
	Francis Barnet Falcon
	Greeves Griffon
1925	Douglas T5
	Douglas T35 Mk 3
1930	Scott Sports
	Scott Autocycle
	Sunbeam Model 1
	Sunbeam Series 2 (80)
	Swallow (Sunbeam) Gadabout
	Triumph Model W
	Triumph TR trials
	Triumph 5TA Super-twin
	Triumph TR6/Austin 7 engine
	Velocette Venom
	Velocette LE
	Velocette GTR
	Vincent Grey Flash
1930s	Ariel Sloper
1952	Ariel Square Four
1958	Ariel Square Four
1958	Ariel VB
1959	AJS C12/31

AJS CSR
AJS Stormer
AJS Model 18
BSA B31
BSA ZB Trials
BSA A10 Rocket
BSA Bantam D7
BSA B40
BSA C15
Corgi

MOTORCARS

AJS saloon
Humber 16/15 saloon
Austin 10
Morris Minor convertible
Austin A30
MG J2
Bond Mini
MG TC2
Ford Model T
Riley Merlin open tourer
Ford Prefect
Standard Big 9
Humber 14/40
Ford Cortina Mk2 Savage
Jaguar XK 150
1927 Humber soft top
Wolseley Hornet

COMMERCIALS
Austin RL van

Admission: adults £2.00; OAPs and children over 5 £1.00. Clubs by prior arrangement; discount for parties.

Betws-y-Coed Motor Museum, Betws-y-Coed, Conway Valley, Gwyneth, LL24 0AH.
Tel. 01690 710760. Curator: Adrian Houghton.

The Museum is located in the centre of Betws. The A5 passes through the village; from it turn off into Station Road, the Museum is signposted. Betws is 25 miles west of Llangollen.

The Motor Museum was created from the private collection of the Houghton family, and is housed in the stone outbuildings of Betws Farm, which overlooks the River Llugwy in the centre of Betws-y-Coed. Varied exhibits include famous marques and more recent classic cars, scale models and motoring memorabilia.

Open: daily from Easter to the end of October, 10.30am to 6.00pm, including Sundays. There's a souvenir and model shop and disabled access. Pay and display parking adjacent. Coaches free.

MOTORCARS		MOTORCYCLES	
1914	Ford Model T open wagon	1947	Triumph Speed-twin
1924	Bentley 3 litre Red Label	1948	Ariel square four
1924	Morris Bull Nose	1962	Norton SS
1927	Austin 7 Chummy	1962	Triumph Tiger 100
1927	Standard Stratford tourer	1969	BSA Bantam 175cc
1928	Austin 7 Gordon England open	1970c	Triumph Tiger Venturer trials
1934	Aston Martin Mk II saloon		
1934	Bugatti type 57	Plus various mopeds - Raleigh, Mobylette, etc.	
1934	Riley MPH open sports		
1935	Ford Model Y saloon		
c1935	MG PA part restored	**MISCELLANEOUS**	
c1933	MG J2 original	Child's racing car	
1936	MG TA	Half-size Model T Fords	
1937	MG SA saloon	Land Speed jet engine	
1946	Rover 10		

Frontispiece of The Betws-y-Coed Motor Museum catalogue artistically illustrates the theme behind this collection: collectable cars of the 1920s, 30s and 40s.
(Courtesy The Betws-y-Coed Motor Museum)

Admission: adults £1.50; children £1.00; concessions £1.00; family ticket £4.00. Group rates by arrangement.

Llangollen Motor Museum, Pentrefelin, Llangollen, Denbighshire, North Wales, LL20 8EE.

Tel. 01978 860324. Curator: Ann Owen.

The Museum can be found one and a quarter miles from Llangollen Bridge, on the A542 towards Ruthin and the Horseshoe Pass. The Museum is on the left, on a left hand bend, across the canal bridge.

Llangollen Motor Museum, formed in September 1980, has a Riley Monaco in its letterhead, which was the first working car acquired by the Museum. It is the Museum's proud claim that all of the cars in its collection are used periodically and are not just static exhibits. Llangollen Motor Museum is housed in a pre-1912 building, which was shown on a period Ordnance Survey map as a fountain pen factory. The Museum also contains a village garage with workshop, reference library, large stores and quiz/work sheets for schools. Ms Owen would prefer that ladies also enjoy the visit, hence, she has introduced a ladies' reading corner. Finally, there's something a little different; a pictorial history of British canals. Repairs are undertaken to older cars and also some restoration. The Museum has a large spare parts store for older cars - sparkplugs a speciality. Older vehicles are bought and sold.

Open: from March to the end of October, Tuesday to Sunday, 10.00am to 5.00pm. November to February, weekends only, 10.00am to 4.30pm. Closed January and Christmas week. The Museum offers a confectionery shop and picnic area and toilets. There's easy wheelchair access to the whole of the Museum, and ample parking.

Ann Owen, second owner of the Museum which came into being in 1980, and a 1925 Vauxhall 30/98.
(Courtesy Llangollen Museum)

MOTORCARS			MOTORCYCLES		
1923	Citroën Cloverleaf	Not reg.	1916	Triumph Model H	HK 9224
1925	Citroën B12 tourer	Not reg.	1928	Raleigh 250cc	EV 2584
1925	Citroën Woody estate	Not reg.	1932	BSA 350cc	JFO 404
1925	Vauxhall 30/98	SV 4182	1935	New Imperial	VN 8255
1931	Standard Big 9, 10hp	GT 7019	1950	BSA C10	JFO 475
1933	Austin 7	ALU 175	1950	Sunbeam S7	RMM 507
1935	Austin 10	APH 131	1956	BSA C12	Not reg.
1933	Morris 8 tourer	TJ 2979	1950	Ariel Red Hunter	XFO 537
1935	Austin Lichfield, 10hp saloon	BXR 411	1960	Triumph Tiger Cub	608 WFM
1936	Morgan F4 (3 wheeler)	JU 7920	1962	Ariel Arrow	Not registered
1939	Ford 8, 7Y FAL 494		1962	BSA Star	EWA 563
1948	Morris Series E, 4 door saloon	JKF 803	1971	Maxton TT race bike,	
1949	AC 2 litre	LJH 211		ex-Charlie Williams	
1955	BMW Isetta	NDY 103	1974	Triumph Trident	KGT 733N
1957	MG Magnette	Not reg.		Sinclair C5	
1962	Austin Healey 3000	161 APO			
1962	Triumph TR 4	73 YKX			
1967	Singer Gazelle	JLC 259D			
1967	Vauxhall Victor 101 de Luxe1.6	JUN 436F			

Admission: adults £2.00; OAPs £1.50; family (2 + 2) £5.00.

Entrance sign, featuring an old Riley, at the Llangollen Motor Museum, Denbighshire.

LLANGOLLEN Motor museuM

Display of model cars at the Llangollen Motor Museum.

A Ford model Y and a 1918 Model T now displayed in what was originally, in 1912, a fountain pen factory. (Courtesy Llangollen Motor Museum)

A Standard Big 9 at the Llangollen Motor Museum.

The Llangollen Motor Museum's delivery van. (Courtesy Llangollen Motor Museum)

Pembrokeshire Motor Museum, Keeston Hill, Haverfordwest, Pembrokeshire, SA62 6EJ.

Tel. 01437 710950. Curator: Cliff Robinson.

The Museum is situated on the main A487 St. Davids Road, 4 miles from Haverfordwest.

Admission: £3 adults; £1 children. Group rates upon application.

Exhibits include approximately 50 cars ranging in date from 1904 to the 1970s. The cars are, in many cases, used by local enthusiasts and the display changes frequently. There are cutaway exhibits of both cars and motorcycles. In addition, 6 bicycles dating from 1890 onwards are on show and there is an outstanding exhibition of some 1500 model cars of the Dinky and Corgi variety, plus other memorabilia to interest all the family.

The Museum is open between Easter and the end of October, and hours of opening are 11.00am to 5.00pm daily, closed Saturdays. Full access for the disabled; a wheelchair is available if required. Toilets, including disabled. There's a cafeteria and a souvenir shop which also sells local pottery. Ample parking. Out of season visits by groups may be possible.

Pendine Museum of Speed, Pendine Sands, Carmarthenshire, SA33 4NY.

Museums Officer: Chris Delaney, Carmarthenshire Museum Service. Tel. 01267 231691. Pendine Museum Tel. 01994 453488.

Location: Follow the A40 dual carriageway west from Carmarthen to the A4066 to Pendine. The Museum overlooks the beach. Pendine is 66 miles west of Cardiff.

This is a new museum, opened in 1996 to commemorate 'BABS,' a 27 litre car driven by J. G. Parry Thomas in 1926 to set a new Land Speed Record of 171.02mph. He crashed the car at Pendine the following year whilst attempting a new record. The Museum overlooks Pendine Sands, the scene of many such record attempts. 'BABS' is only on display during the months of July and August. Other 'borrowed' vehicles are on show, as available, throughout the season, so we are not able to list them in advance. If you are interested you should ring before visiting.

Open: every day of the Easter holiday, then Friday to Monday until the Spring Bank holiday, then seven days a week until the 30th of September. October, Monday to Friday. Opening hours: 10.00am to 1.00pm and 1.30pm to 5.00pm. Closed 1st November until the Easter holiday. There is a souvenir shop, disabled facilities, toilets and car parking.

In the mid-1920s, Malcolm Cambell and J. G. Parry Thomas broke the World Land Speed Record on three separate occasions whilst at Pendine. In March of 1927, Parry Thomas was killed in the same car - 'Babs'- whilst making a further attempt on the record. 'Babs,' until recently, was buried near the sight of the accident. Now restored, she is on loan to Pendine Museum for the summer. (Courtesy Carmarthenshire Museum Service)

Admission: free.

AA Museum, The Stenson Cooke Centre, Norfolk House, Priestley Road, Basingstoke, Hampshire RG24 9NY.
Tel. 01256 492360. Archivist: Michael Passmore.

Basingstoke is about 50 miles southwest of London, and can be reached from junction 6 of the M3. Follow the signs for the North Hampshire Hospital; the AA Museum is located next to the AA Head Office in Priestley Road, near the A340 Tadley Road.

The AA Museum - part of the Automobile Association - contains badges, insignia, road service artefacts, an extensive model collection, telephones, road signs and other AA memorabilia. Many exhibits are unique, like a steel helmet which was issued to patrols during the Second World War, and the first AA member's handbook of 1908.

The Museum is regularly used as a conference centre and is not open on a casual basis. To arrange to view the exhibits, phone Michael Passmore on the above number.

The Collection includes:

1949   MkI swb Land Rover
1961   BMC Minivan

Plus a selection of motorcycles, both solo and combination, which include:

Harley-Davidson
Triumph Tiger
Chater Lea
BSA

Other vehicles in the AA Historic Fleet are maintained and run by AA patrols in various parts of the UK.

Exhibits in the AA Museum.

The World of Country Life, Sandy Bay, Exmouth, Devon EX8 5BU.
Tel; 01395 274533.

Leave the M5 motorway at junction 30 near Exeter, and follow the A376 to Exmouth. From there take the B3178 towards Budleigh Salterton and follow the signs for The World of Country Life.

Billed as an all-weather family attraction, Country Life has lots to offer, including deer parks, a pet centre, adventure playground, working machinery and models, plus a host of other interesting things.

Included in the World of Country Life is a garage in Memory Lane, and a Hall of Transport, where you will find a collection of vintage and classic buses, motorcycles and steam engines.

Facilities include a restaurant, coffee shop, ice cream parlour and picnic areas. There are toilets, a mother and baby room and disabled access. Guide dogs only permitted.

Open: daily from 10.00am from March 29th until October 29th.

Two of the vehicles in the Country Life collection.

Admission: adult £5.25; OAPs £4.75; children £4.00; wheelchair user and helper £3.25; family ticket (2 + 4) £17.50. Special admission offers on Saturdays, excluding the months of July and August: phone for details. Group terms - for parties of over ten - on request.

Index

The Complete Catalogue of British Cars 1895-1975

By David Culshaw & Peter Horrobin
£21.99*

☆ **Revised and updated reprint of a long out of print classic -** *the* **British car Bible**
☆ **Catalogues all of the cars built in Britain from the dawn of the industry until 1975. Many of these vehicles are now prized and collectible veteran, vintage and classic cars**
☆ **Over 1000 photographs**
☆ **Large format hardback with 496 pages**
☆ **A MUST HAVE for every car enthusiast's library**

Contents

The most comprehensive account of British cars ever published, this book presents a huge amount of information - historical as well as technical - in a way which will serve the needs of the dedicated enthusiast and the general reader.

Nearly 700 manufacturers and some 3700 individual models are covered, including technical specifications for most cars. A wide selection of photographs feature all of the major marques and many of the minor ones.

Specification
Hardback • 215x280mm (portrait) • 496 pages • over 1000 photographs • ISBN 1 874105 93 6

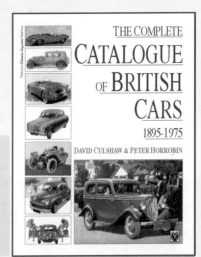

THE COMPLETE
CATALOGUE
of BRITISH
CARS
1895-1975

DAVID CULSHAW & PETER HORROBIN

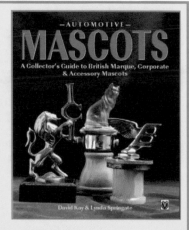